Strategic Survey 2016
The Annual Review of World Affairs

published by

 Routledge
Taylor & Francis Group

for

The International Institute for Strategic Studies

The International Institute for Strategic Studies
Arundel House | 13–15 Arundel Street | Temple Place | London | WC2R 3DX | UK

Strategic Survey 2016
The Annual Review of World Affairs

First published September 2016 by **Routledge**
4 Park Square, Milton Park, Abingdon, Oxon, OX14 4RN

for **The International Institute for Strategic Studies**
Arundel House, 13–15 Arundel Street, Temple Place, London, WC2R 3DX, UK

Simultaneously published in the USA and Canada by **Routledge**
270 Madison Ave., New York, NY 10016

Routledge is an imprint of Taylor & Francis, an Informa business

© 2016 The International Institute for Strategic Studies

DIRECTOR-GENERAL AND CHIEF EXECUTIVE Dr John Chipman

EDITOR Dr Nicholas Redman

ASSOCIATE EDITOR Chris Raggett
EDITORIAL Alice Aveson, Melissa DeOrio, Nick Payne, Daniel Schlappa, Nancy Turner, Carolyn West
MAP EDITORS Alice Aveson, Nick Payne, Nancy Turner, Carolyn West
GRAPHICS CO-ORDINATOR AND RESEARCHER Jo-Anna Halford
COVER/PRODUCTION John Buck
CARTOGRAPHY Martin J. Lubikowski, Kelly Verity

COVER IMAGES Getty Images

PRINTED BY Bell & Bain Ltd, Glasgow, UK

British Library Cataloguing in Publication Data
A catalogue record for this book is available from the British Library

Library of Congress Cataloguing in Publication Data

ISBN 978-1-85743-862-8
ISSN 0459-7230

Contents

Foreword

This is the 50th edition of *Strategic Survey*. The first edition, published in early 1967 and covering the calendar year 1966, was a stapled booklet running to just 39 pages. It had no charts, maps or tables; just black text. The 2015 edition, by comparison, was a perfect-bound book of 432 pages, printed on 120gsm paper, with a gloss-laminated, colour cover. It had 19 full-colour pages of infographics and maps, eight monochrome regional maps and eight colour pages featuring the drivers of strategic change.

The first few editions of *Strategic Survey* were written as a complement to *The Military Balance*. The purpose was to address developments in the strategic policies, doctrine and weapons of the most significant powers – and to attempt to put them into perspective. As the second edition noted, 'Its aim is objectivity but it makes judgments where the evidence supports them.'

That is a credo that IISS publications still live by. At the outset, *Strategic Survey* was highly selective. The first edition did not devote a single page to Latin America or sub-Saharan Africa. The book focused on the superpowers, their respective alliances and arms-control negotiations. It primarily assessed the stability of the international system. While examining that cornerstone issue, it identified those powers acting strategically – and those failing to do so.

Some of the themes of those early editions will be familiar to the modern reader. The first *Strategic Survey* noted the growth of China's potential strategic power, as well as its virulent internal politics; and it pondered whether divergences in US and European interests might prompt Europe to seek greater independent capabilities. One year later, as Reuters noted in a report on the publication, *Strategic Survey* highlighted a growing dichotomy between the increasing military power of the United States and the diminution of its political authority, due to the Vietnam War and race riots at home. That authority and respect, the book noted, had until then been an adjunct to America's military power. Thus, around 20 years before Joseph Nye coined the term 'soft power', *Strategic Survey* was writing about it.

The principal concern of the IISS in its first few decades of existence was the East–West military balance. *Strategic Survey* often reflected that concern, but it was not hidebound in focus or structure. The 1974 edition relegated coverage of the superpowers and detente to just a dozen pages in the middle of the book, to give scope for extensive analysis of the 1973 Arab–Israeli War; the oil-price shock and the Western economic crisis; and conflicts in the Mediterranean region, Africa and Southeast Asia.

In the four decades since then, the publishing industry has changed considerably, especially with the development of the internet and the proliferation of free, instantly accessible information. IISS publications have changed too, with the launch of *Strategic Comments* in 1995, the Armed Conflict Database in 2003 and *The Armed Conflict Survey* in 2015. While *The Military Balance* is concerned with defence and military affairs, and *The Armed Conflict Survey* provides facts and analysis on the world's active armed conflicts, *Strategic Survey* addresses matters of geopolitics, geo-economics and the global and regional orders. It considers how power is distributed and used, and how this distribution and usage are changing.

In 2014 *Strategic Survey* included for the first time the drivers of strategic change, an analytical tool designed to identify trends and events that had the capacity to reshape the world or a region. These drivers centred on factors that could heighten the risk of conflict or death on a large scale; stoke or resolve a conflict; affect the security of large numbers of people; alter security policies and governance; reshape national interests and thus foreign policy and international relations; or create uncertainties about global or regional security.

The 2016 edition of *Strategic Survey* includes the third iteration of these drivers. It also presents a few key metrics of changes in the power of leading states within each region. In 2017, the IISS will aim to develop further its assessment of regional change and risk within the drivers, through greater use of comparable data – for instance, data on income distribution, governance, resource scarcity or access to technology.

These incremental changes are intended to support the core purpose of *Strategic Survey*, analysing the essential aspects of the strategic landscape, as well as the causes and consequences of strategic change. The book mainly focuses on the actions and objectives of the major powers shaping the world and their regions. And it examines the changing environment in which state and non-state actors operate, as well as the security architecture.

The year to mid-2016 suggested that the global architecture was on the cusp of profound change. The United Kingdom's vote to leave the European Union was arguably the first example of an advanced economy calling a halt to globalisation. The establishment of the Asian Infrastructure Investment Bank, following the BRICS Contingent Reserve Arrangement and the New Development Bank, plus the signing of the Trans-Pacific Partnership and negotiations for other regional trade agreements, suggested that the Bretton Woods system was not so much undergoing a major transformation as being fundamentally challenged. In 2017, when the next edition of *Strategic Survey* goes to press, the effects of these developments may be clearer. In the year to mid-2016, there were also significant changes in relations among leading powers, with China growing ever more assertive in Asia and beyond, and Russia projecting force into the Middle East for the first time in its post-Soviet history. By contrast, the US remained wary of deep entanglements in the Middle East and was careful not to overplay its hand in Asia, while Europe struggled to manage internal difficulties and to address external challenges to its security, prosperity and values, particularly on its eastern and southern borders. In sub-Saharan Africa and Latin America, weaker global economic growth and lower commodity prices combined with political change to shake the hierarchy of regional powers, raising questions about the future form and direction of regional cooperation.

Even by the standards of this century, the year to mid-2016 was one of exceptional flux – although some aspects of the future world order came into clearer focus.

Chapter 1

Prospectives

The underpinnings of geopolitics have splintered so much in the past year that the foundations of global order appear alarmingly weak. The year was characterised by a bad-tempered roar against political arrangements seen to be unfair, concocted by others, and out of touch with the current realities of international power or the prevailing winds of domestic sentiment. In this environment, foreign policy became, and will continue to be in 2017, a branch of psychology. Managing competing interests or settling neat balances of power – these clinical tasks of the geopolitician – will be superseded by the need to cope with countries who want their natural position restored, their historical rights as they define them accepted, their 'return to normalcy' acknowledged, their exceptionalism catered to, and their ideology and world view respected. The politics of parochialism now mix with the instincts of nationalism, and both clash with the cosmopolitan world order so carefully constructed by the technocrats of the late twentieth century.

The result is more significant than a popular backlash against the forces of globalisation, with its attendant nostalgic yearnings for a simpler past. Multiple strategic earthquakes have created a situation in which world leaders are in a constant state of crisis control. The institutions that had been created to contain crises are being bypassed or have shown themselves incapable, with the result that conflict management has been renationalised. Unilateralism is the preferred mode of conduct;

stealing a march on the slow-paced deliberative processes of others has become the main strategic gambit.

Russia's foray into Syria, China's activities in the South China Sea, the United Kingdom's exit from the European Union, the interventions of Saudi Arabia and the United Arab Emirates in Yemen – where Iran too was active – all reflected a new 'go it alone' geopolitical trend. With no effective global or regional balances of power to constrain unilateralism, and a pervasive distrust in the ability of institutions to protect national and regional interests, these types of individual actions will continue to multiply. Regional institutions – the EU, the Association of Southeast Asian Nations (ASEAN), the Gulf Cooperation Council (GCC) and others – are fracturing. Global and regional groupings are under threat, as governments struggle to show that they are closer to the concerns of the people over whom they rule and less beholden to international constructs seen increasingly at odds with national interests. It may be that a renationalisation of politics comforts domestic opinion. It does, however, put into reverse efforts of the last half-century to channel political disputes and differences through institutional arrangements.

The next year will likely see more shuffling of the geopolitical deck of cards, an extension of the strategic unease that set in last year, and a frantic drive by major powers in all regions to set new rules of the game and revive old ones. In this context, the apparent strategic dynamism of the East will superficially contrast with persistent strategic arthritis in the West. But, on the whole, the net result will be a grinding of the geopolitical tectonic plates, with no new geopolitical settlement in the offing.

China continued in 2016 to mark its strategic arrival on the world stage with a more persistent and assertive foreign policy. By one estimate, China reclaimed at least 17 times more land in the South China Sea than all other claimant states combined. It continued to insist that territorial disputes be solved bilaterally and not by institutions. It rejected the authority of the UN's Permanent Court of Arbitration (PCA) to rule on its dispute with the Philippines and regularly sought to peel away ASEAN states from any settled consensus on how to engage with China on thorny territorial issues. A champion of multipolarity at the global level, China will continue to strongly emphasise bilateralism in its Asian regional diplomacy. It has also, in its own way, taken the regional issues that affect its core interests to the global stage. While China has always carefully monitored international adherence to the 'One China' policy and punished those who over-empathise with Tibetans, its stance in the South China Sea has now risen to assume equal foreign-policy prominence. States everywhere have been cautioned not to do anything that appears to challenge China's sovereign claims in the region. When the PCA decision comprehensively discounted the validity of China's historical claims and criticised it for the actions it had taken, China stood firm. The South China Sea will therefore remain an area of great contention and competition. The United States will continue to assert its freedom to sail, fly and operate in contested areas, but it will also likely consider other policies to reassure its Asian allies and partners that its 'rebalance to Asia' is sincere and sustainable, and translates into a real capability to maintain a 'rules-based order'. The US at present is not keen to pursue an aggressive policy towards China, but Beijing will still need to tailor its assertions of sovereignty in ways that support its interests without inspiring a regional demand for the US to effectively shift towards a de facto containment strategy.

China's domestic politics in 2017 will have a particular impact on its external stance. Politics are becoming more turbulent as President Xi Jinping's anti-corruption purge bites more deeply into the ranks of the Chinese Communist Party and as leadership changes come closer. In 2017, five of the seven members of the Politburo Standing Committee will be replaced. The slowdown in the economy may make elements of domestic governance more challenging. In the meantime, China's vast geo-economic project, the Belt and Road Initiative, is deepening the country's engagement in the regional politics of the countries that lie along revived trading routes. It is also providing an effective platform for the Asian Infrastructure Investment Bank to demonstrate its vitality and flexibility, and thus showcase how an institution created by China, and with significant international membership, can promote international development. In South Asia, it is clear that Pakistan is being drawn more tightly into China's orbit, just as India is finding the US to be a welcome strategic partner. Elsewhere, China's development of a military base in Djibouti, where traditionally France and the US have maintained a strong presence, indicates China's keen interest – as a newly arrived global power – in deploying military capacity in areas adjacent to its economic interests. In the cyber domain, China is moving to take a greater role in determining how cyberspace and the internet are governed and managed.

As China determines how it will manage its slowing economy, and how it will impose strong party discipline as its senior membership is reshuffled, it will probably continue to develop its international foreign-policy personality so that the question 'what does China think?' is more automatically posed when an international issue is being debated. China is not quite yet seeking to build an alternative world order, but it is backing its own institutions, widening its geopolitical ambitions beyond Asia, and engaging in a firmer 'diplomacy of command' by which it seeks to insist with ever greater firmness that its views be fully taken into account. These are the natural actions of a nascent world power. Yet it will be a very different kind of world power. Unlike previous super-powers, there is no sign that China wishes to export its political system or values, nor is it likely to develop policies aimed at providing global public goods. It will not seek to create or lead an alliance system, but instead to expand an arc of influence in Asia and well beyond. It will try to unpick alliances or state groupings that might attempt to coalesce against its interests. It has done this by seeking to break ASEAN solidarity on the South China Sea issue, and to warn other Asian states that they should not wrap themselves into 'Cold War arrangements' with the US. It will remain highly sensitive to the attempts by others to hedge against the different threats they perceive, and will tend to see the defence strategies adopted by others as uniquely directed against China, even when they have other motivations. China's robust criticism of South Korea's decision to develop a ballistic-missile-defence (BMD) system with the US to counter North Korea's growing capabilities is a case in point. China's long-time perception that regional BMD systems may constrain its own capacities feeds the view that China sees regional security as a zero-sum game, and only through its own eyes. While the rest of the world will indeed ask regularly 'what does China think?', for the foreseeable future China will not reciprocate but rather ask others to respect its perspective as the price of cooperation. And, if China eventually achieves a rebalancing of its economy in favour of consumption and away from dependence on exports, that will ease a constraint on its external behaviour. For countries in Asia and beyond, 'dealing with China' will be a labour-intensive task.

The question 'what does Russia think?' was asked all too infrequently in recent years for Vladimir Putin's taste. That changed in 2014 with the annexation of Crimea, and it changed all the more so in the year to mid-2016 as Russia asserted itself further along its border with NATO states and made itself a key player in the Levant through support for President Bashar al-Assad of Syria. Despite Russian frustration with Assad and the cost of shoring him up, Moscow sees no alternative and feels that its decision has netted strategic gains in the Middle East at the expense of the US. In Europe, the Cold War-like period of tensions in Russia–West relations has now acquired a momentum that will prove impossible to reverse in the short to medium term. Policy decisions taken in 2016 will ensure that the mutual remilitarisation of the NATO–Russia frontier in Northeastern Europe continues unabated. NATO will have deployed its four brigades to front-line states, while the US will spend more than US$3 billion on reinforcing its military presence on the continent. Russia, in turn, has strengthened the Western Military District with more troops and materiel. Neither side will launch a war of unprovoked aggression, but this increasing concentration of forces on both sides of the NATO–Russia divide – in the absence of robust communication and confidence-building regimes – reduces decision-making time, while increasing the possibility of misunderstanding, misinterpretation or accident. That escalatory dynamic has been intensified by a series of incidents and close calls between NATO and Russia in the skies and on the seas, particularly in the Baltic and Black Sea regions. While 2016 saw initial attempts to negotiate mechanisms for managing risks associated with all this close contact, it remains unclear whether Moscow is prepared to back down from its brinkmanship – which came in response to NATO's increased presence along its borders – unless that increase is somehow limited or reversed. Meanwhile, the dispute over the US/NATO BMD system in Romania and, by 2018, in Poland has become an acute concern for Moscow, which might prompt new missile deployments to the Kaliningrad exclave. The BMD issue is becoming increasingly tied up in US–Russia acrimony over the Intermediate-Range Nuclear Forces (INF) Treaty. Russia has charged that the interceptor launchers in Romania, the MK 41 vertical-launch system, could easily be reprogrammed to launch *Tomahawk* cruise missiles, which would constitute a breach of the INF Treaty. For its part, since 2014 the US has alleged that Russia has tested a treaty-busting ground-launched cruise missile.

Yet, despite all these tensions, and those stemming from an unresolved conflict in Ukraine and the 'sanctions war', circumstances will force Russia and the West to try to find ways to cooperate. US President Barack Obama, despite his clear personal dislike of the Russian president, has had little choice but to work with Putin and his government extensively on Syria. So far, all this work has produced limited results, but Obama's successor is likely to have little choice but to continue it. A new American president will have to work ever more closely with European leaders to ensure that there is a united policy towards Russia that firmly deters aggression while keeping the door open to constructive cooperation. The fracturing of Europe's internal politics makes that US engagement with Europe all the more necessary.

If recently the future of Europe was being discussed in the context of a resurgent nationalist Russia and the Greek debt crisis, the decision by the British people to leave the EU (dubbed 'Brexit') in the 23 June referendum portends the biggest change in European politics for a generation. The British population was for many years presumed to be eurosceptic in disposition by a small majority. Full awareness of this fact made calling the referendum a significant risk by those who felt that the UK should remain in the EU. The only psephological questions of consequence in the referendum concerned whether nearly all Remainers would choose to vote and whether an important number of Leavers would choose to abstain. As it turned out, the passion of the Leavers proved stronger than the prudence of the Remainers. It was surprising that so many people were surprised by the result, but particularly stunning that those who had campaigned to leave were as shocked as they were unprepared for the result that they had sought.

British Prime Minister Theresa May has said that she will follow 'the instruction' of the British people to leave the EU. She has accepted that mandate, yet there is no fine print to the 'instruction', and both the UK and the EU are in uncharted territory. No arrangement that any other non-EU state has with the EU is likely to form a useful template. No state has ever left the EU and no state in Europe that has a special arrangement with the EU has the economic, military and diplomatic heft of the UK. The 'Norway', 'Switzerland', 'Canada' and other arrangements so often alluded to may serve as preliminary guides in an intellectual and legal exercise, but they cannot be models for a settlement that will necessarily be bespoke in nature and unique in character. Satisfying the Remainers and the Leavers in the UK will be hugely difficult, but any new deal with the EU will have to be sold in the UK as a 'British' deal. That exceptionalism is exactly what the EU is most concerned about and least ready to concede. This is especially so as EU leaders see the injury of UK departure wrapped in the insult of rejection of the EU postmodern political and economic model. Stripping the emotion out of the divorce talks will be no easy task. And while much of the negotiations will be highly technical in nature, the broader future relationship will need to be kept in constant view.

In the interests of both parties, this will need to be a strategic negotiation: 'we are gone' and 'good riddance' will preferably not be enduring negotiating postures. The aim must be to develop a new economic and political partnership. An EU with more flexible internal arrangements is necessary, as is a more integrated relationship among the eurozone countries. Brexit will change the EU as much as it will change the UK's relationship with the Union. It will require outstanding leadership by the UK, key EU states, the EU Commission and the European Parliament to establish a healthy, mutually beneficial relationship. There is no guarantee that these talks will succeed, as so many interests and constituencies have to be satisfied. This underscores the importance of the prime minister building excellent relations with her principal counterparts, shaping a pragmatic environment for negotiations to effect a complex disentanglement from an institution itself likely in the midst of reinvention. The additional challenge for the UK is that, while it is intensely absorbed in discussions with the EU, it will need to explore and advance special trade and other relations with states beyond Europe. To do both will require a rapid and successful regeneration of the state's capacity to negotiate trade deals. In July 2016, the Confederation of Indian Industry indicated that, while an EU–India trade deal had been held up for many years, a UK–India one could conceivably be negotiated in 12 months. The UK will need that sort of enthusiasm, repeated many times over and executed in fact, not just in aspiration, for its post-Brexit future to be prosperous and inspiring.

As the established structures of Europe are being shaken, the Middle East continues to prosecute its multiple civil wars while coping with a changed economic and fiscal environment. With the Islamic State, also known as ISIS or ISIL, suffering significant setbacks, the battlefield is morphing: the group is progressively less a state defending clear front-lines and more a guerrilla movement mounting surprise attacks and terrorist bombings at home and abroad. It increasingly directs and inspires attacks meant partly to compensate for its own weakening. It is likely to do as much damage when it is losing as when it was winning, including in Europe.

The administration of populations and territories freed from the group's rule in the Middle East will remain contentious. Lack of political engagement in Iraq, distrust of Baghdad and intra-Sunni dynamics will complicate humanitarian relief and reconstruction. In Syria, Western-backed Kurdish forces will struggle to gain the support of Sunni Arab populations. Moving into 2017, the Saudi–Iranian rivalry will remain a driver of regional tension, exacerbating sectarianism and complicating conflict resolution. It will be difficult for Saudi Arabia to maintain a cohesive front against Iran or make significant gains in its proxy conflicts. The fiscal position of the Gulf states will likely improve with rising oil prices, but medium- and long-term economic challenges will intensify. Ambitious reform plans such as Saudi Arabia's Vision 2030 will face implementation obstacles and could provoke some resistance from populations used to the welfare certainties of the last half-century.

While there will remain important pockets of political and economic stability in the region, principally in the GCC states, the conflicts in the Middle East will continue to resonate more widely, not least on the southern shores of the Mediterranean, where the migration challenges of the last year have been so severe. As NATO considers the protection of its eastern flank, it will need to think more about the difficult exposure it has to its south. The diplomatic and military bandwidth of the West will remain sorely stretched.

Robust US intervention in the Middle East's various conflicts remains unlikely. The temptations for military engagement other than in a 'supportive role' are likely to be resisted. The US rebalance to Asia has become an established mantra, and necessary to America's self-image as a resident power in the Asia-Pacific. The commitments made to European security through NATO have a structural and institutionalised quality to them that lends weight to the aims of reassurance and deterrence central to US policy. Still, the world will keenly await the direction that the US takes in 2017 under a new president. When Obama was first elected in 2008, he was initially received as a potentially healing and uniting global force. Relatively quickly, the great weight of expectations placed on his presidency proved untenable. The power of the US has declined, but it remains the geopolitical swing player in the sense that, if it chooses to act decisively, it can still make a difference, but if it chooses to abstain, its absence from a conflict or a diplomatic engagement will also be felt deeply. The selectivity of US engagement abroad makes it hard, however, for the country to sustain its previous reputation as the 'indispensable power'. Its swing-player status is important, especially for formal allies, but the age of US indispensability is perhaps drawing to a close. The US electoral process in 2016 threw up, as was the case in European politics, the concerns of the disaffected and a desire for retrenchment that may limit America's diplomatic extroversion. If so, it may pass up an opportunity, created by the ebbing of the Bolivarian tide in Latin America, for greater engagement in the Western Hemisphere.

Making judgements on foreign-policy trends in the West in the current environment is hugely contingent. Electoral politics in the West have an insurgent quality to them. The domestic licence for expansive, open, engaged international relations is limited and appears difficult to renew. The politics of protectionism is on the rise. While political leaders are consistently looking over their shoulders, alliance politics within the West have become transactional. The scope for strategic thinking and action is shrinking. A sense of strategic malaise is pervasive. The message that globalisation has not been good for everyone, and that there is an unacceptable gap between ruling elites and the people they govern, is clear. Political and business authority needs to reconnect with people. At a time when institutions are in disarray, public-spirited political leadership is vital. Work on the home front in most countries is the priority. Not for the first time in history, stable international relations will depend on wise domestic politics. Understanding geopolitics in 2017 will require careful assessments of the internal dynamics at play in key countries. Once greater confidence is achieved on the home front, perhaps a new effort at intergovernmental institution building can take place. One must hope there is not much delay in renewing that effort, as a world that doubts its regional and global institutions is a world in drift.

Chapter 2
Drivers of Strategic Change

In the following pages, IISS experts seek to highlight developments and themes that have the potential to drive strategic change in individual regions, and in the world as a whole. They do not offer forecasts of specific future events: this annual book remains a review of international affairs covering a 12-month period, in this case from mid-2015 to mid-2016. However, regional experts use their analysis of developments in this and recent years to identify strategic risk factors. This section is not a comprehensive list of risks facing the world, nor does it attempt to assess or quantify threats. World events will remain unpredictable. But we hope our analysis is useful for the identification of key drivers of strategic change.

20
Asia-Pacific

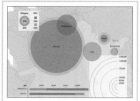

21
South Asia and Afghanistan

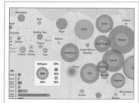

22
Sub-Saharan Africa

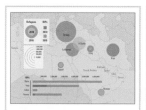

23
Middle East and North Africa

24
Russia and Eurasia

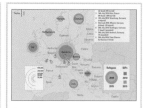

25
Europe

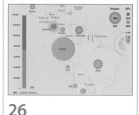

26
Latin America

27
North America

Sources: IISS *Military Balance*; World Bank; UNDESA; UNHCR

Asia-Pacific: drivers of strategic change

- China's deployment of military force and other forms of power in support of its claims in the East and South China seas is raising the prospect of direct confrontation with the United States, as well as US allies and partners in Asia.

- Some countries in Southeast Asia are focusing on domestic issues to the detriment of their foreign policy, undermining the capacity of the Association of Southeast Asian Nations to maintain its political cohesion and autonomy – an effect compounded by China's efforts to prevent the grouping from opposing its activities.

- North Korean nuclear-weapon and missile programmes are forcing Seoul's defence policies into closer alignment with those of Washington and Tokyo – as Japan adopts more extrovert security policies in the region.

- Australia's strong economy, growing military capabilities and alliance with the US could allow it to play a significant security role in the Asia-Pacific, but Canberra is yet to adopt and implement clear policies for dealing with increasing tension in the region.

- Southeast Asia is facing a growing threat from groups and individuals associated with the Islamic State, also known as ISIS or ISIL, and it is possible that the jihadist group will establish a regional affiliate in ungoverned spaces if national counter-terrorism efforts are not sufficiently well coordinated.

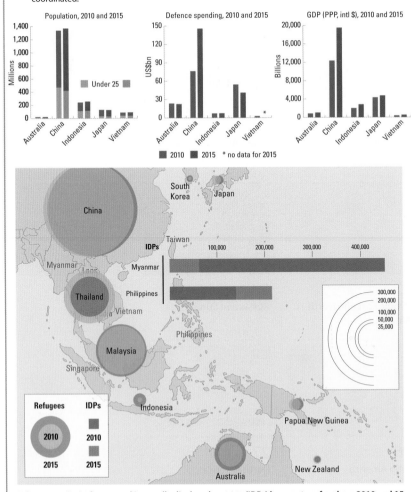

Select countries' refugees and internally displaced persons (IDPs) by country of asylum, 2010 and 15

South Asia and Afghanistan: drivers of strategic change

- Tension between India and Pakistan remains high, as disputes over national security – especially counter-terrorism policy – combine with economic competition.
- Islamabad strengthens its ties with Beijing through the China–Pakistan Economic Corridor, a large-scale infrastructure and investment project that has the potential to change the geo-economic realities in Southeast Asia, bringing the two states' interests into closer alignment.
- Concerned about China's growing influence in South Asia, India is making faltering attempts to improve relations with Bangladesh and other states in the region.
- New Delhi is investing more heavily in its relationships with Washington and the Arab Gulf states through a series of defence and security agreements.
- Prime Minister Narendra Modi is conducting high-tempo economic diplomacy, securing increasing levels of foreign direct investment and leveraging India's fast growth and huge economic potential.
- Afghanistan's security situation is becoming ever more precarious, as the Taliban expands the territory under its control amid the drawdown of Western forces, and Pakistan remains unwilling or unable to restrain the group.

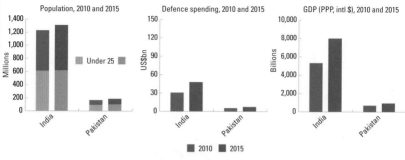

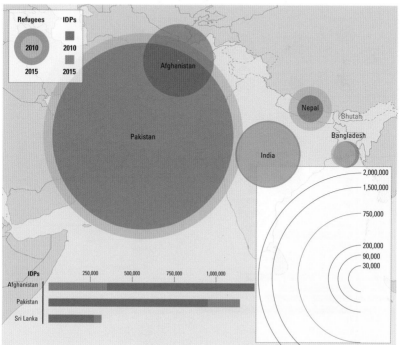

Select countries' refugees and internally displaced persons (IDPs) by country of asylum, 2010 and 15

Sub-Saharan Africa: drivers of strategic change

- The regional security hierarchy is in flux, as economic and political troubles hamper established indigenous powers, and new players China and Saudi Arabia make their presence felt in East Africa.
- Slower global growth and depressed commodity prices are compounding dissatisfaction with governments and mainstream politics, boosting hard-right and hard-left political movements that threaten policy and societal stability.
- Western states are adopting a case-by-case approach to shortfalls in governance, coercing South Sudan while subordinating political values to strategic interests in Ethiopia – a country that is becoming more important as a source of stability in East Africa.
- The African Union is growing more able and willing to support regional peace and security, but is struggling to deal with incumbents who cling to power at the cost of regional stability.
- Support for the International Criminal Court is declining in sub-Saharan Africa, due to the perception that it is unduly interested in prosecuting black Africans – but there is no vision for a regional alternative.
- The international community has adopted the Sustainable Development Goals – which explicitly recognise the link between security and prosperity – as foreign investors become more interested in sub-Saharan Africa and more discriminating in their engagement with states in the region.

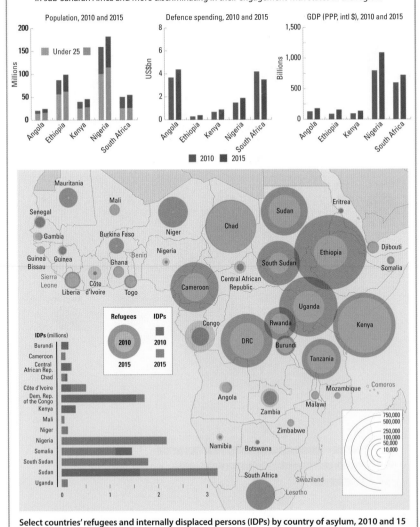

Select countries' refugees and internally displaced persons (IDPs) by country of asylum, 2010 and 15

Middle East and North Africa: drivers of strategic change

- Despite short periods of de-escalation, there seem to be no sustainable political settlements nor outright military victories in sight for the wars in Syria, Iraq, Yemen or Libya, as the humanitarian cost and security repercussions of the conflicts continue to grow.

- Russia's intervention is profoundly shaping the battlefield and diplomacy in Syria, and has positioned Moscow as a central player in broader Middle East dynamics.

- Saudi Arabia and its allies are becoming more assertive in their foreign and defence policies, while attempting to reduce their reliance on the United States as their primary security guarantor.

- Rivalry and proxy conflict between Tehran and Riyadh are intensifying, as Saudi Arabia and its allies fear Iran's regional influence will grow while external powers prioritise the success of the nuclear agreement.

- As it rapidly loses control of territory, the Islamic State, also known as ISIS or ISIL, is becoming more reliant on insurgent tactics, and is building its capacity to conduct attacks outside the Middle East.

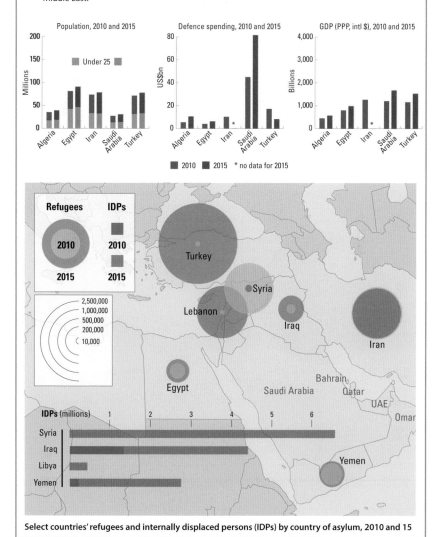

Select countries' refugees and internally displaced persons (IDPs) by country of asylum, 2010 and 15

Russia and Eurasia: drivers of strategic change

- The Russian intervention in the Syrian civil war has placed Moscow at the centre of Middle Eastern diplomacy, demonstrating that Western attempts to isolate Russia have not diminished its great-power status.

- The conflict in eastern Ukraine – and the related international crisis – is continuing with no end in sight.

- Despite high-level engagement, tensions are deepening in Russia's relationship with the West.

- Regional economic turbulence – resulting from low oil prices, an increasingly complex web of sanctions and weak governance – is having wide-ranging effects and is fostering expectations of even greater change to come.

- Russia is seeking to deepen its partnership with China, while Beijing is proceeding cautiously.

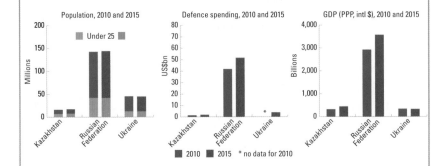

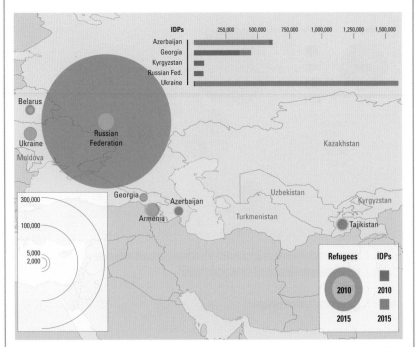

Select countries' refugees and internally displaced persons (IDPs) by country of asylum, 2010 and 15

Europe: drivers of strategic change

- Europeans are increasingly dissatisfied with governing elites, economic stagnation and the large influx of migrants, many of them refugees, across Europe's southern and eastern borders – resulting in the rise of far-right parties in many countries.

- The United Kingdom's referendum vote to leave the European Union threatens the future of the European project and weakens Europe's strategic coherence, while potentially strengthening Germany's position as the de facto leader of the region.

- Among NATO's European member states, the UK and Germany are leading the effort to bolster the Alliance's military presence and capability in the east, in response to challenges from, and incidents involving, the Russian armed forces.

- Europe's intelligence and law-enforcement agencies are collaborating ever more closely to deal with the threat from jihadists, who have carried out a series of high-casualty attacks in France and Belgium.

- A controversial migration agreement between Brussels and Ankara initially helps reduce people trafficking across the Mediterranean, but has the potential to unravel amid court challenges and an increasingly authoritarian trend in Turkey's domestic politics.

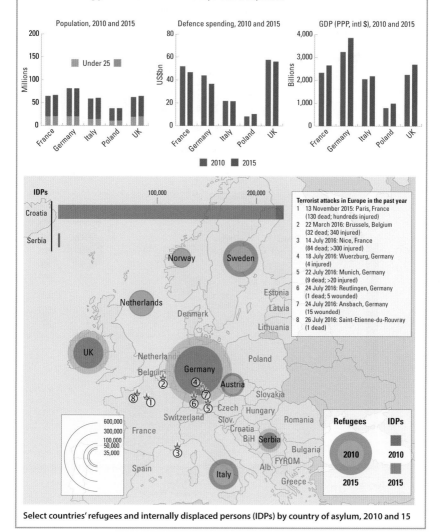

Select countries' refugees and internally displaced persons (IDPs) by country of asylum, 2010 and 15

Latin America: drivers of strategic change

- Mounting economic challenges, corruption scandals and governance failures are stoking public discontent across the region, leading to the fall of some governments and the weakening of others.

- Anti-impunity movements are gaining traction and empowering advocates of reform, but also increasing the likelihood of blowback from embattled political leaders.

- Left-wing politicians are losing support to their centrist or right-leaning rivals, lending momentum to market-friendly regional efforts such as the Trans-Pacific Partnership and the Pacific Alliance.

- Mexico and Central America have little prospect of resolving the violence and instability threatening their security, economic growth and long-term political development – much of it linked to narcotics trafficking and other types of organised crime.

- Deepening economic and political problems in Brazil and Venezuela are diminishing the countries' influence, raising concerns about both the welfare of their citizens and regional stability – and, in Brazil's case, stymying the government's global ambitions.

- The United States has created the basis for a new, friendlier era in its relationship with Latin America, but much rests on the outcome of the country's 2016 presidential elections.

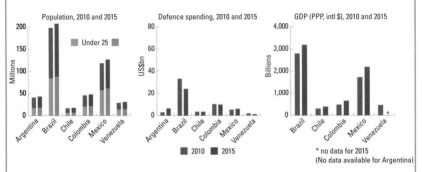

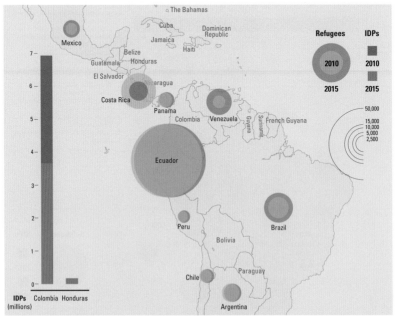

Select countries' refugees and internally displaced persons (IDPs) by country of asylum, 2010 and 15

North America: drivers of strategic change

▨ Coming to the end of his term, US President Barack Obama has reduced America's reliance on military force as an instrument of foreign policy, leading the efforts to secure a multilateral agreement on the suspension of Iran's nuclear-weapons programme and to conduct peace talks in the Syrian civil war.

▨ Under its new Liberal government, Canada is reverting to the kind of multilateralist, pro-globalisation stance that is being challenged in other Western states.

▨ The possibility of radical change to foreign and domestic policy is looming in the United States, as Donald Trump secures the Republican nomination for the 2016 presidential elections.

▨ Many Americans' intense suspicion of ruling elites combines with growing nativist and protectionist sentiment, raising the prospect that US policy will become markedly more inward-looking.

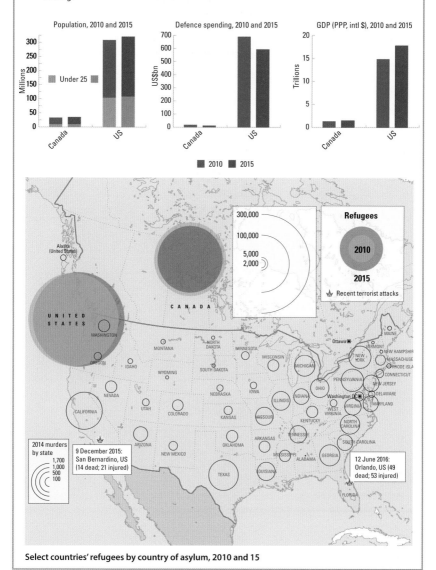

Select countries' refugees by country of asylum, 2010 and 15

Chapter 3

Strategic Policy Issues

The COP-21 Agreement and the Future of Climate-Change Policy

The United Nations Framework Convention on Climate Change's (UNFCCC) twenty-first session of the Conference of the Parties was held in Paris from 30 November to 12 December 2015. COP-21, as the meeting was known, was the most talked-about diplomatic event of the year. The resulting agreement was widely hailed as a great step forward in the diplomatic effort to establish an international policy framework to address the environmental risks associated with emissions of greenhouse gases (GHG). The deal's supporters claim that it has brought the world closer to a trajectory on which human activity will stop increasing GHG emissions by the end of the century.

After the UNFCCC meeting in Copenhagen in December 2009, known as COP-15, the *Guardian* ran the headline 'Low Targets, Goals Dropped: Copenhagen Ends in Failure.' The newspaper reported on COP-21 under the header: 'Paris Climate Change Agreement: The World's Greatest Diplomatic Success.' Some talked of a potential Nobel Peace Prize for Laurent Fabius, the French foreign minister who chaired the conference and mediated the negotiations.

Such a level of enthusiasm is hard to justify. The process behind the Kyoto Protocol (to the UNFCCC) – which was signed in 1997 and defined quantified emissions-limitation and -reduction objectives (QELROs) for the rich world (the so-called 'Annex 1 countries') – died in Copenhagen, and it was not resurrected at COP-21. The Paris agreement builds on the principles established in Copenhagen and a year later in Cancun. These principles are much easier for the parties to agree on than those that underpinned the Kyoto Protocol, but they leave the environmental outcome of the process uncertain.

Saving the planet

The science on which climate-change negotiations rest is full of estimates but clear enough. The combustion of hydrocarbons (coal, oil and natural gas) releases carbon dioxide (CO_2) that had been trapped in previous geological eras, increasing the concentration of the gas in the atmosphere, which reinforces the natural 'greenhouse effect' on the earth's climate. A quick and significant change in the climate – usually summarised as an increase in the mean global surface temperature, although this is a proxy – is almost certain to degrade the environmental conditions that support human life, which could have grave or even catastrophic consequences for parts of the world's population.

To limit its impact on the earth's climate, humankind must reduce its use of fossil fuels – as well as other processes that increase concentrations of greenhouse gases, such as permanent deforestation – to zero by the end of this century. However, the use of fossil fuels has for two centuries been synonymous with industrialisation. Even advanced post-industrial societies are still mostly powered by fossil fuels.

A large proportion of the global population resides in developing states; billions live in poverty. The energy industry can supply fossil fuels to these people in amounts that far exceed the level that the atmosphere can safely take. But carbon-free energy is generally more expensive than carbon-intensive energy, especially when it is used on a large scale.

Any state that opted to significantly reduce its emissions of GHG would incur immediate costs. If no other country followed suit, the global environmental benefit of doing so would be negligible. And, if many states cut emissions, the benefits of doing so will be enjoyed in the distant future and will not be distributed between countries in proportion to the costs incurred. This incentive structure is reminiscent of

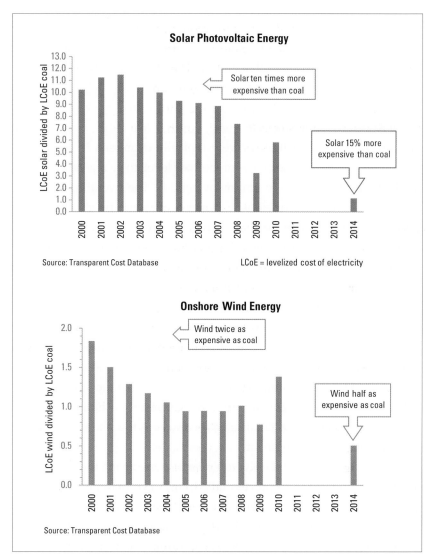

Figure 1 **Costs of Solar and Wind Energy**

the 'tragedy of the commons', in which each actor has an incentive to 'free-ride' on others' efforts, making it almost impossible to reach the collective goal.

This problem calls for an international agreement that allocates the total future stock of emissions among countries – giving them carbon 'budgets' they can spend – and that effectively enforces national obligations. This is what the Kyoto Protocol and the 'post-Kyoto' process tried to do, unsuccessfully. However, the Paris agreement does not. It may allow the world to progress towards a higher level of climate security. Yet it provides no certainty that emissions will be capped at a particular level by any given date.

From Kyoto to Copenhagen

The Kyoto Protocol's QELROs were typically expressed in percentage reductions of GHG emissions from the 1990 level, to be reached between 2008 and 2012 (the first commitment period). The overall objective of Kyoto was to reduce emissions of Annex 1 countries by 5%. There was supposed to be a second commitment period between 2012 and 2020, during which all countries would be bound by quantitative targets.

After the Kyoto Protocol entered into force, international climate politics became polarised. Member states of the European Union, along with countries particularly vulnerable to the potential effects of climate change, defended the environmental integrity of the protocol. The United States, Canada, Japan, Australia and New Zealand supported a flexible approach to Kyoto to cap the implementation costs. Developing states wanted Annex 1 countries to reduce emissions much more aggressively, but resisted suggestions that they themselves should be bound by quantitative targets after 2012, on the grounds that they could not be denied economic development.

The US did not ratify the Kyoto Protocol and Canada withdrew from it. Eventually, the Kyoto process failed for two economic reasons that interact with each other through global trade and investment. Firstly, it was impossible to know with any degree of certainty the cost of reducing emissions; thus, agreeing to absolute emissions reductions in a given time frame (the QELRO approach) meant signing a blank cheque. Secondly, the UNFCCC principle of 'common but differentiated responsibility' among countries, although accepted by all, offered no practical rule for distributing the cost of tackling climate change between developed and developing nations.

The US rejected Kyoto because China was not bound by it. China and India adopted conservative positions in the post-Kyoto negotiations, putting the onus on rich states to drastically cut their emissions. The uncertainty over the cost of addressing climate change, and the impossibility of defining a legitimate rule to share this cost among nations at different levels of development – as well as the weak credibility of international enforcement mechanisms – made the problem politically intractable.

During the 2000s, in parallel with the post-Kyoto negotiations, a rich body of academic literature in applied economics and public policy explored domestic and international climate-policy issues. The literature provided two main lessons. Firstly, the cost of achieving any given goal is reduced by the introduction of market mechanisms, such as trade in emissions certificates. Secondly, it may be sensible to redistribute the uncertainty, so that more falls onto the environmental outcome and less onto the cost of climate-change policies. An international agreement would be easier to secure if the cost was capped, although such a plan would provide no clarity regarding the timing and size of emissions reductions. Economists tend to agree that public investment in research on, and development and deployment of, carbon-free energy technologies is crucial to managing this trade-off, as it has the potential to drastically reduce the cost of future emissions reductions.

At COP-15, the Kyoto architecture collapsed as the political and economic fundamentals behind ten years of international climate politics came to the fore. The EU was marginalised, leaving the US and a few large emerging economies to negotiate a new architecture based on voluntary national commitments by all countries, in exchange for an annual transfer of US$100 billion from the developed world to emerging countries to help the latter invest in emissions limitation and adapt to the impact of climate change. The central element of the Kyoto process, the means by which the international community was supposed to control global GHG emissions – namely, the conversion of the future stock of emissions into national quantified obligations to limit and reduce emissions in a given time frame – was abandoned in Copenhagen. Nearly all climate-policy practitioners and analysts perceived this outcome as a dramatic failure.

From Copenhagen to Paris

The Paris agreement builds on the basic principles established at Copenhagen and Cancun. The key element in the architecture set up by the Paris treaty is a process known as 'pledge and review'. Governments will submit Intended Nationally Determined Contributions (INDCs), or voluntary pledges, to limit or reduce emissions. These pledges will be reviewed by the UNFCCC secretariat. INDCs are intended to be updated every five years, with an increasing level of ambition. The first period of engagement is 2020–25 and the first ex-post reviews of the INDCs will occur in 2027. Consistent with the deal reached in Copenhagen, rich countries agreed to 'mobilise' US$100bn in financing for climate-change mitigation and adaptation. The definition of, and accounting for, this sum is left undefined.

The original aspect of the Paris agreement is that it promotes inter-national scrutiny of national climate-change policies. However, it is unclear whether an international review of national commitments will be enough to place the world on a trajectory consistent with the stabili-sation of CO_2 concentration at a level deemed safe by climate scientists. The INDCs that have already been submitted vary considerably in the way that national commitments are expressed and calculated. This creates complex problems of comparison and aggregation. It will be next to impossible to judge whether one state is promising more or less than another, or even to assess the overall implications of its commit-ments. Finally, it is uncertain how the UNFCCC secretariat will be able to ensure that countries increase the ambition of their commitments over time, and so incur greater costs.

Although the Paris agreement held greater risks for climatic outcomes than national budgets, the text of the deal referred to limiting the global average temperature to 'well below' 2°C, and even mentioned 1.5°C, above pre-industrial levels. Climate scientists estimate that an eventual CO_2 concentration of 450 parts per million would provide a 60% chance of staying below the 2°C line. This concentration is an ambitious target. In 1975 the CO_2 concentration was around 330ppm, and today it stands at 400ppm. The 450ppm target implies deep cuts in the emission rates of developed and developing countries alike. Concentrations compatible with a maximum average warming of 1.5°C are unlikely to be attained without radical technological developments. Given the architecture established in Paris, these ambitious goals should be viewed as merely aspirational.

Technology to the rescue?

The two fundamental issues that brought down Kyoto persist: the uncertainty over the cost of decarbonisation and the intractability of the issue of distributive justice between rich and emerging nations. Rich states were willing to sign the Paris agreement because it did not commit them to meeting an ambitious target at any cost, while emerging states signed it in the belief that they would be able, under the Paris architecture (including INDCs and negotiations with rich countries over financial help), to avoid any significant trade-offs between the cost of energy supply and their global environmental commitments. According to modelling by economists at the Massachusetts Institute of Technology, the implicit carbon price behind the Chinese and Indian INDCs is zero; in other words, their initial commitments to the Paris process involve only steps that they would have taken anyway.

The Kyoto process faltered on the two fundamental issues; the Paris process dealt with them by transferring the uncertainty to the global environment and letting nations determine their own burden. These two problems would be alleviated if the cost difference between carbon-intensive and carbon-free energy largely disappeared. This would eliminate the collective-action challenge associated with global climate change.

Thus, the Paris agreement will achieve little by itself; its effectiveness will be defined by the evolution of energy economics and technology. The continued fall in the absolute and relative cost of clean energy, rather than the Paris accord, will phase out fossil fuels because it will allow cost-conscious governments to switch to clean energy and commit to ambitious national targets under the Paris process.

As suggested by Figure 1, the cost differential has fallen dramatically in the past 20 years (although Figure 1 compares wind and solar power in some of their most favourable locations, and does not include the cost of compensating for intermittent generation, compared to coal plants that can be built anywhere and generate on demand).

One of the promising developments in Paris was the pledge by 20 countries representing 80% of global energy research and development to double their spending in the area within five years. Another was the creation of the Breakthrough Energy Coalition by Bill Gates and 28 other private investors.

COP-21 was greeted enthusiastically because it appeared to offer redemption after the failure of the Kyoto process at COP-15. Yet it offers a fundamentally different approach. On the positive side, the Paris deal acknowledged the fundamental uncertainties over the cost of addressing climate change, the distributive-justice issue between rich and emerging countries, and the practical difficulties of forcing national emissions obligations on sovereign countries. Moving away from the politically intractable Kyoto process was therefore a positive development.

Nonetheless, the new treaty provides no certainty that CO_2 will be prevented from rising to dangerous levels. This suggests three possible future scenarios. Firstly, negotiators may try to make the Paris process less flexible (or ambiguous), with the result that it becomes politically intractable. Secondly, the outcomes of the Paris process may fall far short of what is required to save the planet. Thirdly, clean energy may become more affordable and useful (especially as the cost of managing inter-mittency drops dramatically), meaning that economies will have little incentive to burn fossil fuels. This would enable governments to commit to emissions reductions via the Paris process that are large enough to stabilise GHG concentration at a level that does not endanger the planet.

Geo-physical Change and Systemic Instability

On 12 December 2015, in Paris, the United Nations Framework Convention on Climate Change's twenty-first session of the Conference of the Parties (COP-21) ended with commitments from 195 countries. Simply having reached an agreement was widely regarded as a hard-fought win for diplomacy. In the wake of the conference, the burden shifted to signatory states to fulfil pledges on reducing carbon-dioxide emissions, support adaptation financing and implement five-year plans, among other measures.

It will be some time before the real-world outcomes of the Paris agreement become apparent. The deal aims to limit the global average temperature rise to 'well below 2 degrees Celsius' (since the beginning of the industrial age) by the end of the century. This is supposed to be done by cutting net emissions. However, judging by the agreement's own scientific parameters, current commitments would result in a rise closer to 3°C.

Additionally, the temperature projections are primarily derived from calculations based on greenhouse-gas emissions. They do not account for dynamics such as the albedo effect – in which dark surfaces absorb more solar radiation than light surfaces, as applies to the exposure of darker soil or water through the retreat of Arctic ice – or other climate-feedback mechanisms. Nor do they incorporate a potential major political shift in one of the key signatory countries. In the United States, for instance, Republican presidential candidate Donald Trump has promised to 'cancel' the Paris agreement if elected. Also, for many of the nations involved, the relative costs of renewable energy and fossil fuel will be major determinants of whether their commitments are implemented.

The COP-21 captured a moment in time: a flash of global political will to address specific aspects of a complex challenge. It will take years to see whether that will can be sustained. Yet, in the year to mid-2016, the potential for systemic instability caused by broader environmental change (including, but not limited to, climate change) was clearly on display.

According to the World Meteorological Organization, 2015 was the warmest year on record. It also saw an unusually wide range of extreme weather events, some exacerbated by the strong El Niño event of 2015–16. Heat waves killed around 2,500 people in India and roughly 1,600 in Pakistan. Heavy rains in China between May and October affected around 75 million people. Yemen was hit by a hurricane-strength cyclone for the first time since records began. On 6 August, Marrakech received 13 times its monthly rainfall in one hour. South Africa had its driest year on record. The Arctic experienced its smallest sea-ice annual maximum extent. The eastern North Pacific Basin was hit with three simultaneous major hurricanes for the first time in recorded history. The eastern North Pacific and North Atlantic basins saw a record North Pacific hurricane, which caused damage as far as east Texas. The United Kingdom experienced severe flooding in December 2015 and the following month. The extremes continued further into 2016, with record-breaking heat waves in India, and severe floods in Europe, Sri Lanka and Bangladesh. In Paris, the Louvre was closed and works of art moved to high ground as the Seine rose exceptionally high.

Physical infrastructure

The picture is much more complex than simply climate change. Globally, the physical environment is changing in myriad, often interconnected, ways. While the rainfall that triggered the flooding in the UK was record-breaking, it affected many more people than it otherwise might have because some areas in flood plains had been built over – not only putting homes in harm's way, but also decreasing the ground's capacity to absorb water. The decision to build in these areas therefore increased vulnerability at a time of growing extremes.

Additionally, infrastructure tends to be built on the assumption, often false, that physical conditions will remain constant. For example, several major cities are sinking at the same time that seas are rising. Between 1900 and 2013, mean cumulative subsidence was 2 metres in Jakarta, 1.13m in New Orleans, and around 1.25m in Bangkok and Manila. They are all still sinking.

Largely built on sediment in an active delta, parts of Shanghai have subsided by 2m since 1921. The subsidence was mainly caused by efforts to pump out groundwater from the area, a practice that became more widespread as the city grew. Beijing is trying to control the subsidence partly through artificial recharge, with mixed results. The effect is exacerbated by massive infrastructure projects that add weight to the already unsteady ground, block natural groundwater recharge and create water flows that can accelerate erosion. Shanghai is also in a typhoon pathway. Even without a climate change-linked rise in sea level, Shanghai is at increasing risk of suffering the same fate as New Orleans beneath Hurricane Katrina.

Given Shanghai's political and economic importance to China, and China's political and economic importance to the global economy, it is possible that a major environmental event in Shanghai could have far-reaching implications. As such, a comprehensive strategic assessment of potential threats should look beyond just climate change to 'geo-physical' change (involving larger, more complex global changes in the physical world), and examine how these geo-physical changes interact with geopolitics and geo-economics.

The new dynamics resulting from this interaction are now coming to the fore in a range of sectors. In the same way that physical infrastructure is usually built on the assumption that the surrounding environment will not change, legal, financial and defence infrastructures are established on the premise that they will interact with a constant physical world. This is far from true – as is becoming increasingly apparent.

Legal infrastructure

Legal infrastructure is particularly susceptible to unexpected changes in the physical environment. Most agreements that govern the physical world are founded on the status quo. As this world changes, these agreements become unstable, threatening to erode the rule of law. For instance, almost all countries – the main exception being the US – have ratified the United Nations Convention on the Law of the Sea (UNCLOS), which defines clear parameters for a state to claim a maritime exclusive economic zone (EEZ). In its most simple form, a state can claim a 200-nautical-mile EEZ from its coastal baseline. This means that every habitable island can provide a level of dominion over an area 200nm in every direction from its shores. As a consequence, the Republic of Kiribati – a Pacific island country home to around 100,000 people scattered over hundreds of islands – can claim as much of the planet's surface as India. Under UNCLOS, every little rock in the South and East China seas, and elsewhere, is worth contesting. To this end, some countries are building up semi-submerged reefs, calling them islands and making claims.

Critically, the convention fails to take account of what will happen if a coastline or island changes after a claim map is submitted and approved. This lacuna is becoming ever more important. While new islands create one set of challenges, disappearing islands create another.

Most of Kiribati's islands are only a couple of metres above sea level, making them susceptible to flooding. They could be rendered uninhabitable through gradual erosion over decades; a severe storm that causes irreparable damage; or the infiltration of salt water into their fresh-water aquifers, which could kill plant life, speed up erosion and require water to be shipped in, or expensive desalination plants constructed.

Aware of its vulnerabilities, the country has been buying land in Fiji in case it needs to relocate its population. At COP-21, Kiribati President Anote Tong publicly thanked Fiji for its willingness to take in the people of Kiribati. This leads to serious questions for UNCLOS. If an island in Kiribati disappears, and its citizens relocate to another country, does Kiribati lose its claim on that island's EEZ? If – in the most extreme case – the entire population relocates, does it cease to exist as a country?

These considerations have general and specific implications. Generally, a decision on Kiribati could set a precedent for islands everywhere, including those in the Indian Ocean, the Caribbean and even the Florida Keys. Specifically, each island has value, and some are strategically important. One island in Kiribati was home to a Chinese tracking station tasked with monitoring US activity in the Marshall Islands. Kiribati shut it down. However, if Kiribati or any other country in a strategically important location faces an existential crisis and needs funds to relocate (as is conceivable), it will be open to any viable offers. These offers could involve outside powers building facilities on its territory.

Geo-physical change is also putting strain on water-sharing and fisheries treaties. Most agreements for sharing river water apportion it by a fixed amount rather than as a percentage of flow. The contested, if technically in force, 1959 United Arab Republic and Sudan Agreement for the Full Utilization of the Nile Waters assessed the entire flow of the Nile river, as measured at the Aswan High Dam, to be approximately 84 billion cubic metres per annum, with a loss due to evaporation and other factors of around 10bcm per annum. The total remainder of the flow was divided between Sudan (18.5bcm per annum) and Egypt (55.5bcm per annum). This meant that, should the river flow decrease, due to a drought or any other change, one or both of the parties would be aggrieved. It also meant that Ethiopia, which is upriver and outside the treaty, was allocated no water and had no interest in dredging the Nile or otherwise working to keep the river flow healthy.

In the year to mid-2016, there was an urgent push to re-examine the Nile agreement. In this case, instead of geo-physical change triggering political change, political change was triggering geo-physical change. Egypt and Sudan had both used their regional influence to try to maintain the status quo. But with Sudan distracted by civil conflict and Egypt thrown into turmoil by the Arab Spring, Addis Ababa seized the opportunity to begin constructing the long-planned, massive Grand Ethiopian Renaissance Dam on the Nile. The dam is designed to provide hydro-electric power to Ethiopia, enhancing its new-found role as a zone of relative stability in the region and giving the country a seat at the table in negotiations over new water-sharing agreements. However, if these agreements are based on the allocation of fixed amounts of water rather than a percentage of the flow, they are likely to create further tension in years to come. Intra-state water-sharing agreements are also coming under pressure, including those in India and the western US. Both countries have experienced increasingly tense demonstrations over water rights, with no resolution in sight. Some public figures have tried to use the disputes to gain political advantage. During campaign speeches in California, Trump engaged with the issue by declaring that 'there is no drought'. Making his pitch directly to the agricultural sector, he stated 'believe me, we're going to start opening up the water, so that you can have your farmers survive'. The science behind his promise is unclear.

Similarly, fisheries agreements tend to rest on the assumption that they are regulating a static environment, and that the same types of fish will stay in the same waters forever. They are also coming under strain, with cascading consequences. In 2013–14, shoals of herring and mackerel followed the northward movement of cold waters into the EEZ of the Faroe Islands, prompting the government of the islands to unilaterally claim its right to fish them. The move incurred the wrath of the European

Union, which claimed the fish were covered under its fisheries agreements. The Faroe Islands government stood its ground and, as a result, was temporarily boycotted by all EU nations – including Denmark, of which the Faroe Islands are an overseas division. While the disagreement was eventually resolved, it spurred the Faroe Islands to look for other partners and to open in 2015 a permanent representative's office in Moscow. In this way, an environmental change can cause legal confusion that, if politically mismanaged, results in unintended, potentially strategic, shifts. Around the globe, carefully negotiated agreements are at risk of coming undone due to transformations in the physical world they govern.

Financial infrastructure

Like their legal counterparts, economic systems are struggling to adapt to environmental shifts. In some cases, this relates to financing that is closely tied to the physical world – such as farming subsidies – and that fails to account for changing water availability and temperatures. These changes can confine producers to a specific use of crops or land regardless of whether it is appropriate to new conditions, with adverse effects for productivity. Moreover, some financing arrangements are designed to provide returns on time frames long enough to be affected by environmental change, but include no provisions for this change. For example, while nuclear power plants are built to last for at least 50 years, many fail to factor in changes in water availability, rising river temperatures (which decrease cooling capacity) and other limiting factors. In Europe and the US, some of these facilities have been forced to shut down temporarily because their designs are unable to accommodate extreme temperatures.

The insurance sector is the most vocal, cross-cutting area of business to be affected by changes in the physical world. After incurring significant losses, it realised the difficulty of trying to predict future risk in the physical world by relying on historical data. Inflation-adjusted insurance payouts from weather-related events have risen from an annual average of around US$10bn in the 1980s to approximately US$50bn in the past decade.

According to 'The Impact of Climate Change on the UK Insurance Sector', a report published in September 2015 by the Bank of England's

Prudential Regulatory Authority, the industry faced at least three types of risk. The first of these related to physical threats such as flooding, which could involve not only damage to property, but also knock-on effects including resource scarcity and disruptions in global supply chains. The second risk arose from the transition to a low-carbon economy, with the scale and speed of repricing carbon-intensive assets. The third risk resulted from potential claims against those perceived as responsible for climate-change damages. In the context of liabilities, the insurance sector was mostly concerned about successful suits against emitters, along the lines of cases holding tobacco companies responsible for health problems among smokers.

The insurance sector is actively trying to lower its exposure to environmental change. Around the world, it is trying to respond to risk using measures such caps on liabilities, self-insurance and the transfer of risk onto the public – as it does with the US government's National Flood Insurance Program. Funded by the taxpayer, the programme subsidises insurance in flood-prone areas and is more than US$24bn in debt.

Governments are also being asked to help lower insurers' risks and facilitate lower premiums as a 'public good'. In April 2016, after years of negotiation between the UK government and the insurance sector, Flood Re, a major reinsurance fund, was launched in England and Wales. Created in part through levies on the insurance sector, it is expected to facilitate lower premiums for up to 350,000 properties at risk of flooding. That means houses not at risk of flooding may pay slightly more for their insurance to subsidise lower premiums for those in flood plains. However, the safety net will not cover properties built after 2009 because Flood Re aims to encourage rigorous and responsible planning decisions.

This hints at another area of potential liability for the insurance sector: claims against planning authorities for using flawed zoning regulations, resulting in houses built on flood plains being designated safe and insurable. This has been a particular problem in the UK in the last few years as some cash-strapped councils have rezoned and allowed construction in marginal areas. The risk that tens of thousands of mortgaged homes could flood – becoming uninsurable and impossible to resell, and thus technically worthless – adds to the potential debt bomb in the UK financial system. The effect could be seen in the US after Hurricane Katrina.

Despite a year-long moratorium on foreclosures following the hurricane, tens of thousands of properties were abandoned.

Defence infrastructure

The defence sector is interlinked with geo-physical change in many ways, including through deployment, training, procurement and site stability. Militaries are often deployed to manage domestic emergencies caused by extreme weather, as well as to support humanitarian-relief activities overseas. If done well, as with Indian assistance to Nepal following the country's 2015 earthquake, these deployments can help build, or reinforce, ties between states. In that case, India's support was not only effective, but also compared favourably with that provided by China – making a broader point in the rivalry between the countries. In contrast, a poorly executed deployment can have lingering negative repercussions. This could be seen in New Orleans in 2005, when US combat troops who had no appropriate training, and who had recently returned from the war in Iraq, were sent to aid the city's civilian population.

As training and procurement form a part of effective deployment, governments must weigh a range of factors when determining whether they are capable of responding to environmental change. These considerations include whether militaries are properly trained and equipped to deal with civil emergencies caused by extreme weather events; whether civilian governments understand when and how to use their armed forces during crises; and, given the length of time required to procure major military systems, whether the effects of geo-physical change are properly weighed in assessments of future requirements. Icebreaking capability provides an example of how considering environmental change can affect procurement. Judging that increased access to the Arctic would be desirable given the changing conditions there, China commissioned in January 2016 its second icebreaker, the *Hai Bing* 722, which would be assigned to the navy's North Sea Fleet. Russia already has a large, active fleet of icebreakers – including some that are nuclear-powered – and is ordering more. Meanwhile, the US last commissioned a heavy icebreaker around 40 years ago.

There are also challenges in site stability. For instance, the US National Intelligence Council estimated in 2008 that more than 30

American military installations were at risk from rising sea levels. Based on that finding, the 2010 Quadrennial Defense Review noted that the Department of Defense 'must complete a comprehensive assessment of all installations to assess the potential impacts of climate change on its missions and adapt as required'. Unfortunately, that task has proven difficult.

One reason for this is that the locations of installations are highly political. Due to the fact that bases create jobs and draw investment, members of Congress usually resist efforts to move any such facility out of their districts. As a result, bases that were severely damaged by a weather event have been rebuilt in the same location, often against the advice of the military. For example, in 1992 Hurricane Andrew severely damaged Florida's Homestead Air Force Base. In 1995 the Base Realignment and Closure Committee recommended shuttering the facility, partly because of its vulnerable location. But state and federal politicians successfully lobbied to have it rebuilt – at a cost of more than US$100m. In 2005 around 50% of Mississippi's Keesler Air Force Base, which was supposed to provide assistance to the state in the event of a hurricane, was flooded by Hurricane Katrina. The facility had to be evacuated, drawing critical logistical support away from the civilian rescue effort. It suffered US$950m in damage, and was soon rebuilt in the same location. In June 2016, nine soldiers drowned in Fort Hood, when their vehicle was caught in extreme floods in a location previously thought safe.

The true complexity of the challenge posed by environmental change can be glimpsed by weaving together the many strands of problems. For instance, the US government could be sued for liability if a flood damaged houses covered by National Flood Insurance after it closed a nearby military base due to the facility's vulnerability to such an event. The homeowners could argue that the government knew the site was dangerous, but effectively encouraged them to stay there by subsidising their insurance, thereby distorting their understanding of the risks.

Moreover, a rise in sea level or increase in storm intensity that led to the evacuation of an island in Kiribati could also imperil military installations in Diego Garcia and Guam. It might also swamp China's highly prized, low-lying artificial islands in the South China Sea. Were such a change to occur, a military that had planned for the eventuality would have a distinct advantage over one that had not.

Across systems, the assumption that the physical environment is essentially static, at a time when it evidently is not, creates a range of new vulnerabilities. These can combine with economic and political factors in a cascade that leads to nasty strategic surprises. The most successful governments will be those that strive to understand environmental changes, and to be ready for them when they arrive.

The Drift Away from Nuclear Disarmament

Barack Obama's visit to Hiroshima on 27 May 2016, the first by a sitting US president, was perhaps a final exhortation in a nuclear-policy legacy that started with great promise. In Prague in April 2009, he had memorably called for a world free of nuclear weapons. In between these bookends, however, actual progress towards this goal makes for a slim book. Deployed strategic warheads and delivery systems were reduced by Washington's 2010 New START Treaty with Moscow. The July 2015 Iran nuclear accord, implementation of which began in January 2016, will bottle up Iran's nuclear-weapons options for the next decade or more – if the deal holds. Also on the positive side, the security of civilian nuclear facilities worldwide has been strengthened due to the attention given to them by Obama's four Nuclear Security Summits, although the threat of nuclear terrorism has arguably increased.

The impact of the last such summit, hosted by Obama in spring 2016, was diminished by a Russian boycott, a consequence of heightened East–West tensions. There are no arms-control talks between the two nations that possess 93% of the world's 15,000 or more nuclear weapons. Russia rejected Obama's offer for further cuts to deployed strategic warheads, and to address non-deployed and non-strategic weapons, on the grounds that more reductions would be impossible without discussing a variety of other issues, particularly America's ballistic-missile-defence systems and superiority in long-range conventional strike weapons. Russia's interventions in Ukraine and loose talk of nuclear war-fighting sparked commentaries about a new nuclear arms race and a return to the Cold War.

Nuclear-modernisation programmes undertaken by both sides – as well as those by other nuclear-armed states – and mutual accusations of violating earlier agreements left arms control in limbo, if not decay. Adding to the gloom, there has been no halt to North Korea's nuclear-weapons programme; no break in the nuclear-arms competition in South Asia; no progress towards implementing the Comprehensive Test-Ban Treaty (CTBT), signed 20 years ago; and no navigation of the impasse on negotiating a Fissile Material Cut-Off Treaty, which arms-control advocates have had at the top of their wish list for just as long. Instead, in Europe, Northeast Asia and South Asia, the nuclear pendulum is swinging away from disarmament. Possessing no nuclear arms, the vast majority of states would prefer otherwise. They promote recognition of the humanitarian consequences of using nuclear weapons, and often seek to outlaw such systems by means of a ban. Opposition to such legislation until conditions are ripe is one of the few areas in which Russia and its nuclear-armed Western adversaries agree.

Successes in reducing nuclear dangers

In his historic visit to Hiroshima, President Obama reaffirmed his commitment to pursuing the peace and security of a world without nuclear weapons. Actual progress towards nuclear disarmament has been meagre and largely limited to two steps in 2010: the treaty to slightly reduce US and Russian arsenals and a minor reduction in the role of nuclear weapons in US national-security policy.

Obama's one signal achievement – the conclusion and implementation of the agreement to block all of Iran's potential paths to a nuclear weapon for a decade and more – included the most intrusive verification regime of any non-proliferation measure ever negotiated. The accord was hammered out bilaterally between Iran and the United States, and then endorsed by the other powers formally engaged in the negotiations (China, France, Germany, Russia and the United Kingdom, plus the European Union). It reduced Tehran's uranium-enrichment and plutonium-production capabilities in exchange for the lifting of UN and EU sanctions, plus the extraterritorial measures that had allowed the US to block much of Iran's foreign trade. Because foreign banks remained cautious about servicing such trade, however, Iran has benefited less from the deal than expected. On the other side, the US and some of its partners were unhappy about the acceleration of Iranian missile development, which was not addressed by the deal. The loud dissatisfaction with the deal expressed by Republican Party presidential candidate Donald Trump leaves a sword hanging over Obama's foremost non-proliferation achievement.

The president could also claim to have strengthened global efforts to reduce the risk of nuclear terrorism. Despite tightening the security of civilian nuclear facilities through the 2016 Nuclear Security Summit,

Obama's efforts fell short of the goal he had announced in Prague: securing all vulnerable nuclear material around the world in four years. In particular, the 83% of nuclear materials in the non-civilian sector were deemed too sensitive to touch. There are still no legally binding comprehensive international standards for the security of even civilian nuclear facilities. Russia's boycott of the 2016 Washington summit amid deteriorating East–West relations undercut the achievements that were made at the summit. Among these were greater attention to the threat that terrorists would use radioactive materials, such as those contained in industrial and medical devices, to construct dirty bombs. Awareness of the danger was magnified by news that the supporters of the Islamic State, also known as ISIS or ISIL, who set off bombs in Brussels a week before the summit had also been targeting nuclear facilities in Belgium. Obama spoke of the 'real risk' of the terrorist group acquiring a nuclear weapon.

Ongoing stalemates

There has been a marked increase in most of the nuclear challenges that confronted Obama when he took office. The worst of these is posed by North Korea, which conducted its fourth nuclear test on 6 January 2016. Producing an explosion of similar magnitude to those in its previous tests, the device could not have been a hydrogen bomb as North Korean leader Kim Jong-un claimed. Yet it is likely that progress was made towards developing a boosted weapon small enough to fit the nation's ballistic missiles. Those systems now include the intermediate-range mobile system called the *Musudan*, which was successfully tested on 22 June after four failed tests in spring. A submarine-launched missile that had a partially successful test in April could also be included. These systems helped North Korea advance towards the nuclear capability it believes will deter the US. South Korea responded by considering the introduction of the US Terminal High Altitude Area Defense, sparking concern in Beijing about the impact of the system's radar capabilities on Chinese strategic forces. China thus accepted tougher UN sanctions on North Korea, but there remained doubts about how strictly these measures would be implemented.

Pakistan and India continued a slow but steady nuclear arms race, with India more focused on China and Pakistan relying on strategic systems to compensate for growing conventional inferiority vis-à-vis India. In October 2015, Pakistan rejected an informal US proposal to halt its introduction of tactical nuclear weapons, which many countries consider to be destabilising, and to limit the range of its missile systems in return for access to civilian nuclear technology. Meanwhile, suggestions for India–Pakistan bilateral talks were shelved, and the sides continued to stockpile weapons-grade plutonium. India is also expanding its uranium-enrichment capability. Global efforts to cap such production by means of a Fissile Material Cut-Off Treaty started in the early 1990s, but were stymied by Pakistan's veto of a motion to begin negotiations on the measure at the Conference on Disarmament in Geneva.

The other long-standing multilateral arms-control quest – for a Comprehensive Nuclear Test-Ban Treaty – will remain unfulfilled for as long as the US and seven other countries refuse to take steps towards its ratification. Given that the US Senate was controlled by Republicans who viewed the treaty with scepticism, securing the two-thirds approval needed for US ratification seemed an impossible dream, so Obama chose not to pursue it.

Bilateral arms-control aspirations also remained unfulfilled. New START will restrict the US and Russia to 1,550 deployed strategic warheads each by 2018, a goal that Washington met in October 2015 and that Moscow is on track to meet. While the treaty lowered warhead limits by one-third compared to earlier treaties, overall US nuclear forces have only been reduced by 13% during Obama's presidency – the smallest proportion under any US leader since the end of the Cold War. Following the agreement on New START, the US sought to negotiate down to 1,000 deployed strategic warheads and to bring non-strategic nuclear weapons and reserve strategic weapons into the equation, but Russia refused. Moscow stated that it would not make further cuts or even enter into new negotiations unless they were joined by China, France and the UK, and entailed binding limits on US ballistic-missile defence and other conditions.

At the Munich Security Conference in February 2016, Russian Prime Minister Dmitry Medvedev said the world had entered a 'new Cold War'. The following month, former Russian foreign minister Igor Ivanov rated the risk of nuclear confrontation as higher than in the 1980s. On the other side of the Atlantic, former US secretary of defence Bill Perry went further, saying: 'the danger of a nuclear catastrophe today is greater than during the Cold War'. This pessimism was among the reasons that the *Bulletin of the Atomic Scientists* moved its iconic doomsday clock up to three minutes before midnight.

From a Western perspective, heightened nuclear tension is due to Russian aggression in Ukraine and subsequent nuclear scaremongering by the Kremlin. The NATO secretary general's annual report for 2015 stated that Russian exercises have included simulated nuclear attacks against NATO allies and partners. At least there was no repeat of the direct nuclear threats that Russian officials had made in spring 2015, when a Russian ambassador warned Denmark that joining NATO's missile-defence system would make the Danish navy a legitimate target for a Russian nuclear attack, and President Vladimir Putin said he had considered putting nuclear weapons on combat-ready status following the invasion of Crimea.

Yet Russian leaders repeatedly signalled their nuclear capability. In November 2015, Putin said on national television that Russia would have to strengthen its strategic nuclear forces in response to US-led missile defences in Europe. The TV camera then zoomed in on a piece of paper in the hands of a Russian general describing plans for a cobalt-covered nuclear bomb. Codenamed *Status*-6, it would be delivered by a torpedo and was designed to 'create an extensive zone of radioactive contamination' to make an enemy's coast uninhabitable. Such systems were necessary, Russian officials later said, to counterbalance America's enormous advantages in conventional weapons and development of a prompt global strike capability. Given that the US has a ninefold advantage in defence spending, nuclear weapons are central to Russia's ability to deter the US and to its sense of remaining a superpower.

Nuclear-modernisation programmes

Russia started recapitalising its nuclear weapons earlier than other nuclear-armed states, all of which are also modernising their strategic forces. Moscow is building a new generation of nuclear bombers, eight new ballistic-missile submarines and 400 intercontinental ballistic missiles (ICBMs) and submarine-launched ballistic missiles. In May 2016,

Russia announced plans to deploy a heavy ICBM called RS-28 *Sarmat*, which will replace the R-36 *Satan*. The new missile will carry a payload of up to 10 tonnes and, in the words of one Russian broadcaster, be capable of 'wiping out parts of the Earth the size of Texas or France'. A new generation of long-range missiles carrying multiple small warheads (a capability Obama dropped for stability purposes early in his tenure) is also in development. In an alleged violation of the Intermediate-Range Nuclear Forces (INF) Treaty, Russia also reportedly tested a ground-launched cruise missile at intermediate range.

Justifying their build-up, Russian strategists point to Washington's plans to modernise all three legs of its nuclear triad, which independent experts have forecast will cost US$1 trillion over 30 years – three times the official estimate. Russia charges, improbably, that the US also violated the INF Treaty with its missile-defence installations in Europe due to the interceptor launchers' similarities to ship-based cruise-missile launchers. More plausibly, Putin said in April 2016 that the US had failed to fulfil a 2000 bilateral agreement on the disposal of excess weapons-grade plutonium. This was because, on cost grounds, the US halted its construction of a plant to turn the plutonium into mixed-oxide fuel, and instead considered alternative methods of plutonium disposal that Russia has yet to accept. Washington's concerns about what some see, correctly or not, as an increasing Russian willingness to use small-yield nuclear weapons are mirrored by Moscow's worry that the US will be tempted to employ the smaller, more precise weapons it is developing.

The nuclear-modernisation plans of the US involve five classes of weapons. Several models of the B61 gravity bomb are being merged to produce the B61 Model 12, which has an adjustable yield, as well as a new tail section and steerable fins to increase accuracy. Critics dispute the government's claim that the weapon will have no new capabilities. In addition to the bombs and modernised facilities to produce and maintain their nuclear components, the US will upgrade all delivery systems with a new penetrating bomber, new land-based ICBMs, new ballistic-missile submarines and new long-range cruise missiles. Called the long-range stand-off missile, the last of these employs hypersonic-glide technology to penetrate missile defences and can carry either conventional or nuclear warheads – although an enemy that manages to detect their arrival would not be able to discern the difference, and might therefore launch a retaliatory nuclear strike.

In the mix of what US Secretary of Defense Ashton Carter calls a 'return to great power competition', China is also modernising its nuclear forces. New long-range strategic bombers entered service in 2009. More recently, China began deploying solid-propellant road-mobile ICBMs, flight-testing a new generation of ICBMs and re-engineering missiles to carry multiple warheads. The triad is completed by a fledgling force of ballistic-missile submarines that provide a near-continuous at-sea strategic deterrent. China is also developing a hypersonic-glide vehicle. And China may be revising its nuclear doctrine through measures such as a stated policy of 'improving strategic early warning' for nuclear forces. This suggests a move away from China's long-standing stated policy of 'no first use' of nuclear weapons. Many analysts see this policy shift and the development of new nuclear forces as a response to perceived US encirclement of China. Like Russia, China also worries about America's technological advantages.

France and the UK are also modernising their nuclear forces. Among other enhancements, France is extending the range of its submarine-launched ballistic missiles, and replacing its nuclear-armed *Mirage* 2000Ns with the new *Rafale* F3 fighter jet. Britain has yet to finalise a replacement for the four *Vanguard*-class submarines that provide its sole nuclear-strike capability, named the 'Trident programme' after the ballistic missiles carried by the boats. Trident opponent Jeremy Corbyn, who was elected to lead the Labour Party in September 2015, declared soon after taking up the role that he would never launch a nuclear strike as prime minister. This put him at odds with his own shadow defence secretary and shadow home secretary at the time.

Push for disarmament in the Southern Hemisphere

While Corbyn's anti-nuclear stance made him an outlier at home, elsewhere in the world he would have found himself in good company. Most countries possess no nuclear weapons and seek to hold the nuclear-armed states to their obligation under the Non-Proliferation Treaty to eliminate their nuclear arsenals. Many nations – particularly those in the Southern Hemisphere, where nuclear-weapons-free zones prevail – also want to agree on a deadline for this process. Even some NATO allies were pulled in this direction by their citizens' aversion to nuclear weapons. The global push for disarmament has taken on a new dimension, with an increasing emphasis on the catastrophic humanitarian consequences of nuclear-weapons use. In fact, the trend is to drop the word 'use' and to declare nuclear weapons illegitimate, along with the concept of nuclear deterrence.

Increasingly well-attended international conferences on these humanitarian consequences were hosted by Norway, Mexico and Austria in March 2013, February 2014 and December 2014 respectively. The nuclear-weapons states boycotted the first two events, but the US and the UK were among the 158 countries officially represented in Vienna. India and Pakistan also attended the latter conference, as did China, in an unofficial capacity. A total of 127 nations have endorsed the host's 'Austrian Pledge' – subsequently called the 'Humanitarian Pledge' – to pursue effective measures to 'fill the legal gap for the prohibition and elimination of nuclear weapons'. In December 2015, the UN General Assembly adopted the pledge in the form of a resolution that won support from 139 nations. Most nuclear-armed states and US allies voted no, but some abstained, including Japan, Greece, Iceland, Norway and Portugal – as did China, India and Pakistan.

A lawsuit against the world's nuclear powers brought by the Republic of the Marshall Islands, the site of 67 US nuclear tests in the 1940s and 1950, lends moral support to the disarmament push. Filings in the International Court of Justice (ICJ) claimed that the nine nuclear-armed states had violated customary international law by not engaging in negotiations on nuclear disarmament. The UK, India and Pakistan – the three of the nine that accept the compulsory jurisdiction of the ICJ – claimed in response that they have strong records of support for disarmament. Their preliminary objections were heard in April 2016; if the court sides with the Marshall Islands, the merits phase of the lawsuit will ensue. Nonetheless, it is hard to envision how the ICJ could rule in favour of the plaintiff in a way that would be effective and enforceable.

The UN General Assembly voted in December 2015 to establish an Open-ended Working Group on the legal measures needed to establish a world without nuclear weapons, which was scheduled to meet for up to 15 days in 2016. A boycott by all of the nuclear-armed states undermined the practicality of the exercise. Many of the attendees advocated the negotiation of a legally binding treaty to ban nuclear weapons, which would not apply to the states that chose not to accept it. Recognising this reality, the advocates of a ban treaty seek to stigmatise the possession of nuclear arms. Their models are the 1997 Mine Ban Treaty and the 2008 Convention on Cluster Munitions, which outlawed these forms of weaponry and deemed their use incompatible with the principles of international humanitarian law. As a result, some states eventually gave up their land mines and cluster munitions.

Nuclear arms belong to a very different category of weapons, however. Their destructive power makes them uniquely attractive as weapons of last resort and national insurance. The states that have given up these weapons have done so either as a result of regime change, as was the case in South Africa, or due to state dissolution – as was the case with Belarus, Kazakhstan and Ukraine after the fall of the Soviet Union.

Uncertain future of the nuclear order

One cause of the breakdown in East–West relations is the Russian government's fear that it will be targeted by US-backed regime change, given that Washington was seen to promote 'colour' revolutions in other former Soviet states. The eastward expansion of NATO and the EU exacerbated that fear. NATO missile interceptors in Romania, which became operational in May 2016, and Poland, scheduled to come online in 2018, are seen as the latest provocation. Putin warned that, as a result, those countries may now be in Russia's cross hairs.

Moscow's opposition to the deployment of missile-defence systems in former Warsaw Pact countries is based not so much on the limited capabilities of the SM-3 Block IB systems in question, which are too slow to pose a threat to Russian strategic ballistic missiles, as on the potential for subsequent upgrades. Russia fears that the low-velocity systems will someday be replaced by faster interceptors, and that the missile batteries can be modified for offensive use. If so modified, the location of the sites could conceivably give the US the ability to conduct 'decapitation' strikes without resorting to a massive strategic exchange. Washington has sought to address this concern by offering to put forward an agreement on missile-defence transparency and cooperation. Limits on certain future capabilities could also be negotiated. Yet Russian demands for legally binding measures are rejected because of the strong opposition to limiting missile defence from the Republican-controlled US Congress.

If arms control is to have a future, it may need to prioritise unilateral measures. At Hiroshima, Obama declined to follow the advice of arms-control advocates who wanted him to announce a halt to some aspects of the US nuclear-modernisation programme, such as the long-range stand-off project, or to at least declare that he was taking America's ICBMs off high alert. Serving his last few months in office, Obama had no political constraints on such executive decisions, but could not ignore a strategic constraint. In the face of Russia's belligerent nuclear rhetoric, a one-sided US move towards disarmament would be seen as a weakness to be exploited. The situation calls for negotiated measures – if only both sides were willing to negotiate. Moscow shows no interest in doing so.

With Putin firmly ensconced for the foreseeable future, the next US president will be inclined to de-emphasise disarmament. Rather than removing the 200 or so remaining US tactical nuclear weapons from Europe and Turkey, the debate in NATO countries has shifted towards what further capabilities should be added to deter potential Russian aggression against the Alliance's eastern members. In the arms-control realm, there is a critical need to devise future rules for the use of new nano-, cyber and space technologies. Yet perhaps the best that can be achieved for now is the preservation of past gains: keeping Russia in the INF Treaty and in adherence with its CTBT pledge, as well as extending New START beyond 2021.

If the next US president is not Hillary Clinton, however, no prediction is safe. Donald Trump is unlikely to implement all of his campaign pledges – or even most of them – should he reach the White House. Yet his isolationist inclinations could see a reduction of the US military presence in Europe and Northeast Asia, if he could overcome resistance from the military and from the establishment members of his own party. One might hope that Russia would respond to such a retreat with reciprocity, but the more probable response is triumphalism. There is more reason to hope that American allies would not follow the astonishing nuclear policies Trump advocated on the campaign circuit, such as encouraging Japan and South Korea to obtain nuclear weapons of their own to reduce the US burden of deterring North Korea. If not, the nuclear order could be in for a dangerous shake-up.

Technology and Future Conflict

In May 2016, a team set up by the chief of staff of the US Air Force published 'Air Superiority 2030 Flight Plan'. The document warned that

> emerging integrated and networked air-to-air, surface-to-air, space and cyber-space threats, as well as aging and shrinking fleets of US weapons systems, threaten the Air Force's ability to provide air superiority at the times and places required in the highly contested operational environments of 2030 and beyond.

The document starkly supports the proposition that, for the United States and other Western powers, the character of conflict will change significantly in the next two decades. Crucially, the changes will conspire to undercut many of the advantages that leading Western military powers have come to rely on. This will shape defence and security planning and strategy, as well as political judgements over military intervention, and could dramatically change the risk–benefit calculus over whether to engage in conflict.

As Carl von Clausewitz wrote, the nature of conflict is enduring. But the ways and means of engaging in conflict, its character, can change dramatically over time and across different contexts. The character of conflict is affected by developments in technology and political dynamics within societies. This is true between separate conflicts, and also within a single conflict as it evolves – as has been grimly apparent in the campaigns that Western powers have fought in Iraq and Afghanistan in the last decade and a half.

These gruelling counter-insurgency campaigns have seen unconventional opponents challenge technologically superior Western forces. In developing a response, Western policymakers relied heavily on continued dominance in the air domain. And, in planning for other contingencies, they counted on their command of the naval domain to project power at a great distance from home bases with near impunity. Those assumptions of dominance look increasingly tenuous.

The military-technological drivers of this change promise (or threaten) profound upheaval. The proliferation of advanced military capabilities, including among non-state actors, is likely to close the technology gap between the West and the rest. So, just as the West has found that the land has turned into a contested domain, the traditional 'global commons' of the seas, air and space are set to follow suit. To compound this problem, cyberspace is becoming a crucial and contested war-fighting domain in its own right.

Technological development will lead to significant advances in the capabilities and use of unmanned systems across the air, sea and land domains. Emerging technologies such as directed-energy weapons (including lasers) and hypersonic systems (which travel at Mach 5 or more) will also have a major effect. Improvements in the speed and precision of weapons will dramatically shorten the time that commanders in the field and politicians in government have to respond. And the advent of autonomy and artificial intelligence is likely to transform the battlespace further, although it remains unclear when this will occur. Today's unmanned systems rely on human decision-making, but they may eventually be replaced by those able to 'think' for themselves – or, in the case of the simpler autonomous systems that are also likely to become more widely used, be pre-programmed to carry out many basic supporting military missions around the battlefield. In Western states, there remain significant legal and ethical impediments to using technology for certain tasks, including weapons release; that is not necessarily the case for other countries and non-state actors.

Accelerating change

Major powers have sought to adjust to and influence these changes in different ways. In November 2014, Chuck Hagel, then US defence secretary, unveiled what immediately became known as the US Third Offset Strategy. The strategy aims to protect the United States' competitive military advantage by creating transformational new technologies through domestic innovation. It recalls the 'offsets' of the 1950s and 1970s: the Eisenhower administration's successful effort to counter Soviet conventional superiority with the New Look nuclear build-up; and, two decades later, the creation of revolutionary conventional capabilities with precision-strike, stealth, and intelligence and reconnaissance systems.

In late 2015, China unveiled elements of an ambitious defence-reform programme designed to cut military personnel by 300,000 while producing a more integrated and networked command structure better suited to the Information Age. Meanwhile, the United Kingdom's November 2015 Strategic Defence and Security Review (SDSR) sought to strengthen military readiness for crisis response. The document also included plans to bolster the country's fleet of unmanned aerial vehicles; improve the equipment of special forces; recruit 1,900 more intelligence personnel; and double investment in cyber security over five years. The German defence ministry announced in April 2016 that it would create a dedicated cyber and information command, comprising 13,500 personnel drawn from other military services and organisations.

Western powers' concerns about the technology challenge primarily focus on China. Multiple prototypes of Beijing's stealthy Chengdu J-20 heavy fighter are now flying, and the aircraft is expected to enter service in 2020. If successfully deployed, it will form a major part of the Chinese military's capacity to contest the air environment at extended range. In this sense, the J-20 will be important to China's developing capabilities in anti-access/area denial (A2/AD), guided weapons and maritime power projection. And, while 'A2/AD' was until recently a US label placed chiefly on Chinese ambitions, Washington and its allies have come to use it elsewhere – particularly in the context of NATO and Russia. Vice Admiral James Foggo III, commander of the US 6th Fleet, co-authored in June 2016 an article entitled 'The Fourth Battle of the Atlantic'. The piece drew parallels between the submarine threats to Allied navies in the two world wars, Soviet submarine operations in the Cold War and the renewed activity by a technologically advanced Russian submarine force.

It is unclear to what extent submarine sorties have increased due to the growing assertiveness of Russia's navy. Given that the force has fewer boats than the Soviet Navy, the activity may be limited in comparison to the Cold War era, but it is much greater than it was in the 2000s. The scale and implications of Russian military investments and activity may be tempered by Moscow's ability to fulfil its modernisation plans in light of significant economic difficulties (see *Strategic Survey 2015*). Nonetheless, like China, Russia is deploying increasingly advanced systems.

This could be seen in October and December 2015, when Russian forces launched *Kalibr* cruise missiles at targets in Syria from relatively small surface warships in the Caspian Sea and then from a submerged Russian *Kilo*-class diesel-electric submarine (SSK) in the Mediterranean Sea. Although some of the missiles landed in Iran, these events underscored the fact that the West no longer has a monopoly on this type of capability. And it showed how weapons once limited to high-end platforms such as nuclear-powered attack submarines were being deployed more widely. Platforms such as modern SSKs are also proliferating, especially in the Asia-Pacific. And the use of A2/AD capabilities is also becoming more common, including by non-state actors. A decade ago, Hizbullah's strike on an Israel Navy corvette off the Lebanese coast using a C-802 anti-ship missile showed how this development could affect the outcome of a conflict.

The US and its allies may maintain an absolute technological advantage for some time. At the 2016 IISS Shangri-La Dialogue, US Secretary of Defense Ashton Carter insisted that due to decades of unmatched investment and operational experience, as well as the prospect of future innovation, 'it will take decades or more for anyone to build the kind of military capability the United States possesses'. Nonetheless, the air and naval domains will be contested in a manner unseen since the end of the Cold War, and this shift will have profound implications.

For instance, the US and its allies must contemplate having to fight to gain access to operational spaces such as the Baltic Sea and the South China Sea, as well as within them. This will inevitably have an impact on alliances and partnerships, as well as on potential adversaries.

As a consequence, attrition and survivability will become increasingly important issues for Western air and naval forces. The West's strategic response to the human and other costs of the land campaigns of the last two decades has involved a reluctance to deploy 'boots on the ground' in future conflicts. The prospect of increased losses in the air and naval domains could further dampen its appetite for intervention, although technological advances, particularly in unmanned systems, will help tip the balance back the other way.

The West's recent focus on counter-insurgency and power projection has come at the cost of maintaining an advantage in conventional war-fighting tactics and capabilities. In offensive air capabilities, anti-ship systems, artillery and other indirect-fire weapons on land, the US and its allies are facing the possibility of being outranged and outweighed by rival states. For example, Russian and Chinese brigades have more than twice the number of artillery systems deployed by their equivalent US and NATO formations, and the Russian and Chinese systems have a greater range and payload than those of their Western counterparts. The US Navy's anti-ship missiles have a shorter range than systems developed by China, Russia and India. As a result, the US is pursuing several short- and long-term initiatives designed to redress the balance. These include a programme to develop an anti-ship version of the *Tomahawk* land-attack cruise missile (which has a range of 1,600 kilometres), scheduled for initial deployment in around 2021, as well as air- and surface-launched versions of the Long-Range Anti-Ship Missile currently under development.

The US Navy is also set to pursue the concept of 'distributed lethality'. Instead of relying, as in the past, on a few high-value capital ships such as aircraft carriers for its offensive power, the force will aim to spread offensive missile systems widely throughout its fleet. Whereas in the last two decades the navy has focused principally on how to achieve effects on land, it now has to consider how best to complicate the calculations of an opponent in the context of something that has not been on the horizon in recent times: a war at sea.

Although the capability of individual platforms has improved, this may not be enough to compensate for an overall lack of numbers. Among European NATO powers, the UK and France have invested significantly in advanced combat aircraft and associated systems, accepting the trade-off of quantity for quality. Since the beginning of *Operation Desert Storm* against Iraq in 1991, the number of combat aircraft in their air forces has fallen from 475 and 579 to 194 and 271 respectively. In a contested air environment with a more level technological battlefield, militaries will once again require sufficient numbers of systems to compensate for attrition.

Militaries forced to adjust their calculations on the balance between quality and quantity will make different judgements. In the US, the Pentagon is curtailing its plans for a relatively cheap and ubiquitous warship design, the littoral combat ship, in favour of investment in more advanced capabilities. In the UK, the 2015 SDSR changed the course of frigate procurement, cutting planned procurement of high-capability Type-26 frigates from 13 to eight in favour of a cheaper general-purpose design to be built in greater numbers in the long term.

Another distinction that could become increasingly open to question is that between high- and low-end security tasks. Some states choose to focus on the latter because it suits their national interests and allows them to avoid the extra expense of investing in the most capable platforms and systems. But, due to the proliferation of advanced capabilities among non-state actors such as transnational criminal groups, it could become more difficult to conduct tasks heretofore seen as focused on law enforcement and crisis management rather than war fighting.

There is a divergence among NATO members over whether Russia, with its advancing A2/AD capabilities, is a greater threat than the movement of non-state groups and terrorism around the arc of crisis along the southern and eastern edges of the Mediterranean. Each would appear to suggest a different set of defence-capability responses. But, in a world in which even people traffickers may have increased access to advanced technologies, while non-state groups gain some of the resources and capabilities traditionally monopolised by states, many low-tier security tasks will become more demanding and require more powerful capabilities.

Emerging technologies and cyberspace

In the operations of land, sea and air forces, it will become increasingly common to combine unmanned and manned capabilities. Technology will eliminate or reduce the human element in some of the most hazardous missions, such as those involving complex urban environments, mine countermeasures or the penetration of advanced air defences. In all the traditional war-fighting domains, this will inevitably alter the relationship between military personnel and their adversaries, as well as the ways in which they engage in combat. The potential to mitigate the risk of casualties among one's own forces, even in more contested war-fighting scenarios, will also affect the risk–benefit calculus of political and military decision-makers as they weigh issues of military intervention and engagement.

Another potentially transformative technology is directed-energy weapons, which may be finally coming of age (see *The Military Balance 2015*). These systems currently have limited operational capabilities. For example, in the Persian Gulf, the US Navy equipped an outdated amphibious ship, the USS *Ponce*, with a trial laser weapon that could be used to defend against small drones, helicopters or speedboats. Over the coming decade, advanced laser technology might play a growing part in the protection systems of land, sea and air platforms – whether they be armoured vehicles, warships or combat aircraft – contending with advanced missile threats.

In an era of contested battlespace, directed-energy weapons could thus have a significant influence on the development of a new offence/defence arms race. More advanced lasers could provide the only effective defence against offensive missiles that are becoming faster (sometimes hypersonic) and more prevalent. And, unlike expensive missile interceptors – which cost US$1 million each or more, and whose stocks could be quickly depleted – advanced directed-energy weapons could prove to be relatively cheap per shot, with the number of shots limited only by the defender's ability to generate energy.

Increased speed and complexity, and the resulting requirement for quick decision-making, will reinforce the value of networked systems and investment in data analytics. However, networked capabilities will face a growing number of threats. Improving the inbuilt resilience of these systems will provide one solution to this problem. Military units will also need to learn, or perhaps relearn, how to operate and make decisions in situations in which their command-and-control networks have been disabled or impaired. The threats to these networks will come from directed-energy weapons such as radio-frequency systems and other electromagnetic-warfare capabilities, and the growing contestation of space will likely make satellites another vulnerability.

Artificial intelligence or autonomy could be key in confronting some of these challenges, especially in relation to network vulnerabilities and the speed of decision-making. But, in this area, technological development may already be outpacing the debate in the West over the cultural, ethical and legal concerns over its use in conflict. There is also a risk that such technologies will become available to adversaries who do not face similar constraints.

Perhaps the most significant looming change to the future character of conflict concerns the emergence of cyberspace as a fully fledged domain of confrontation. Missions in cyberspace will be an integral part of military operations. Part of the challenge in the domain is that the lack of warning time for, and the difficulties of attributing, attacks further blurs the distinction between conflict and peace. The cyber capabilities of the Islamic State, also known as ISIS or ISIL, and other militant groups appear to be relatively limited. Nonetheless, governments are investing in cyber power. There have been several highly publicised cyber incidents – including operations against US government and private networks – that have exacerbated fears over the potential strategic impact of disabling attacks on critical national infrastructure (CNI).

Military planners will have to take into account domestic CNI cyber vulnerabilities when proposing military options to policymakers. How to respond to a cyber attack creates several problems, not least in weighing proportionality. When will the use of military force be justified? What are the risks of rapid escalation? For Western societies in particular, the deployment of offensive cyber capabilities raises the spectre of cyber 'collateral damage' (resulting from the unintended destruction of essential humanitarian services).

Fears of a cyber attack are perhaps analogous to concerns over the development of air power up to the 1930s. In that era, amid the rise of dictatorships in Europe, the pervading fear that 'the bomber will always get through' shaped public opinion on, and the attitudes of democratic leaders to, confrontation and war. As was the case with the air threat then, efforts to counter the cyber threat will mitigate some of this risk.

Cyberspace will therefore be a new factor in calculations on, and perceptions of, A2/AD capabilities. A combatant could deny an adversary access to any area of operations by crippling their home logistics and support infrastructure, thereby sabotaging through cyber means their ability to project military power.

The experiences of the past decade and a half have forced an evolution in what might be termed 'the Western way of warfare', even if this approach continues to centre on asymmetric technological advantages. Prospective technological change will create significant opportunities to strengthen both the Western way and some of these advantages. However, as advanced technology proliferates against a backdrop of intra-state violence, hybrid warfare and resurgent inter-state confrontation, challenges to the strategic assumptions of the US and its allies are likely to overshadow these opportunities.

Chapter 4

Asia-Pacific

In the year to mid-2016, China's increasingly robust assertion of its interests exacerbated geopolitical tension throughout the Asia-Pacific. Important long-term strategic objectives drove the country's strident behaviour in its maritime littoral, not least its construction of artificial islands and military infrastructure in the South China Sea. These objectives included eroding the United States' role as the pre-eminent power in the region; securing control of hydrocarbon, fishery and other maritime resources; protecting sea lines of communication; increasing its capacity to project military power throughout the Asia-Pacific; and protecting the national nuclear deterrent as it gained a submarine-launched component. However, there is also a degree of consensus among countries in the region that China's foreign policy in its littoral and towards its neighbours is closely linked to the state of its domestic economy and politics. Beijing may have capitalised on the vulnerabilities of the West, particularly the US, since the 2008 global financial crisis – as well as the resulting sense of flux in the global distribution of power, notwithstanding Washington's 'rebalance' to the Asia-Pacific since 2012. But there is growing concern that China's economic difficulties, together with political tension in the lead-up to important changes in the Politburo planned for 2017, will accentuate President Xi Jinping's tendency to pursue hardline regional policies.

China's concerted efforts to advance its interests across the Asia-Pacific increased the strain on its relationships with not only the US

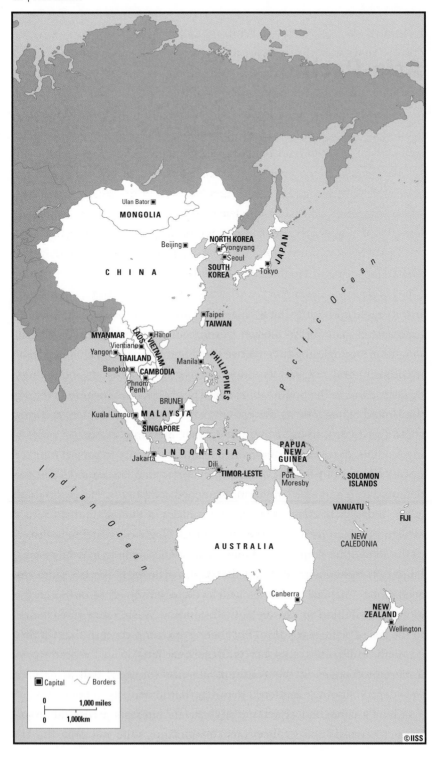

but also other Asian states. While Xi called for a 'new type of major power relations' with America and a new Asian security architecture, there was a growing perception that China sought to undermine and ultimately overturn the existing regional order. As a consequence, other countries had little appetite for these formulations, despite the appeal of Chinese investment, trade and economic initiatives such as the Asian Infrastructure Investment Bank. Relations with Tokyo remained fragile, as Beijing not only played up historical issues but also maintained pressure on Japan in the East China Sea. While Beijing was unhappy with North Korea's fourth nuclear-weapon test in January 2016, ties with Seoul – which seemed to strengthen in 2015 – deteriorated after the Republic of Korea (ROK) improved its security relations with the US, and the deployment of the Terminal High Altitude Area Defense (THAAD) anti-missile system on South Korean soil became more likely. Beijing's relations with Taiwan also became more difficult in January 2016, when a presidential election brought to power Tsai Ing-wen, the candidate of the pro-independence Democratic Progressive Party. There was renewed friction in the relationship between China and India over their disputed land border, and New Delhi's concern about the growing Chinese naval presence in the Indian Ocean provided impetus for closer Indian security cooperation with both the US and Japan.

There were doubts about whether the next Japanese government would continue the Abe administration's major defence and security reforms. Although they had only been partially implemented, the reforms had significant results. The passage of 11 security bills and related amendments in September 2015 allowed Japanese forces to undertake a wide range of UN missions. The new guidelines on security cooperation with the US effectively recast the bilateral alliance in global terms, while identifying new areas of military cooperation directly relevant to Tokyo's unease about threats from North Korea and China. Japan also relaxed its defence-export restrictions. Australia rejected a Japanese proposal to build the country's new submarines, but it seemed likely that this new freedom to export military equipment could boost Japan's influence in Southeast Asia. This could involve the supply of maritime-reconnaissance aircraft and naval vessels to Southeast Asian states, which sought to bolster their capabilities in the South China Sea.

This reflected Japan's interest in supporting Southeast Asian countries – particularly the Philippines, with which it shared concern over China's ambitions and assertive policies in the maritime domain. Moreover, Tokyo's security links with the ROK grew with their mutual interest in responding to the military threat from North Korea. While the Sino-Japanese diplomatic relationship became more stable, Tokyo remained wary of China's activities in the East China Sea and the country's efforts to expand its strategic footprint through the Belt and Road Initiative. In view of this, Japan competed with China to build infrastructure such as railways in Southeast Asia and India.

Despite their common membership of the Association of Southeast Asian Nations (ASEAN), Southeast Asian countries maintained distinct strategic orientations. Some ASEAN members – notably the Philippines and Vietnam, but also Brunei and Malaysia – were claimants to, and occupied, features in the South China Sea. Yet Cambodia, Laos, Myanmar and Thailand had a smaller stake in developments there. While China claimed in mid-2015 that it had halted reclamation activities in the Spratly Islands, it soon emerged that the country was constructing important military infrastructure on newly expanded islands. Faced with Beijing's strengthening position in the South China Sea, the US conducted naval patrols and overflights designed to assert freedom of navigation, and enhanced its support for Southeast Asian armed forces and coastguards. Washington also boosted naval and other military deployments to facilities in the Philippines and Singapore, and attempted to promote ASEAN unity at events such as the Sunnylands summit in February 2016.

However, ASEAN has been unable to formulate a strong common position in response to China's activities in the South China Sea. Some Southeast Asian governments – now including those of Indonesia and Singapore – were anxious about developments in the sea. At the ASEAN Summit held in November 2015, they demonstrated enough solidarity to express serious concern over the matter. But China successfully used its economic power to play on the equivocation of some Southeast Asian governments, thereby undermining ASEAN's capacity to oppose Beijing diplomatically. The election of Rodrigo Duterte as Philippine president, and the possibility that he might be tempted to enter into a pragmatic bilateral deal with China over conflicting claims in the South China Sea, has further undermined expectations of ASEAN unity.

Some governments in the region are also worried about the threat from jihadists linked to the Islamic State, also known as ISIS or ISIL, such as Southeast Asians who fought for, or otherwise supported, the group in the Middle East. The fear was that they would return home to carry out terrorist attacks in Indonesia, Malaysia or other countries. An assault in Jakarta on 14 January 2016, the first in Southeast Asia connected with ISIS, encouraged the intelligence and security forces of Indonesia, Malaysia and nearby states to cooperate more closely to disrupt terrorist plots. There is persistent anxiety among Southeast Asian governments and security agencies about the possibility that ISIS will establish a foothold in the southern Philippines by exploiting the area's weak governance structures, as well as its jihadist and criminal networks.

Australia remained a potentially important strategic actor in the Asia-Pacific, despite its relatively small population and geographical separation from the rest of Asia, by dint of its economic dynamism, close alliance with the US and increasingly powerful military capability. With these advantages, the country had the potential to become an important strategic actor in the Asia-Pacific. Yet the government led by Malcolm Turnbull, who became prime minister in September 2015, has conveyed mixed signals on Australia's future role in the Asia-Pacific. The February 2016 Defence White Paper repeatedly emphasised Australia's interest in supporting the international rules-based order and its concern over Chinese activities in the South China Sea. However, Turnbull's government was ambivalent about supporting US freedom of navigation operations; rejected the plans of the previous prime minister, Tony Abbott, to purchase the country's new submarines from Japan; proved unable to reach agreement with Washington on the allocation of costs for the construction of infrastructure to support US Marine Corps deployments to Darwin; and appeared unconcerned about a Chinese company's lease on the port of Darwin. Australia's strategic predicament epitomised that of the broader region: despite widespread appreciation of the dangers associated with rising tension over security matters, there was a reluctance to take measures that might result in a more hard-edged confrontation, and to take sides in the competition between the US and China.

China: uncertainty in Beijing

Across Asia, politicians and analysts have long worried about the potential impact of domestic turbulence in China on the country's foreign policy. The risk of large-scale unrest remains low: the security forces are quick to suppress demonstrations and prevent them from spreading. But there is growing anxiety in the region about the possibility that economic difficulties in China, or struggles within its elite, may encourage the country's leaders to pander to popular nationalism as a means of boosting their support. The Chinese Communist Party is preparing for sweeping leadership changes in a congress scheduled for late 2017. This has unleashed a power struggle in which competing politicians will be on guard against charges by rivals that they are failing to defend China's interests abroad. One of the accusations that led to the downfall in 1987 of Hu Yaobang, Deng Xiaoping's one-time successor-designate, was that he was soft on the Japanese. No Chinese leader wants to repeat that mistake.

The economy looked set to provide little good news. In 2015 China's GDP grew by 6.9%, the slowest rate in a quarter of a century. That figure was in line with what the government had been hoping to achieve: the leadership acknowledged that the days of relentless double-digit expansion were over, and that a change was needed from growth fuelled by wasteful investment to a more sustainable, consumption-driven mode of development. But officials worried that a massive build-up of debt (to nearly 260% of GDP by the end of 2015, up from 150% a decade earlier) would cause growth to slow much more sharply. Few countries have emerged unscathed from such a rapid increase.

Disagreements over the economy have centred on whether to engage in more debt-inducing stimulus or to carry out tough reforms that may slow short-term growth but help avoid a crash. The debate has exacerbated political feuding in the lead-up to the 2017 party congress, where leaders will appoint a new Central Committee of around 370 members. The committee will meet immediately afterwards to confirm the composition of a new Politburo. Of the seven current members of the Politburo's Standing Committee, all but two (President Xi Jinping and Prime Minister Li Keqiang) are due to retire. Although he is seemingly more powerful than any Chinese leader since Deng – if not Mao Zedong – Xi is unable to dictate the outcome of the congress without a fight. The president's sweeping campaign against corruption has aggravated some of his colleagues, including those allied with Jiang Zemin, who stepped down as party chief in 2002 but remains, even at the age of 89, a significant force in Chinese politics.

This combination of economic uncertainty and political tension will increase the risk of instability, both within the leadership and on the streets. Middle-class Chinese, hitherto a bulwark of support for the party, are likely to become increasingly anxious about the party's ability to create prosperity. Blue-collar workers may protest against the economic reforms that Xi claims to favour, especially those that involve cutting the staff of loss-making state firms. Despite heavy censorship, social media promises to play an important role in linking disaffected individuals and mobilising them to exert pressure on the government.

Asian countries' anxiety about China's foreign policy have been heightened by their sense that the West is preoccupied with its own economic and political difficulties: sluggish growth, terrorism and the impact of an influx of refugees into Europe. There might be little appetite in the West for a robust response to China should it attempt to play to nationalist sentiment at home by acting aggressively in its dealings with other Asian countries. America's 'rebalance' to Asia under President Barack Obama has been broadly welcomed in the Asia-Pacific, but many Asian leaders fear that America has become distracted by its acrimonious presidential race, and that Chinese leaders may take advantage of this opportunity.

Since the onset of the global financial crisis in 2008, China's external behaviour has changed markedly – especially in Asia, where it has become more assertive in its territorial disputes with neighbours. This resulted from a perception within the elite, as well as the general public, that the global balance of power is shifting and, specifically, that the West suffered a body blow from the financial meltdown while China continued to rise (albeit with the help of colossal stimulus spending). Chinese leaders have been probing weaknesses in America's formal and informal alliances in Asia, especially those in the East and South China seas. It has become increasingly apparent that their long-term goal is to displace American power in the Western Pacific, and to establish China as the new regional hegemon.

Xi has been closely associated with this strategy. In 2012, a few months before his appointment as general secretary, he became the head of a new 'Maritime Rights Protection Leading Small Group', which was set up by the party to oversee its claims in nearby seas. Xi would have been a key player in China's move that year to take control of Scarborough Shoal, a rocky outcrop in the South China Sea also claimed by the Philippines. He would also have taken the decision to send coastguard vessels on frequent patrols in territorial waters around the Japanese-controlled Senkaku/Diaoyu Islands, following Tokyo's nationalisation of three of the features. Since becoming president, Xi has overseen a massive effort to build islands on submerged reefs in the South China Sea claimed by the Philippines and Vietnam. This undertaking has alarmed these countries and others in the region, as well as the US, which responded by sending military aircraft and vessels close to the islands as a challenge to Beijing.

Xi has tried to prevent disputes in the East and South China seas from escalating into military confrontations with other states, particularly the US. Indeed, he has overridden the demands of nationalists at home that he seize the Senkaku/Diaoyu Islands, and the stand-off between China and Japan over them has largely settled into a choreographed routine. Both countries avoided sending naval vessels to the area until June 2016, when China did so for the first time, thereby risking an escalation of its confrontation with Japan.

China has shown no willingness to abandon its island-building programme in the South China Sea. The country responded angrily to a July 2016 ruling by the Permanent Court of Arbitration (PCA) at The Hague that undermined China's vaguely defined claim to most of the South China Sea. The court largely upheld a case lodged by the Philippines that challenged China's rights to territorial waters and exclusive economic zones around features in the Spratly Islands, an archipelago in the south of the sea. The PCA ruled that the features in the Spratlys did not count as islands and therefore could not generate such rights under the UN Convention on the Law of the Sea.

China's immediate response was measured, aiming to show its defiance of the tribunal's decision without risking immediate confrontation with the Philippines or other claimants to territory in the South

China Sea. China had long expected such a verdict – hence its efforts in the months before the ruling to strengthen its presence in the South China Sea by accelerating the island-building programme and turning reclaimed land into military outposts.

Beijing may start building military facilities on Scarborough Shoal. The Philippines would regard such a move as a considerable provocation, and the US is believed to have warned China that it would be seen as a threat to US interests.

The Chinese public likely favours tough action by the government in the South China Sea. But Chinese censors were quick to delete posts on social media calling for public protests against the tribunal's verdict. It appeared that Xi did not want public displays of nationalism to complicate his decision-making. He may worry (as some Chinese scholars privately do) that China's behaviour in the region is causing serious damage to its image in Southeast Asia; demonstrations in Chinese cities by angry nationalists would cause even greater reputational harm.

Xi has also shown some restraint in his dealings with Taiwan. China responded relatively calmly to the January 2016 victory of Tsai Ing-wen in Taiwan's presidential election. President Tsai, who took office in May 2016, belongs to the Democratic Progressive Party, which China abhors. Xi may try to step up economic pressure on Taiwan to force her to accept the notion that Taiwan is part of 'one China', but he appears reluctant to resort to the kind of sabre-rattling that Beijing engaged in during the 1995–96 Taiwan Strait Crisis, much less to mount an invasion.

Similarly, Xi still appears eager to find at least some areas of common ground with the US – for example, on climate-change policy and in efforts to persuade North Korea to abandon its nuclear-missile programme (he seems to have moved much closer to the US position that North Korea's nuclear ambitions pose a serious threat to global security). Xi appears keenly aware that China's economic welfare is closely entwined with that of the US. He does not want a conflict that may put even greater stress on China's economy and thus exacerbate social tension at home.

Despite the nationalist tone of some of his rhetoric, Xi appears to regard nationalism as a double-edged sword that can be wielded to great effect in domestic political struggles, but that risks causing considerable harm to the user if mishandled. The security forces keep anti-Japanese groups under close observation and discourage nationalist demonstrations. Some of the most ardent nationalists in China are linked with neo-Maoist groups that were supportive of Xi's jailed rival Bo Xilai. The president does not want them, or the many other disaffected elements of society, to use nationalism as a cover for an attack on his leadership.

The build-up to the 2017 congress was likely to place great strain on the leadership, especially as Xi's grip on power may have been far less secure than many observers supposed. Should the conflict among the elite become more open, as happened during the Tiananmen Square protests in 1989, then China's behaviour abroad could become far less predictable. However, if Xi ensures that his allies fill key positions after the congress, his strategy in the East and South China seas is likely to remain assertive but measured. Although China's neighbours would continue to be concerned about this approach, they could draw some comfort from it as a signal of stability within the country.

China's developing great-power diplomacy

Throughout the year to mid-2016, diplomacy in the Asia-Pacific was characterised by shifting alignments, new coalitions and increasing tension. This was primarily due to China's intensified competition with the US, Japan and India, and a limited expansion of cooperation between Beijing and Moscow.

China continued to challenge the US alliance system in Asia. At meetings with President Obama in September 2015 and March 2016, Xi called for China and the US to implement his concept of a 'new type of major power relations'. Yet Washington had quietly begun to distance itself from the idea the previous year – out of concern that to do otherwise would require an unacceptable accommodation of Chinese interests in the region, including the loss of US spheres of influence. In an address to the UN General Assembly on 28 September, Xi put forward a parallel concept of a 'new type of international relations'. This appeared to be designed to promote a multilateral approach to security that rejected the 'Cold War mentality' of bilateral alliances. To avoid a strong US reaction, Chinese Foreign Minister Wang Yi reassured the US during a visit to Washington in February 2016 that China did not seek to replace America as a global superpower.

Xi repeated his call for a new Asian security architecture in Beijing in April 2016, when he spoke at the foreign ministers' meeting at the Conference on Interaction and Confidence Building Measures in Asia. His rhetoric was more moderate than it had been at the 2014 iteration of the summit, where he appealed for 'Asian people to uphold Asia's security' and to 'completely abandon' old security concepts such as the US bilateral alliance system.

China's relations with the Republic of Korea (ROK) markedly improved in 2015, before faltering the following year. South Korean President Park Geun-hye had stood alongside Xi and Russian President Vladimir Putin on 3 September at China's military parade to commemorate the 70th anniversary of the end of the Second World War. In December, China and the ROK resumed bilateral talks on the demarcation of their exclusive economic zones (EEZs), the China–ROK Free Trade Agreement came into effect and the Chinese and South Korean defence ministers announced the establishment of a military hotline. However, these developments came shortly before a series of setbacks in the China–ROK strategic trust-building that Xi and Park had prioritised since 2013. Xi avoided speaking by phone to Park in the days following 6 January 2016, when North Korea conducted its fourth nuclear-weapon test. Beijing also reacted negatively to heightened US–ROK alliance cooperation in response to growing security threats from the North. China's disapproval was particularly evident following the initiation on 4 March of formal talks on the deployment of the Terminal High Altitude Area Defense (THAAD) anti-missile system to South Korea, and the largest-ever annual US–ROK military exercises the same month. Due to its heavy-handedness on these issues, Beijing lost some of the gains it had made in its relations with Seoul.

In October 2015, worries about China's declining influence on North Korea prompted Beijing to send fifth-ranking Politburo member Liu Yunshan to Pyongyang's celebration of the 70th anniversary of the Workers' Party of Korea. But the abrupt recall of North Korean leader Kim Jong-un's favourite band, just before it was to perform in Beijing in December, underscored the persistent tensions between the sides over the North Korean nuclear programme. After learning that the performance included a video of North Korea's 2012 missile launch, the

Chinese leadership reportedly informed Pyongyang that senior party leaders would not attend, leading to the cancellation of the event.

Beijing's willingness to support UN Security Council Resolution 2270, which includes the most severe sanctions ever enacted against North Korea, reflected its growing frustration with Kim's defiance of Chinese calls for denuclearisation of the Korean Peninsula. The decision improved Beijing's relations with Seoul, Tokyo and Washington, and to some extent eased the security competition in Asia between China on one side and the US and its allies on the other. After the annual meetings of China's National People's Congress and the Chinese People's Political Consultative Conference in March 2016, Beijing signalled that it still needed to maintain a modicum of stability in its political ties with Pyongyang. Foreign Minister Wang said at the press conference following the meetings that China and North Korea 'enjoy a normal state-to-state relationship built on a deep tradition of friendship'. He added that if the North 'seeks development and security, we will be prepared to help'. On 1 June 2016, Xi indicated his possible willingness to improve ties with Pyongyang when he met with Ri Su-yong, a former foreign minister said to be a close confidant of Kim Jong-un.

China's relations with Japan remained stable yet fragile due to historical and maritime issues, as well as the countries' contest for influence in the Asia-Pacific. High-level bilateral interactions between them were rare in the run-up to the 70th anniversary of the end of the Second World War, but gradually resumed in late 2015 and then gained momentum. In early November, Chinese Prime Minister Li and Japanese Prime Minister Shinzo Abe joined Park for their first trilateral summit since 2012, issuing a Joint Declaration for Peace and Cooperation in Northeast Asia. In December, Xi and Abe held a four-minute conversation on the sidelines of the Paris climate-change conference, having ignored each other during the G20 meeting and the Asia-Pacific Economic Cooperation summit in November. The following April, Wang hosted Fumio Kishida in Beijing – the first visit by a Japanese foreign minister to China in four and a half years. Wang laid out firm conditions for improved ties that included respecting each other's legitimate interests and concerns in regional and international affairs, and a requirement that Japan 'face up to and reflect upon history and follow the one-China policy to the letter'.

Unease over historical issues spiked at the end of 2015, when China criticised an agreement between Seoul and Tokyo aimed at resolving a dispute over Japanese forces' sexual enslavement of Korean women during the Second World War. China was also incensed by Japan's growing involvement in the South China Sea, including the participation of the Japan Maritime Self-Defense Force in a trilateral military drill with the US and the Philippines off Subic Bay; the visit of a Japanese submarine to the Philippines in April as part of a naval flotilla that sailed on to Vietnam's Cam Ranh Bay base; Tokyo's decision to lease five aircraft to Manila for use in patrolling the South China Sea; and the announcement of plans for a joint naval exercise involving Japan, the US and India near the South China Sea in 2016. As chair of the G7, Tokyo drew Beijing's ire when the G7 foreign ministers issued a major statement on maritime security at their April 2016 meeting in Hiroshima. Nonetheless, the G7 heads of state endorsed the statement the following month.

China Coast Guard (CCG) ships continued to make frequent incursions into the 12-nautical-mile territorial sea around the disputed Senkaku/Diaoyu Islands, with Beijing sending large, well-armed ships that would have a considerable advantage in a stand-off with Japanese law-enforcement vessels. There was an increase in Chinese military activities in airspace close to Japan – particularly above the East China Sea, where the countries' Air Defence Identification Zones (ADIZs) overlap. These zones require all aircraft flying through them to submit their flight details to the relevant country's authorities. Japan reportedly scrambled its fighters to intercept Chinese military aircraft a record 571 times in 2015.

Beijing's assertive approach to the South China Sea became the most contentious issue in the Asia-Pacific. In mid-2015, China raised hopes that tension might be lowered when it announced the completion of its land-reclamation activities. Wang reaffirmed this commitment at the Association of Southeast Asian Nations (ASEAN) Regional Forum ministers' meeting in August, pledging to build facilities that provide 'public goods'. During his meeting with Obama in Washington the following month, Xi stated that Beijing had 'no intention to militarise' the Spratly Islands.

However, this claim was at odds with subsequent events. In November, China started operating J-11 fighter aircraft from Woody

Island in the Paracel Islands. The country then landed two civilian aircraft on Fiery Cross Reef in the Spratlys in January, and deployed advanced HQ-9 surface-to-air missiles in Woody Island in February. China also reportedly built an advanced radar system on one of its newly built islands, Cuarteron Reef. In March, there were back-to-back incidents involving Chinese intimidation of Southeast Asian states. The CCG used ramming tactics to prevent an Indonesian law-enforcement vessel from detaining a Chinese trawler that encroached on Indonesia's EEZ off the Natuna Islands. China referred to the area as 'traditional Chinese fishing grounds' falling within its ambiguous 'nine-dash line' claim. A few days later, a CCG cutter escorted around 100 Chinese fishing boats into Malaysia's EEZ, near the Luconia Shoals.

In March, Chinese activity around Scarborough Shoal raised concerns that Beijing might reclaim land at the feature, which lies around 120nm away from the main Philippine island of Luzon. Beijing may have been deterred from dredging temporarily, although some observers expected it to eventually turn Scarborough Shoal into another military outpost. General Fan Changlong – vice-chairman of the Central Military Commission and one of China's top military leaders – made a quiet visit to Fiery Cross Reef in April. A Chinese military transport aircraft landed on the outpost later that month, ostensibly to rescue injured workers.

China harshly criticised the US decision to conduct three freedom of navigation operations less than 12nm away from Chinese-occupied features in the South China Sea in October, January and May, but did not directly interfere with the missions. Beijing presented the operations as evidence that Washington was the primary source of regional tension. In May, two Chinese fighter jets allegedly conducted an unsafe intercept of a US surveillance aircraft off China's coast. This was the first such incident since September 2015, when the countries signed an agreement on the rules of behaviour governing aerial encounters.

Diplomatic friction over the South China Sea intensified as a decision neared in the Philippines' case in the Permanent Court of Arbitration. In late October 2015, the United Nations Arbitral Tribunal ruled that the case was 'properly constituted' under the UN Convention on the Law of the Sea, and accepted its jurisdiction on several issues. Hearings on the merits of the case were held in November and December, despite

Beijing's refusal to participate in the proceedings, and its insistence that any ruling would not apply to China. Chinese leaders attempted to enlist friendly states in support of their position. In May, China's foreign ministry claimed to have won endorsements from 40 countries – although some of them, including Fiji and Slovenia, publicly denied taking sides. China's assertive diplomacy drew unusually strong criticism from a senior Singaporean diplomat, who charged Beijing with trying to split ASEAN.

Following the election of Rodrigo Duterte as Philippine president in May, Beijing encouraged Manila to return to bilateral negotiations over the dispute. Duterte's loyalties and policies were less clear than those of his predecessor, Benigno Aquino III, who had brought the case before the court at The Hague. As a gesture of goodwill, China permitted Filipino fishermen to return to their traditional grounds at Scarborough Shoal, although it was unclear whether this would last. In the meantime, the US conducted its own diplomatic push to encourage like-minded states publicly to declare support for the resolution of maritime disputes through legal mechanisms, and to implement fully binding decisions by courts and tribunals under the United Nations Convention on the Law of the Sea. At the annual IISS Shangri-La Dialogue held in June, US Secretary of Defense Ashton Carter called for building a 'principled security network' based on shared principles, and charged China with erecting a 'Great Wall of self-isolation'.

During the presidency of the Kuomintang's Ma Ying-jeou, Beijing and Taipei had made progress in developing cross-Strait relations. Their efforts culminated in a historic meeting between Xi and Ma on 7 November 2015 in Singapore. But the election of Tsai in January 2016 introduced a new degree of uncertainty into Sino-Taiwanese relations. While she pledged to preserve the status quo and took numerous steps to reassure Beijing that she would not pursue *de jure* separatist policies, China remained suspicious. To show his dissatisfaction with Tsai's unwillingness to endorse the principle that the two sides of the Taiwan Strait belong to 'one China', Xi restored China's relations with Gambia (which had broken off ties with Taiwan two years earlier); reduced the number of mainland tourist groups travelling to Taiwan; broke an agreement to import milkfish from Taiwanese suppliers; and threatened to suspend cross-Strait official and semi-official communication mechanisms.

China actively courted Russia as a geopolitical partner opposed to US global predominance, a source of advanced defence technology and a supplier of natural resources. However, this marriage of convenience failed to evolve further than strengthened military and economic ties, due to enduring Russian concerns about becoming China's junior partner in Asia, as well as Beijing's reluctance to be associated with Moscow's risky interventions in Syria and Ukraine.

In August 2015, the Russian Pacific Fleet and the People's Liberation Army (PLA) Navy staged their largest joint exercise to date, deploying 22 naval vessels, 20 aircraft, 40 armoured vehicles and 500 marines. Held in international waters off Russia's eastern coast, *Joint Sea II* 2015 was also the countries' first exercise in the Sea of Japan, and the first to include a joint amphibious-assault drill. This continued a trend of increasingly complex joint exercises and improving inter-operability since Beijing and Moscow began conducting regular joint naval drills in 2011. In April 2016, the Russian and Chinese defence ministries announced that their countries would hold more ground and naval exercises in 2016 than ever before, and the following month China and Russia conducted their first joint computer-enabled missile-defence exercise.

Russia also agreed on two major arms sales to China after a decade of strained relations between their defence industries. Under pressure from Western financial sanctions and the drop in the global oil price, Moscow decided in April 2015 to put aside its concerns about Chinese reverse-engineering and signed a US$3-billion contract for the sale of the S-400 air-defence system, widely regarded as employing the world's best surface-to-air missiles. China made an advance payment in March 2016 for at least six S-400 battalions. Deliveries were scheduled to begin in the first quarter of 2017. In November 2015, Beijing and Moscow signed a US$2bn deal for the supply of 24 Sukhoi Su-35 combat aircraft to the PLA Air Force. Industry sources revealed in February 2016 that China would receive the first four of these advanced fighters in late 2016. China will be the first foreign operator of both systems, which will significantly improve Chinese defence capabilities and indigenous research and development. The deals were equally important to Russia, as Beijing's purchases accounted for nearly one-quarter of the country's arms sales in 2015.

Moreover, China received Russian support in opposing US-backed security initiatives in the Asia-Pacific. Moscow approved UN Security Council Resolution 2270 sanctions in January and even threatened military intervention against North Korea in March, after Pyongyang warned that it might carry out pre-emptive nuclear strikes on its opponents. In April, however, Moscow joined Beijing in protesting against the proposed deployment of THAAD systems on the Korean Peninsula, arguing that this would threaten Russian security, as well as stability in the region. The same month, Russian Foreign Minister Sergei Lavrov appeared to side with China on the Philippines' arbitration case at The Hague. He outlined Moscow's position that disputes be 'resolved directly between the countries involved … without any interference from third parties or any attempts to internationalize these disputes'.

China and Russia agreed in July 2015 to admit India and Pakistan as full members of the Shanghai Cooperation Organisation (SCO), ratifying an agreement to do so at its annual summit held in June 2016. Russia, China, Kazakhstan, Tajikistan, Uzbekistan and Kyrgyzstan held a traditional counter-terrorism exercise under the auspices of the SCO in September, before convening their first joint exercise to address terrorists' use of the internet, in Xiamen in October. In November, SCO defence officials gathered in Bishkek to plan the biennial *Peace Mission* exercise in 2016. Beijing also attempted to build security arrangements in Central Asia outside the SCO framework. During a visit to Kabul on 1 March 2016, PLA Chief of Staff General Fang Fenghui proposed the creation of an 'anti-terror regional alliance' consisting of Afghanistan, China, Pakistan and Tajikistan – a list from which Russia was conspicuously absent.

China and India avoided open rivalry despite the emergence of new sources of friction in their relationship, as New Delhi moved closer to Washington and its allies in Asia. In September 2015, Chinese and Indian forces once again confronted each other in the Depsang Plains in Ladakh, along the Line of Actual Control, their disputed border. A five-day stand-off over the construction of a PLA surveillance structure close to the border eventually resulted in a senior-level meeting and agreement to de-escalate the situation. China and India held the 19th round of high-level talks on their border dispute in April 2016, but little progress was made, with India interested in border delimitation and China more focused on confidence-building measures. In October 2015, the PLA and the Indian Army conducted their fifth annual counter-terrorism drill, which involved more than 300 soldiers, at Kunming Military Academy in southwestern China. However, the undertaking was overshadowed by the Japan Maritime Self-Defense Force's participation in the annual India–US *Malabar* naval exercises in the Bay of Bengal during the same month. Chinese submarines were increasingly active in the Indian Ocean, making port calls in Sri Lanka and Pakistan. As a consequence, during Carter's visit to New Delhi in April, the US and India agreed to start navy-to-navy discussions on anti-submarine warfare. They also reached a preliminary agreement on military logistics that would grant the US access to Indian land, air and naval bases. Ostensibly intended to support UN anti-piracy operations in the Gulf of Aden, Beijing announced in November 2015 that it would establish a naval logistics facility in Djibouti, at the mouth of the Red Sea. Construction of the base, China's first overseas, began in February.

There was growing geo-economic competition between Beijing and New Delhi as a result of the US$46bn China–Pakistan Economic Corridor (CPEC). Part of China's Belt and Road Initiative, CPEC will pass through disputed Gilgit-Baltistan in Pakistan-controlled Kashmir. In November 2015, China included CPEC in its 13th Five-Year Plan, and the China Overseas Ports Holding Company took control of 2,000 acres of land at the strategic deep-water port in Gwadar, leased to the Chinese state-owned enterprise for 43 years. With New Delhi having voiced its objections to CPEC in 2015, Pakistan stated in March and April 2016 that India was sending spies to disrupt various aspects of the project. Chinese officials announced in April that work on the Gwadar port expansion was almost complete. The following month, construction began on the US$44-million Pakistan–China Optical Fibre Cable Project running through Gilgit-Baltistan. Vijay Kumar Singh, India's minister of state for external affairs, said that New Delhi was still waiting for Beijing's response to its concerns over CPEC. Following accusations that India had supported an economic blockade of Nepal during the latter's September 2015 constitutional crisis, Beijing and Kathmandu signed a historic oil trade deal in October, ending a monopoly that the Indian Oil Corporation had held for several decades. In March, China and Nepal also signed ten agreements on infrastructure and energy projects for the landlocked nation.

Chinese economic statecraft steadily developed in the year to mid-2016, even as Beijing continued to pursue cooperation and integration with US-led regional and global institutions. In July 2015, the BRICS countries (Brazil, Russia, India, China and South Africa) held their seventh meeting, convened in the Russian city of Ufa. There, they concluded an agreement to begin lending in their local currencies through the New Development Bank by the end of 2016. In April, members of the bank's board met on the sidelines of the World Bank and IMF summits in Washington to approve a US$811m fund for renewable-energy projects. During a meeting of the SCO heads of state in Zhengzhou in December 2015, Li proposed the development of 'specific measures' to create a 'free trade area within the SCO framework'. Most member states welcomed the initiative. When in October officials from the US, Japan and ten other Pacific nations reached a final agreement on the Trans-Pacific Partnership (TPP), China reiterated its interest in ultimately joining the trade pact. At the Asia-Pacific Economic Cooperation summit held in November, Li maintained that the TPP and China's preferred Regional Comprehensive Economic Partnership could complement each other, and suggested that the two agreements could eventually form the foundation of an Asia-Pacific free-trade zone. Probably spurred on by developments in the TPP, Beijing announced its intention to conclude the prolonged negotiations on the partnership in 2016.

The Chinese-led Asian Infrastructure Investment Bank was officially established on 16 January 2016. Germany, India, South Korea and Indonesia secured top spots on the bank's board of governors, suggesting that developing countries and US allies would play an important role in its management. The institution announced in April that its first set of loans would go to 'high-quality, low-cost projects', most of them involving infrastructure in Central Asia. Separately, under the Belt and Road Initiative framework, Chinese firms won contracts from Myanmar in January and April. The first of these was for the construction of a deep-water port in the Bay of Bengal, and the second an oil refinery near the

Dawei special economic zone. Beijing met with a significant setback in February, when Gazprom cut 50% of its funding for the Power of Siberia natural-gas pipeline, scaling back construction plans for the year. Yet neither China nor Russia had moved to cancel the US$400bn energy deal they had signed in 2014, despite worsening conditions in the Chinese and global economies.

Japan: energetic diplomacy

By mid-2016, Prime Minister Shinzo Abe was poised to lead his governing coalition to victory in Japan's Upper House elections on 10 July. Already one of Japan's longest-serving post-war leaders, he was on course to strengthen his position and remain in office until 2018.

Japan's relations with China and the Republic of Korea (ROK) were still marred by persistent tension, albeit while undergoing marginal improvements. There was little change to the strategic competition between Japan and China, increasingly perceived by the Japanese government and security establishment as a 'war by other means' (although not publicly articulated as such).

Domestically, Abe's conservatism and assertive security policies encountered persistent opposition from the traditional left. Although the economy stuttered, Abe's unusually long tenure as prime minister steadied Japanese politics, and compared favourably with the country's recent experience with short-lived premierships. This political stability contrasted even more starkly with the turbulence and populism gathering in Western democracies, a striking reversal of Japan's political fortunes of just five years ago.

The passage of 11 security bills and related amendments through the Diet in September 2015 marked the end of one phase in the Abe administration's efforts to 'normalise' Japan's international security role. Subsequently, the government's focus shifted towards implementing the legislation, although Abe's ultimate political objective remained to revise the constitution, specifically Article 9, which outlaws war. He had consistently expended political capital to put in place a new legal framework for Japan's defence and security, despite attempts by opposition parties to disrupt proceedings in the Diet, and high-profile street protests against the new legislation. However, such resistance was less intense than suggested by some media reports. Japanese citizens largely accepted the government's case for reform.

However, proposed amendments to collective self-defence restrictions were watered down to ensure support from the Liberal Democratic Party's coalition partner, Komeito. As a result, the new security legislation fell short of allowing the Japan Self-Defense Force (JSDF) to engage in collective security arrangements under a UN mandate. Nonetheless, Japanese peacekeeping troops had been authorised to use weapons to protect other countries' units, as well as civilians engaged in peacekeeping efforts. The range of UN missions in which the JSDF could take part was expanded to include naval minesweeping, as well as other activities. Japanese forces' rules of engagement continued to have strict limits. But the legislation allowed the Japanese military far more latitude than it had during Abe's first term as prime minister in 2006–07.

The government also made efforts to implement the revised Guidelines for US–Japan Defense Cooperation. The changes to the guidelines centre on the assertion that Japan's peace and security 'cannot be defined geographically'. They rebrand the alliance as global in scope, and as encompassing the space and cyber domains. On one level, this merely acknowledged the reality that the US and Japan had long cooperated 'out of area', across a broad spectrum of defence and security activities. But Tokyo struggled to accept the expansion of the alliance's geographical scope, given the deterioration in Japan's immediate strategic environment since 1997, when the guidelines were last revised.

Concern over potential threats from China and North Korea implicitly shape many of the areas identified in which the revised guidelines have enhanced US–Japan cooperation. They include air and missile defence; intelligence, surveillance and reconnaissance; maritime security; air and sea interdiction; and capacity-building. Southeast Asia and the South China Sea are increasingly likely to fall within the operational ambit of the guidelines.

In late 2015, Japan gave conflicting political signals about whether it was prepared to join the United States in conducting freedom of navigation patrols in the areas of the South China Sea where China had built islands. The Abe administration ultimately settled for diplomatic expressions of support for the US rather than making an operational contribution. Tokyo's caution owed much to its desire to avoid exacerbating tension in the East China Sea. Nonetheless, the Japan Maritime Self-Defense Force (JMSDF) maintained a consistent presence in the South China Sea, making high-profile deployments of surface vessels, submarines and aircraft, and conducting port visits to Southeast Asian countries such as the Philippines and Vietnam.

Japan's concerns about maritime security grew in June 2016, when a Chinese naval vessel entered Japan's territorial sea off the southern prefecture of Kagoshima, the first such incident since 2004. The incursion came soon after a Chinese warship followed a small Russian Pacific Fleet flotilla near the Senkaku/Diaoyu Islands. This was the first time that the People's Liberation Army Navy had sailed within the 24-nautical-mile contiguous zone of the islands. Tokyo was particularly worried by the possibility that Russia and China had coordinated their activities.

The most important institutional innovation made by the revisions to the Guidelines for US–Japan Defense Cooperation was an alliance-coordination mechanism. The system was introduced to address the absence of an overall joint command structure, a long-acknowledged weakness in the alliance in comparison to the compact between Washington and Seoul. The coordination mechanism was used for the first time in January 2016, immediately after North Korea's fourth nuclear-weapon test. That incident also triggered recently agreed information-sharing arrangements between the US, Japan and the ROK.

Cooperation between the US and Japan continued to deepen in many areas, benefiting from Abe's strong personal commitment to national security and the centralisation of decision-making powers around the new National Security Council structures – under the supervision of National Security Adviser Shotaro Yachi. In May 2016, US President Barack Obama's historic visit to Hiroshima, where he attended a wreath-laying ceremony, underscored the health of relations between the US and Japan.

The most significant challenges to the countries' alliance emanated from Okinawa. As three-quarters of all Japan-based US forces are stationed there, the island is pivotal to their relationship. It emerged in February 2016 that, following tortuous negotiations, the relocation of the US Marine Corps air station from Futenma to another location within

Okinawa would be delayed by two more years. Okinawa Governor Takeshi Onaga, who had pursued a vigorous campaign against the base since he was elected in late 2014, forced the delay in the hope that this might prompt a more distant relocation. As a result, the move will not take place until 2025 at the earliest. The development was embarrassing for Abe, particularly as it went against commitments that he had made on the issue. In May 2016, the murder of an Okinawan woman, allegedly by a former US marine who had worked on the base, further inflamed anti-Americanism on the island.

Although the new defence guidelines put in place an updated steering framework for the alliance, they are not legally binding, and their implementation depends on political commitment in Japan. As long as Abe remains in power, the current momentum in alliance cooperation is likely to be maintained. Abe's conservative brand of nationalism, the main source of the controversy surrounding his leadership (particularly in Japan), did nothing to lessen his commitment to the alliance with Washington as Japan's most effective counterweight to China. Therefore, the US has sought to strengthen the relationship as much as possible under Abe – recognising that if a less defence-minded leader takes office in 2018, Japan's legislative security framework will probably be implemented more slowly or reinterpreted more narrowly.

In 2015, Japan's defence industry appeared to have a major opportunity to expand, after the Abe government relaxed restrictions on arms exports to strengthen Tokyo's budding security partnerships in the Asia-Pacific. Yet the sector had mixed fortunes during the year that followed, as Japan sought to gain a toehold in a crowded international arms market. The largest disappointment came in April 2016, when Japan lost the opportunity to design, build and supply Australia's A$50-billion (US$38bn) future submarine. The contract had been widely expected to go to Japan, as the seal on the improved relationship with Australia personally fostered by Abe and then-prime minister Tony Abbott. However, their close political alignment became irrelevant in September, after Malcolm Turnbull challenged and replaced Abbott.

Closer security cooperation between Japan and Australia had also received Washington's blessing. The countries' roles as the northern and southern anchors of the US alliance system in the Western Pacific have been especially apparent in the maritime domain. For example, Japan and Australia have independently pursued amphibious military capabilities and made commitments to acquire the F-35A Joint Strike Fighter. Canberra staunchly defended its decision to award the submarine contract to a French firm as the best technical choice. But, due to Japanese expectations and Australia's mishandling of the politics of the deal, the decision dealt a blow to the budding strategic partnership, while undercutting Japan's technological prestige just as it re-entered the international arms market.

Despite some lingering suspicion and resentment about the contract publicly expressed by Minister of Defense Gen Nakatani, Tokyo's relationship with Canberra remained sufficiently broad that their security relationship appeared likely to recover. Reciprocal submarine visits and naval exercises between Japan and Australia continued throughout the year to mid-2016. Yet putting the security partnership back on track promised to require careful diplomatic work, as well as creativity in identifying new areas for cooperation. Meanwhile, Japan had dwindling hope of boosting its defence-industrial ties with India through the export of its US-2 amphibious search-and-rescue aircraft.

Despite these setbacks, Japan announced in May 2016 a groundbreaking arrangement to lease retired TC-90 maritime-patrol aircraft to the Philippines, marking modest progress in its efforts to extend its influence in Southeast Asia. More significantly, reports surfaced the following month that Vietnam might purchase several Japanese P-3C aircraft to boost its maritime-patrol and anti-submarine-warfare capabilities in the South China Sea. It appeared that Japan had an opportunity to capitalise on the capacity-building requirements of Southeast Asian countries, particularly those with claims in the South China Sea. This could take the form of defence exports or strategic assistance in civilian maritime law enforcement and domain awareness.

Japan also had growing involvement in Indian infrastructure projects, including those for roads and railways – and, potentially, for power generation in the remote, undeveloped Andaman and Nicobar Islands. The trend suggested an effort by New Delhi and Tokyo to pursue joint development projects as an alternative to China's Belt and Road Initiative, with a view to balancing Beijing's growing civilian and military presence in the

Indian Ocean. By mid-2016, Tokyo's interest in forging capacity-building and defence links with Southeast Asia had been a theme of Abe's foreign policy for several years, building on a strong economic foundation. As Japanese corporations diversified away from China – primarily for commercial rather than strategic reasons – Southeast Asian countries became the primary focus of redirected investment. In 2015, Japanese companies invested US$20bn in Southeast Asia, double the amount of Japanese foreign direct investment in China and Hong Kong combined.

Japan and China competed economically in South and Southeast Asia, as seen in Tokyo's unsuccessful bid to construct a US$5bn high-speed railway on the Indonesian island of Java. China won the contract in October 2015 (although the deal subsequently ran into difficulties). Two months later, New Delhi opted for Japan rather than China in a US$15bn deal to construct a high-speed railway between Mumbai and Ahmedabad. The decision emphasised a growing strategic undercurrent to high-profile infrastructure projects across Asia. In May 2015, the Japanese government pledged US$110bn in assistance for such projects over five years.

The intensifying competition with China for major infrastructure deals also led Japan to ease its high standards for extending overseas assistance, dropping its well-established policy of requiring host governments to guarantee loans. The effect of this rivalry on Tokyo's diplomatic priorities became even more evident in March, when Abe welcomed Zimbabwean President Robert Mugabe on a state visit.

Japan's strategic threat perceptions continued to converge with those of several other countries in the Asia-Pacific. Tokyo repeatedly articulated its interest in freedom of navigation and secure trade, underlining its dependence on sea lines of communication running through Southeast Asia. It provided strong diplomatic support for the Philippines' legal challenge to Chinese maritime claims in the South China Sea, and closely observed the proceedings at the Permanent Court of Arbitration at The Hague. Under then-president Benigno Aquino III, Manila had moved to intensify its security cooperation with Japan and the US, due to concern about China's large-scale land-reclamation activities in the Spratly Islands and assertive approach to dealing with Southeast Asian countries that had competing claims. As part of this, the Philippines welcomed Japan's new security legislation, hosted port calls by the JMSDF and acquired Japanese equipment for its coastguard and armed forces.

Partly due to continuous US diplomatic efforts, Japan's relations with the ROK also began to improve, having been frosty for much of President Park Geun-hye's tenure. In August, Abe delivered his most conciliatory speech towards Seoul to date, in commemoration of the 70th anniversary of the end of the Second World War. This made it easier for Park to reciprocate, and the countries subsequently reached an agreement on the issue of Korean women who had been sexually enslaved by Japanese troops during the conflict. Seoul described the deal, under which Japan apologised and provided an unofficial compensation fund, as 'irreversible' if it was completely fulfilled. But many in the ROK heavily criticised the agreement for favouring Japan, and for going over the heads of civil-society groups and the surviving victims.

Despite the partial and flawed nature of this rapprochement, North Korea's fourth nuclear-weapon test in January 2016, and subsequent rounds of missile tests, forced Seoul, Tokyo and Washington into closer security cooperation. The tests confounded Park's hopes that China would be able and willing to restrain the North, and led the ROK to approve the deployment of the US Terminal High Altitude Area Defense anti-missile system on South Korean soil, prompting a major counter-lobbying effort by Beijing. The decision fell within the ROK's shift towards emphasising its alliance with the US, and adopting a more receptive stance on Japan – as signalled by the countries' joint naval missile-defence exercise in June.

Nonetheless, there was a thaw in Sino-Japanese relations, resulting in greater contact between high-level officials in Tokyo and Beijing. The sides persisted in their drawn-out discussions on military confidence-building measures, although they had yet to reach a final agreement on the issue. Japanese Foreign Minister Fumio Kishida's visit to Beijing in April 2016 marked a high point in the developing relationship. Yet the rivalry continued, and China's naval incursions into waters near the Senkaku/Diaoyu Islands in June, as well as the high tempo of its activities in the East China Sea, largely undermined any sense of progress.

Despite growing alignment between Beijing and Moscow, and Russia's poor relations with G7 states, Abe remained committed to diplomacy with the Kremlin. In May, this effort culminated in a visit to Sochi, where he held discussions with President Vladimir Putin. Abe clung to the notion that Japan could carve out a strategic relationship with Russia and reach a bilateral agreement to settle their long-running territorial dispute over the southern Kuril Islands/Northern Territories. The prime minister hoped that, by reaching out to Russia independently of the West, he could enlist Moscow's help in counterbalancing China. However, the endeavour appeared to be increasingly unrealistic: Russia showed no sign of compromising on the territorial dispute with Japan, nor of restraining its increasing naval and air activity near Japanese territory. Regardless of these trends, Japan and Russia continued to discuss the territorial dispute and a possible peace treaty in bilateral talks, while Abe and Putin planned to hold another meeting in Vladivostok in September 2016.

Korean Peninsula: Pyongyang undermines strategic patience

The most consequential security development on the Korean Peninsula in the year to mid-2016 was the fourth nuclear-weapon test by the Democratic People's Republic of Korea (DPRK), held on 6 January. This followed tests in 2006, 2009 and 2013. Combined with the country's continued missile tests, this activity reaffirmed the DPRK's commitment to developing a nuclear-weapons capability that could credibly threaten not only neighbouring adversaries such as the Republic of Korea (ROK) and Japan, but also the United States. By June 2016, monitoring agencies concluded that Pyongyang had restarted reprocessing plutonium at its Yongbyon facility, indicating its desire and capacity to make more nuclear bombs using two methods (the other being uranium enrichment).

The DPRK's actions reinforced the widespread view that it has no intention of trading its nuclear weapons for promised economic benefits. Seoul declared that it would abandon 'trustpolitik' in favour of a tougher approach to North Korea, even at the risk of antagonising China. This created openings for deeper security cooperation with the US and Japan. Washington spoke of the DPRK nuclear-weapons challenge with a new urgency. And Beijing made another step towards pressuring the country to denuclearise.

Pyongyang claimed that its fourth test involved a hydrogen bomb. The ability to build a thermonuclear weapon, which uses a combined fission–fusion reaction and can be hundreds of times more destructive than an atomic bomb, would be a startling technological advance by the DPRK. However, outside measurements detected an explosion similar in size to the 2013 test, suggesting the fourth test involved a less advanced boosted-fission device.

Three tests showed that the DPRK could fire a missile from a submerged submarine, although in each case the missile failed early in its flight. Between April and June, the country held six test firings of the intermediate-range, road-mobile *Musudan* missile. The first five were outright failures, but the sixth missile flew 400 kilometres. This followed the country's second successful satellite launch, on 7 February. Since the satellite-launch vehicle is a multi-stage, long-range rocket, security analysts regard these launches as tests for developing an intercontinental ballistic missile (ICBM).

Against this background, it became impossible for South Korean President Park Geun-hye to maintain trustpolitik, an inherently contradictory policy that she described as 'promoting inter-Korean confidence on the one hand, while refusing to accept a nuclear North Korea and responding more firmly to provocations'. Both elements of the policy had come under strain in August, when two ROK soldiers were maimed by mines on the South Korean side of the border. After an investigation into the incident determined that North Koreans had planted the devices, Seoul responded by restarting propaganda broadcasts into the DPRK using loudspeakers located near the border, a practice discontinued 11 years earlier. In retaliation, Pyongyang fired four rockets in the direction of the loudspeakers and threatened a larger attack if South Korea did not silence them by a set deadline. Seoul held firm, returned fire with an artillery barrage and refused to comply. Instead of attacking, Pyongyang agreed to high-level negotiations. After a gruelling 43-hour meeting, the two sides' delegations emerged with an agreement that in essence represented a victory for the ROK. While Seoul said that it would end the loudspeaker broadcasts on the condition that the North avoided provocations, the DPRK expressed regret for the injuries to the soldiers, pledged to 'lift the semi-war state' and agreed to conduct more cross-border family reunions, a long-standing South Korean objective.

The other element of Park's policy, promoting inter-Korean confidence, was symbolised by the Kaesong Industrial Park. The ROK government remained committed to the project despite the mine incident and past provocations. Located just inside the North Korean border, Kaesong was a North–South joint venture in which over 50,000 North Koreans worked under the management of 100 South Korean companies. Advocates of the scheme saw it as a way to expose North Koreans to marketisation and South Korean soft power, thereby stimulating the growth of a North Korean middle class. But its critics pointed out that Kaesong was hermetically sealed from the rest of the DPRK, and that the state took most of the workers' pay. Park had maintained the ROK's commitment to Kaesong through difficult times but, after the fourth nuclear-weapon test and the 7 February satellite launch, her patience was exhausted. Seoul announced on 10 February that it was withdrawing its citizens from Kaesong. Park's stated rationale for the move was that North Korean earnings from the project were feeding the DPRK's nuclear and missile programmes. Closing Kaesong may have been necessary to gain Chinese acquiescence to a tougher sanctions package after the fourth nuclear-weapon test, as Beijing complained that Seoul had no grounds to demand such a move while it allowed such a glaring exception. During her 16 February address to the National Assembly, Park announced that trustpolitik was finished. 'The existing approach and good intentions will by no means work', she said. 'From this moment on, the government will employ tougher and more effective measures' to achieve denuclearisation, Park continued, while attempting to protect the South from various forms of harassment from the DPRK, including terrorism and cyber attacks.

Following the fourth nuclear-weapon test, US military leaders expressed stronger concern than they previously had over the progress Pyongyang was making towards developing nuclear weapons and ballistic missiles. In early 2016, with the US election campaign well under way, the Republican Party presidential candidates took full advantage of the nuclear-weapon test to castigate the Obama administration – and particularly former secretary of state and leading Democratic Party presidential candidate Hillary Clinton – for its failure to stop North Korea from threatening the US with a nuclear attack. Like Seoul, Washington implemented its own sanctions on the DPRK, in addition to those imposed by the UN Security Council. In June, the US Department of the Treasury designated North Korea a jurisdiction of primary money-laundering concern, a move that could largely prevent North Korean banks from accessing the international financial system. This was the most powerful sanction the US government had imposed on the DPRK. In July, Washington announced sanctions against North Korean leader Kim Jong-un personally, along with ten other North Korean officials, as punishment for their role in the regime's human-rights abuses. Pyongyang's official news agency called the move 'an open declaration of war against DPRK' and 'the worst crime that can never be pardoned'.

Military pressure on Pyongyang from Washington and Seoul noticeably increased in the first half of 2016. Although the joint US–ROK *Key Resolve* and *Foal Eagle* military exercises are held annually, their iterations in March and April 2016 were larger than any that had come before. Significantly, the exercises reportedly included simulated raids by special forces to capture North Korean nuclear facilities and to destroy the DPRK leadership – presumably in keeping with the classified Operations Plan 5015 adopted in 2015.

The fourth nuclear-weapon test also prompted China to toughen its policy on North Korea. While Beijing has publicly affirmed that it wants North Korea to denuclearise, this objective comes second to maintaining stability on the Korean Peninsula. In practice, this means preventing the collapse of the regime led by Kim Jong-un. As a consequence, China has been unwilling to exert severe pressure on the DPRK, despite the anger of Chinese leaders over Pyongyang's failure to heed their advice. Throughout 2015, Beijing continued to keep Pyongyang at arm's length. Chinese President Xi Jinping has yet to meet Kim. In October, China sent Liu Yunshan, the fifth-ranking member of the Politburo Standing Committee, to represent China at the ceremony commemorating the 70th anniversary of the Korean Workers' Party. The gesture was China's most significant show of respect since Kim became president in late 2011. Some foreign analysts concluded that Liu's visit halted a planned North Korean rocket launch. If so, the effect was temporary.

China's foreign ministry stated that the DPRK had not provided advance warning of the 6 January nuclear-weapon test. A Chinese television station reported that the resulting blast generated tremors in northeastern China, causing cracks in the grounds of a high school and forcing teachers to evacuate the building. On 5 February, Foreign Minister Wang Yi publicly warned the DPRK against a reportedly imminent rocket launch. North Korea openly defied Beijing, conducting a launch two days later. China's outrage at the incident was reflected in the sanctions package devised by the UN Security Council. As had been the case following previous North Korean nuclear-weapon tests, the council haggled behind closed doors for several weeks, before unveiling Resolution 2270 on 3 March. The measure is unusually stringent, indicating a greater sense of urgency in Beijing about the need to denuclearise North Korea. It greatly restricts imports of minerals from North Korea (a crucial source of revenue for the regime); requires all UN member states to inspect DPRK cargo passing through their ports; limits the DPRK's access to the international banking system; and prohibits the sale of aviation fuel to North Korean entities. If fully enforced – especially by China – these sanctions could put Kim's government under serious strain.

Beijing continued to call for a negotiated settlement, proposing parallel negotiations over both denuclearisation and a peace treaty between the DPRK and the US. The latter is a perennial objective of the DPRK, which believes that such a treaty would further its demands for the withdrawal of US forces from South Korea and the dissolution of the US–ROK military alliance, including the accompanying guarantees of extended nuclear deterrence. For this reason, as well as North Korea's proven unwillingness to negotiate over its nuclear weapons in good faith, neither Washington nor Seoul seriously considered the Chinese proposal.

North Korean belligerence complicates China–ROK relations

Beijing and Seoul had been growing closer throughout 2015. During China's September 2015 parade to commemorate the 70th anniversary of the end of the Second World War, Park sat near Xi, with only Russian President Vladimir Putin between them, while DPRK representative Choe Ryong-hae sat near the end of a row of minor dignitaries. Chinese and ROK legislators also consulted on a plan for their navies to conduct a joint anti-piracy exercise in the Gulf of Aden. To some observers, it appeared that Seoul was moving into Beijing's orbit.

Yet, with the fourth nuclear-weapon test, the ROK moved decisively in favour of deploying the Terminal High Altitude Area Defense (THAAD) system, a serious irritant for China. Washington wants to deploy THAAD in the ROK to help defend against approximately 1,000 North Korean missiles that could hit the South. China has strongly opposed the move, stating that it would 'undermine China's security interests', as defence spokesman Wu Qian put it. Although THAAD is built to shoot down missiles in their terminal phase (rather than in the early or middle stages of flight), Beijing apparently worries that THAAD's X-band radar could detect ICBM launches inside Chinese territory, potentially weakening its nuclear deterrent in relation to the US. Moreover, opposition politicians in South Korea have complained that THAAD would fail to stop a DPRK missile attack, fray the ROK's relationship with China and deepen South Korean dependence on the US. In the months leading up to the fourth nuclear-weapon test, Seoul said that it was undecided about THAAD, claiming that Washington had made no official request for the system's deployment.

However, in late January 2016, ROK Minister of Defense Han Min-koo hinted that his country was moving towards the deployment of THAAD. Beijing reiterated its opposition, with the Chinese ambassador to South Korea stating that years of carefully cultivated ROK–China relations 'could be destroyed in an instant' if Seoul went ahead. Park's government proceeded anyway, and the US and the ROK jointly announced in July that the system would be deployed. The Chinese responded with boilerplate criticism, reflecting their awareness that the battle was lost months earlier. Yet THAAD still faced domestic opposition in South Korea.

Relations between South Korea and Japan underwent a modest improvement due to the unifying effect of a common enemy. The South Korean and Japanese foreign ministers announced in December 2015 that they had resolved the issue of Japanese forces' sexual enslavement of Korean women during the Second World War. Tokyo agreed to provide ¥1 billion (US$9.2m) to fund a Korean foundation that would assist surviving victims, and Japanese Prime Minister Shinzo Abe telephoned Park to offer yet another Japanese apology. Moreover, following the fourth nuclear-weapon test, Japan, the ROK and the US declared that they planned to increase their efforts to share military intelligence related to North Korea. They held a joint missile-defence exercise off Hawaii in June 2016. The undertaking marked a cautious revival of Japan–ROK security cooperation (albeit in partnership with Washington) after a proposed bilateral agreement to share defence intelligence crumbled in 2012, following intense criticism from South Korean citizens.

Despite the external turmoil he caused, Kim appeared to be firmly in control of the DPRK. Although he is notorious for ordering the execution of high-ranking leaders, several senior figures thought to have been purged returned to public view during the year. Much speculation attended Kim's call for a congress of the Workers' Party of Korea in May 2016. Since this would be the first official meeting of the entire DPRK political elite in 36 years, it might have signalled Kim's intent to announce a major change of course. But the meeting proved uneventful: Kim received the new title of chairman of the party, but there were no significant changes to domestic or foreign policy. During a long speech that praised the country's nuclear-weapons programme, Kim put forward the idea of North–South military talks to ease tension between the sides. The gesture was unusual because Pyongyang typically disparages Seoul as a puppet government and demands bilateral talks with Washington. Nonetheless, the ROK government immediately dismissed the proposal as meaningless given that the North was unwilling to discuss denuclearisation.

In contrast, in April 2016, South Korea held a pivotal National Assembly election that weakened Park's position. Only a few months before the vote, her domestic rivals appeared to be in disarray, with the main opposition party splitting in December over a factional dispute. Park's conservative Saenuri Party seemed poised for a decisive victory, with some analysts arguing that it had a chance to gain a 180-seat super-majority in the 300-seat legislature. But such assessments underestimated the electorate's dissatisfaction with the economic programme implemented by Park. Saenuri emerged from the polls with only 122 seats, while liberal opposition groups the Minjoo Party and the People's Party won 123 and 38 seats respectively. Since South Korean presidents are allowed only one term and Park no longer had the legislative support to push forward her domestic agenda, some commentators pronounced her a lame duck despite the fact that her tenure would not end until February 2018. Barring a dramatic policy change by Pyongyang, North–South relations seem likely to remain locked in a cold war in the interim, given the deep hostility between the Park government and the Kim regime. However, the 2016 legislative-election result increases the chance that the ROK's next president will be relatively liberal, and perhaps more willing to offer concessions to Pyongyang.

These developments had a variety of effects on regional security. On the positive side, Seoul's show of resolve during the aftermath of the landmine incident probably decreased the chance that Pyongyang would return to its previous tactic of extorting concessions through lethal provocations, a potential trigger for war.

Seoul also confirmed the limits to its accommodation of Beijing. The ROK's planned deployment of THAAD strengthened its alliance with the US, demonstrated impatience with the lack of effective Chinese action to alter Pyongyang's behaviour, and expressed the will to stand up for South Korean interests despite pressure from Beijing. China's sharp reaction to the THAAD announcement reminded Seoul of the perils of becoming vulnerable to domination by China.

Japan, the ROK and the US were closing ranks in the face of a growing challenge from North Korea, while Beijing called for negotiations without preconditions and viewed regional security cooperation as 'anti-China'. Yet China drew closer to the US–ROK position on North Korea. The DPRK's provocations and steadily advancing weapons programmes also undercut important Chinese interests by increasing the possibility of war on the peninsula and creating opportunities for the US to display strategic leadership.

Overall, the regional security environment continued to deteriorate. North Korea spent another year insisting that its status as a nuclear-weapons state was permanent and non-negotiable, while DPRK technicians moved closer to fielding a reliable nuclear-armed ballistic missile. The North's drive for a nuclear-missile capability has only negative effects, acting as a potential source of nuclear technology and material for terrorist groups and rogue states. Its possession of nuclear weapons also strengthened the arguments of the minority of South Korean politicians and opinion-makers who believed that the ROK should acquire a matching capability. Both Beijing and Washington are strongly opposed to such a development, not least because it would increase the likelihood that Japan would follow suit. In the meantime, Pyongyang has failed to enhance its security, due to the growing international pressure created by its nuclear aspirations and threats. In view of this, the DPRK's nuclear-weapons and missile advances increasingly appear to have achieved only pyrrhic victories.

Southeast Asia: the South China Sea challenge

Developments in the South China Sea were dominated by two issues in the year to mid-2016. The first was the completion of China's reclamation activities on seven features in the Spratly Islands, and the activation of facilities on these artificial islands, enabling the People's Liberation Army Navy (PLAN) and the China Coast Guard (CCG) to increase their presence in the South China Sea. The development generated further tension with the other claimants and stakeholders in the sea – especially the United States, which began using warships and aircraft to challenge China's jurisdictional claims.

The second major issue was the decision by the Permanent Court of Arbitration (PCA) at The Hague that it had jurisdiction to rule on a case submitted by the Philippines in January 2013 to challenge the legality of China's claims in the South China Sea. In anticipation of the PCA's ruling on 12 July 2016, China and the US sought to rally international opinion in support of their respective positions. Rodrigo Duterte's victory in the May 2016 Philippine presidential elections compounded uncertainty about the impact of the ruling on the dispute, as he had issued contradictory statements on the South China Sea during his campaign.

It became increasingly clear that the disagreement transcended issues of territorial sovereignty over tiny atolls, maritime jurisdiction and access to natural resources, and that the South China Sea was the principal arena of strategic competition between China and the US in Asia. The ten-member Association of Southeast Asian Nations (ASEAN) largely failed to manage the dispute and lower tension among the parties. As a consequence, its actions appeared to be ever less relevant to events in the sea.

In April 2016, Singaporean Minister of Defence Ng Eng Hen articulated the concerns of many senior officials and analysts in Southeast

Asia that, in an era of rising defence budgets (partly driven by increasing tension over maritime disputes) and the emergence of more capable armed forces in Asia, 'miscalculation or missteps [could] precipitate serious tensions and even physical conflicts'.

Artificial islands, FONOPs and growing US–China competition

In June 2015, Beijing announced that it had ceased reclamation activities in the Spratlys. The US government reported that, since beginning work in late 2013, China had reclaimed 3,200 acres of land and transformed seven tiny features into artificial islands. Beijing tried to counter criticism of these activities by arguing that it had the sovereign right to undertake them. The primary purpose of the multibillion-dollar construction effort, China argued, was to improve the living conditions of personnel stationed on the atolls, as well as to provide international public goods such as lighthouses, search-and-rescue facilities, and meteorological outposts.

However, publicly available satellite imagery revealed that the projects under construction on the artificial islands – which included airstrips, helipads, barracks, radars and other surveillance equipment – appeared to be primarily designed to support military operations. The US intelligence community estimated that, once completed, the infrastructure on the islands would enable China to deploy important military capabilities, facilitating operations by the Chinese navy and the CCG throughout the South China Sea. In January 2016, the airfield on Fiery Cross Reef began accepting civilian flights, followed by military aircraft a few months later. The facilities on the artificial islands were expected to become fully operational by the end of 2016.

In responding to international criticism of its actions in the South China Sea, the Chinese government contended that it had legitimate maritime rights in the area, while underplaying the tensions, which it blamed on other parties. Furthermore, while China insisted that its sovereignty over the South China Sea was 'indisputable', and that it had to uphold territorial integrity and legitimate rights and interests, the country also claimed to be resolving the dispute through peaceful dialogue and negotiations. Senior Chinese officials repeatedly characterised the situation in the South China Sea as stable, provided reassurances that freedom of navigation was not under threat and promised not to militarise the dispute – a pledge made publicly by President Xi Jinping to his US counterpart, Barack Obama, when they met in Washington in September 2015. China viewed itself as acting with self-restraint while other countries – especially the US and its allies, such as Japan and the Philippines – heightened tension and militarised the dispute.

As the reclamation projects advanced, the dispute led to growing rancour between Washington and Beijing. Senior US officials appeared to address China when they stated that the claimants should clarify their claims in keeping with international law; pursue their claims without resorting to force, bullying or coercion; uphold freedom of navigation and overflight; and cease unilateral, destabilising actions such as reclamation work. They also warned China not to undertake reclamation work at Scarborough Shoal – effectively annexed by the country in 2012 following a showdown with the Philippines – or to declare an Air Defence Identification Zone over the South China Sea, as it had over parts of the East China Sea in 2013.

In response to China's island-building and generally more assertive behaviour in the South China Sea, the US took steps to deter further Chinese encroachment. Washington attempted to bolster its leadership and credibility, exercised its maritime rights and strengthened the military capabilities of its allies and partners in the region.

In a highly anticipated move, the US conducted three freedom of navigation operations (FONOPs) in the South China Sea by sailing warships within 12 nautical miles of features occupied by China: at Subi Reef in October 2015; at Triton Island (in the Paracel Islands) in January 2016; and at Fiery Cross Reef in May 2016. In addition, the US also conducted several freedom of overflight operations above the South China Sea. The purpose of these naval and air missions was to demonstrate the Obama administration's pledge that the US military would 'continue to fly, sail, and operate wherever international law allows'. The FONOPs were largely symbolic, and although China criticised them as 'provocative' and a violation of its sovereignty, Chinese warships restricted themselves to shadowing the US naval vessels and warning the vessels to leave the area. The US indicated that the frequency and complexity of future FONOPs would increase. Japan, Australia and several other countries reportedly considered conducting their own FONOPs. If the

Chinese military adopts a more robust response to future FONOPs, the risk of a dangerous incident at sea or in the air will rise. These risks came into sharp relief in May and June 2016, when the US stated that Chinese fighter aircraft had conducted unsafe intercepts of US surveillance flights over the South and East China seas.

The US also stepped up capacity-building support for, and strengthened defence ties with, key Southeast Asian countries. For example, under the Department of Defense's Maritime Security Initiative, the US has earmarked US$425 million over five years for Indonesia, Malaysia, the Philippines and Vietnam to improve their maritime-domain awareness. This was intended to enhance these countries' ability to monitor and respond to Chinese naval activity in contested waters. Washington paid greater attention to the Philippines and Vietnam – the countries most affected by Chinese assertiveness in the South China Sea over the preceding five years – than to other Southeast Asian states. In March 2016, the US and Philippines began conducting joint naval patrols in the South China Sea; and, under the Enhanced Defense Cooperation Agreement (approved by the Philippine Supreme Court in January 2016), the US military would maintain a rotational presence at five military bases in the Philippines. During a trip to Hanoi in May 2016, President Obama announced that the US would lift a decades-old arms embargo on Vietnam, paving the way for closer defence cooperation between the countries. In December 2015, Singapore agreed to host rotational deployments of US P-8A *Poseidon* aircraft, which are designed for maritime surveillance and anti-submarine warfare. Washington has also tried to promote ASEAN solidarity on the South China Sea. In February 2016, at the conclusion of a summit held in Sunnylands, Obama and all ten ASEAN leaders issued a declaration that reaffirmed their commitment to the peaceful resolution of disputes through legal and diplomatic processes, freedom of navigation and overflight, and non-militarisation and self-restraint.

The US and China repeatedly accused each other of provocative behaviour, militarising the dispute and raising tension throughout the year to mid-2016. In high-level meetings, senior US and Chinese officials talked past each other, merely reiterating their respective positions. At the 15th IISS Shangri-La Dialogue, held in Singapore in June 2016, when US Secretary of Defense Ashton Carter remarked that through its actions

China risked creating a 'Great Wall of self-isolation', China's delegation leader, Admiral Sun Jianguo, responded that the US was interfering in the South China Sea dispute, encouraging smaller countries to 'bully' China, and that America manifested a 'Cold War mentality'. Sun ended his speech with the ominous comment that 'we do not make trouble, but we have no fear of trouble'.

Both Washington and Beijing have vital interests in the South China Sea. For the US, the dispute is about maintaining leadership and credibility in the Asia-Pacific, as well as the unimpeded operation of its military ships and aircraft. For China, it is about righting perceived historical grievances, protecting its territorial and jurisdictional claims, and – in the long term – achieving primacy in Asia by gaining strategic advantage. Accordingly, the dispute will almost certainly remain a point of contention between Washington and Beijing regardless of which candidate wins the US presidential election in November 2016.

Southeast Asian responses

The Philippines and Vietnam have been on the front-line of the disputes in the South China Sea. However, tension between Hanoi and Beijing eased somewhat. Although China again deployed the large drilling platform Haiyang Shiyou 981 into waters contested by Vietnam in January and April 2016, this action did not trigger a major crisis in bilateral relations as it had in May 2014. Nonetheless, Vietnam remained critical of China's actions in the South China Sea, and repeatedly accused Beijing of violating its sovereignty.

Relations between the Philippines and China continued on their downward spiral. Beijing continued to refuse to participate in the proceedings at the PCA, arguing that the tribunal had no jurisdiction because the case concerned issues of territorial sovereignty (on which only the International Court of Justice can adjudicate) and that China had withdrawn in 2006 from compulsory dispute resolution in matters concerning the delimitation of maritime boundaries. In July 2015, the tribunal convened a hearing on jurisdiction, and in October rejected China's arguments and ruled that it had jurisdiction. In November, the judges began examining the merits of the case. The ruling of the PCA was largely in favour of the Philippines. Specifically, the court found that 'there was no legal basis for China to claim historic rights' to resources within its 'nine-dash line'; none of the features claimed by China were capable of generating an exclusive economic zone (EEZ); China had violated the Philippines' sovereign rights in its EEZ, including through the construction of artificial islands; and China had caused 'severe harm' to the marine environment through its land-reclamation activities and construction of islands. In the run-up to the verdict, Australia, Japan, the European Union, the United Kingdom and the US called on all parties to abide by the ruling. However, China accused those countries of 'meddling' in the dispute and tried to rally international opinion in support of its own position that the dispute should be resolved bilaterally by the claimants. In mid-June, China stated that it had the support of 60 countries, although the majority of them were not maritime powers and had no stake in the dispute. Following the ruling, a Chinese foreign-ministry spokesman described the PCA as a 'law-abusing tribunal' and claimed that Beijing would not recognise the court's decision. Another spokesman described the ruling as 'illegal and invalid'.

One important uncertain factor that might influence the course of the dispute is the stance of the Duterte administration in the Philippines. An unconventional politician from Mindanao, President Duterte took office on 1 July. Discerning his policy on the South China Sea was difficult due to the contradictory statements he made during and after the election campaign: that he was willing to de-emphasise the Philippines' sovereignty claims if China financed and built a railway network in Mindanao; that China should not violate Philippine sovereignty and he would personally plant a Philippine flag on Scarborough Shoal, even at the risk of being killed; and that the claimants – together with the US, Japan and Australia – should engage in multilateral talks but, if these were unsuccessful, Manila should talk to Beijing about the joint development of resources. Duterte's policy towards the US was also unclear. Despite recognising Washington's central role in maintaining regional stability, he has indicated that the Philippines should not rely on the US in its dispute with China, and that Manila should 'chart its own course'. China reacted positively to Duterte's victory, and in a congratulatory message Xi expressed hope that the two countries could put bilateral relations back on track. In the weeks following the election, media reports suggested that the CCG had stopped harassing Philippine fishermen at Scarborough Shoal. On taking office, Duterte appointed former president Fidel Ramos to visit Beijing to start a discussion on the dispute. China appeared to be delaying any substantive moves in reaction to the PCA ruling until it had a clearer sense of whether negotiations with Duterte's administration were possible and likely to bear fruit.

Malaysia and Indonesia played unusually prominent roles in the dispute during the year to mid-2016. Both countries were forced to respond to the growing presence of Chinese fishing trawlers, supported by CCG vessels, in their EEZs: Malaysia at Luconia Shoals (100 kilometres off the Sarawak coast) and Indonesia off the Natuna Islands, whose EEZ overlaps with China's 'nine-dash line' claim. While Malaysia merely monitored the presence of Chinese fishing vessels, the Indonesian authorities moved to detain those it deemed to be fishing illegally. In March 2016, a CCG vessel intervened to prevent the Indonesians from seizing a Chinese trawler. In response to the upsurge in Chinese fishing activities in their EEZs, Indonesia and Malaysia de-emphasised the incidents as mere fishing problems rather than as part of the wider South China Sea dispute, perhaps in an attempt to preserve cordial relations with China, an important trade and investment partner. But, at the same time, they tried to address the concerns of nationalists at home by underscoring their commitment to protecting maritime rights, including by strengthening their military forces in affected areas. As the facilities on China's artificial islands become operational, and Chinese fishing fleets – protected by the CCG and the PLAN – move into southern areas of the South China Sea, Malaysia and Indonesia could be drawn further into the dispute.

ASEAN's increasing irrelevance?

As tension rose in the South China Sea, and the rhetoric between Washington and Beijing became more barbed, ASEAN expressed growing frustration at the deteriorating situation. But the organisation also struggled to maintain its unity and relevance.

At its 27th Summit, held in November 2015, ASEAN stated that it 'shared the concerns expressed by some leaders on the increased presence of military assets and the possibility of further military outposts in the South China Sea'. And at the ASEAN foreign ministers' retreat, held in February 2016, the participants commented that they

> remained seriously concerned over recent and on-going developments and took note of the concerns expressed by some members on the land reclamations and escalation of activities in the area, which had eroded trust and confidence, increased tensions and may undermine peace, security and stability in the region.

Use of the phrases 'some leaders' and 'some members' indicated differing levels of concern over China's construction of artificial islands. This lack of unity has been a perennial problem for ASEAN, one made worse by increasing tension over the past few years. In Phnom Penh in November 2012, ASEAN unity collapsed over the South China Sea and, for the first time, the leaders of the organisation's member states were unable to issue a final communiqué. Since then, ASEAN has maintained a semblance of solidarity, although there have been exceptions. For example, in November 2015, ASEAN's defence ministers – and those of its six 'dialogue partners', who make up the ASEAN Defence Ministers' Meeting–Plus – were unable to agree on a final statement. The primary disagreement was between China and the US, but divisions within ASEAN contributed to the lack of consensus.

ASEAN unity over the South China Sea is fragile and, while China did not create the divisions between claimants and non-claimants, it has repeatedly tried to exploit them for its own ends. In April 2016, Chinese Foreign Minister Wang Yi announced that it had reached a 'four-point consensus' with three ASEAN members – Cambodia, Laos and Brunei – on the South China Sea, claiming that the dispute was not an issue between ASEAN and China, and that it could only be resolved by the parties directly concerned. The diplomatic gambit was widely seen as Beijing's attempt to pre-empt a joint statement by ASEAN in support of the PCA's ruling. However, the move backfired: several senior Singaporean diplomats, including former ASEAN secretary-general Ong Keng Yong, accused Beijing of interfering in the organisation's internal affairs. More damagingly, Cambodia and Brunei denied having ever agreed to the consensus.

As the security situation in the South China Sea deteriorated, there was a loss of confidence in the conflict-management process between ASEAN and China, designed to reduce tension, build trust and foster cooperation. The sides had little to show for their continuing discussions on the implementation of the 2002 Declaration on the Conduct of Parties in the South China Sea (DoC), or the development of a legally binding Code of Conduct. In August 2015, Singapore became the country coordinator for ASEAN–China relations and, as a long-time advocate of the Code of Conduct, pledged to secure the agreement within its three-year term. As an interim measure designed to reduce the risk of conflict before the Code of Conduct was signed, Singapore suggested extending the Code for Unplanned Encounters at Sea to include the coastguard vessels that have been used by some of the claimants, especially China, to enforce their claims in the South China Sea. This non-binding set of protocols sought to prevent dangerous incidents between naval vessels, and was signed in 2014 by the 21 members of the Western Pacific Naval Symposium, including China and eight ASEAN members. However, Beijing reacted coolly to the proposal from Singapore, and there was no progress at the 11th Senior Officials Meeting on Implementing the DoC, held in Singapore in April 2016. The lack of unity within ASEAN was apparent once again at a special meeting of foreign ministers from the organisation and China, held in Yunnan Province in mid-June. ASEAN issued a statement that repeated its 'serious concerns' over land reclamation and the militarisation of the dispute, issuing a direct rebuke to China's position that the problem was not one between ASEAN and China by asserting that 'we also cannot ignore what is happening in the South China Sea'. The statement was subsequently retracted for 'urgent amendments'. A joint press conference between the Chinese and Singaporean foreign ministers was called off, and individual member states were left to issue their own statements. The incident further undermined ASEAN's credibility, as did Cambodia's decision to block any mention of the PCA ruling in the communiqué of the ASEAN Ministerial Meeting in late July 2016.

Regardless of whether they are claimants in the South China Sea, ASEAN states are highly concerned at the prospect of the growing Sino-American rivalry playing out in Southeast Asia. They are also concerned about the potential emergence of a condominium in which matters of regional security would be decided by Washington and Beijing without the participation of Southeast Asian governments. Therefore, ASEAN members endeavour to shape and control the regional security agenda, and want the major powers to defer to what the organisation called its 'centrality'. Given the current trajectory of the dispute, this aspiration appears to be increasingly divorced from reality: Sino-American strategic competition in Southeast Asia – centred on the South China Sea – is increasingly dividing and marginalising ASEAN.

ISIS and Southeast Asia

Local terrorist groups with potential links to the Islamic State, also known as ISIS or ISIL, and foreign fighters returning from Syria and Iraq, are a growing source of concern for governments in Southeast Asia. In the year to mid-2016, the region experienced an increase in apparent cross-border linkages between local jihadists, as well as between these jihadists and their counterparts in the Middle East. There were several attacks in Southeast Asia linked to ISIS or ISIS-aligned groups.

While ISIS has not announced the establishment of a Southeast Asian *wilayat* (province), the existence of capable and ideologically aligned non-state armed groups, ungoverned spaces and weak state institutions in the region – particularly in the Mindanao–Sulawesi–Sabah triangle – provide the conditions for such a declaration in the near future. Around 700–800 Southeast Asians, most of them Indonesians and Malaysians, are thought to be in Syria and Iraq. Many of them have joined the Indonesian-language Katibah Nusantara lid Daulah Islamiah (Malay Islamic Archipelago Battalion of the Islamic State), which was established in Syria in 2014. However, not all of these people are fighters; some are housewives, children or other non-combatants. At least 100 Indonesians have returned from Syria and are being monitored, according to the country's intelligence agency. The returnees cannot be prosecuted for fighting abroad under existing legislation.

The first ISIS-inspired attack in Southeast Asia, and the first major attack in Indonesia since 2009, came on 14 January 2016 in Jakarta, when four terrorists attempted to carry out a complex *fedayeen*-style attack in the centre of the capital. Four civilians were killed, as were the four attackers, while 26 others were injured. Bahrun Naim, an Indonesian member of Katibah Nusantara, planned and helped fund the attack. Naim appears to have ordered the attack to demonstrate his credentials as a candidate for the leadership of a potential Southeast Asian ISIS affiliate, as part of a process of 'outbidding' other rivals that might result in further attacks. For instance, three men arrested on 8 June 2016 for planning suicide bombings in Surabaya, on the Indonesian island of Java, reportedly have links to Abu Jandal, another Indonesian in Syria.

Naim is associated with Abu Wardah, better known as Santoso, the leader of Mujahedin Indonesia Timur (MIT). The group, which has sworn allegiance to ISIS, is mainly concentrated in Poso on the northern Indonesian island of Sulawesi. Jakarta regards the group as a major threat, and has intensified operations against it. By May 2016, Santoso and his followers were reportedly cornered in an area of five square kilometres, encircled by more than 2,000 police and military personnel. In late June, Indonesia's national police chief, General Badrodin Haiti, said Santoso 'must' be captured before the scheduled end of the operation in August. On 19 July, Coordinating Minister for Political, Security and Legal Affairs Luhut Pandjaitan announced that Santoso had been killed the previous day. But the MIT is also active elsewhere in Indonesia. On 21 December 2015, the security forces had arrested nine suspected terrorists and former Jemaah Islamiah members, including a potential suicide bomber, who were allegedly planning attacks in Jakarta on Christmas Day and New Year's Eve.

Indonesia has detained many terrorism suspects, but its deradicalisation programmes have been largely ineffective. In August 2015, the country's officials stated that 90 of 600 former inmates convicted of terrorism offences had resumed militant activities. Saud Usman Nasution, head of Indonesia's national counter-terrorism agency, announced in September 2015 that 'cooperative' terrorist convicts would be separated from those deemed to be 'radical'. The clerics Abu Bakar Bashir and Aman Abdurrahman – a central figure in the Indonesian jihadist network – have made pronouncements from, and met associates in, their cells for some time. But the government attempted to curtail this behaviour in February 2016, moving them from Nusa Kambangan prison, off the southern coast of Java, to other jails.

Despite these developments in Indonesia, the southern Philippine island of Mindanao remained the place in which a Southeast Asian ISIS affiliate was most likely to be established. The underdeveloped region is home to capable jihadist groups who have pledged allegiance to ISIS. Militants from Indonesia, Malaysia and other countries are frequently in contact with Philippines-based groups, underlining the transnational nature of the threat. On 27 November 2015, eight members of the ISIS-aligned Ansar al-Khilafah Philippines died in a clash with security forces in Palimbang, in Mindanao. One of these figures was Ibrahim Ali Sucipto, who allegedly had links to Jemaah Islamiah and the MIT. A second Indonesian MIT member also died in the battle. A Moroccan fighting with the Abu Sayyaf Group (ASG), Mohammad Khattab, was killed in a large clash with security forces on the Sulu Sea island of Basilan in April 2016. The Philippine armed forces claimed that Khattab was trying to link local groups with international terrorist organisations, and ISIS used its news agency, Amaq, to declare that it had carried out the attack. Isnilon Hapilon, the ASG leader in Basilan, has also sworn allegiance to ISIS, as have other leaders in his group.

Furthermore, many Moro Muslims in Mindanao were disappointed by the government's failure to conclude a peace process with insurgent group the Moro Islamic Liberation Front (MILF) in 2015. The organisation's leadership, which remained committed to maintaining its ceasefire with Manila, warned of 'growing restlessness and frustration' in the ranks that could cause renewed violence and prompt its members to join extremist groups. Ansar al-Khilafah Philippines is led by former MILF commander Muhammad Jaafar Maguid, also known as Commander Tokboy. And the Bangsamoro Islamic Freedom Fighters (BIFF), a MILF splinter group opposed to negotiations, has also declared its allegiance to ISIS. The jihadist–criminal Maute group, led by former MILF members, engaged in clashes with security forces in February 2016 in Butig, in Lanao del Sur, where it raised the ISIS flag.

In Malaysia, the security forces foiled several apparent terrorist plots. Ten Malaysians with suspected links to ISIS, including five members of the security forces, were arrested in August 2015. Another Malaysian arrested in August was an auxiliary police officer working as a luggage screener at Kuala Lumpur International Airport, a position in which he could potentially allow explosives to be brought on board an aircraft. Dozens of other suspects were also arrested.

Malaysian Defence Minister Hishammuddin Hussein said in November 2015 that he and several other senior government figures were on an ISIS kidnapping-target list. The version of the group he referred to likely comprised radicalised locals or even members of Katibah Nusantara. While often less capable than jihadists in the Middle East, remotely radicalised terrorists inspired by ISIS pose a significant risk in Southeast Asia, as they do in Europe and the United States. A Saudi Arabian preacher, Sheikh Aaidh al-Qarni, was shot and injured in the Philippines in March 2016. While the attacker's motive was unclear, *Dabiq*, the ISIS magazine, had identified Qarni as a target for lone-wolf attackers.

There is also a less obvious transnational link with ethnic Uighur Muslims from the restive Chinese region of Xinjiang. Two Uighurs were among the four people arrested after a small bomb attack in central Bandung, in West Java, on New Year's Day, and two Uighur members of the MIT were killed in a March 2016 battle with the security forces. One of the reasons for this development is that many Uighurs who flee Xinjiang travel through Southeast Asian countries, particularly Malaysia and Thailand. Like Southeast Asians, some Uighurs also go to Syria to fight, and Poso may be a waypoint where they receive training. The 17 August 2015 bombing at Bangkok's Erawan Shrine also had a Uighur connection, although the Thai government claimed that the assault was unrelated to jihadism.

While terrorism is not an existential threat in Southeast Asia, Singaporean Minister of Defence Ng Eng Hen has described the phenomenon as a 'gathering storm'. The risk of transnational terrorism in the region significantly increased in the year to mid-2016, raising the real possibility that ISIS would establish an affiliate in the region. Such a move could change the strategy of Southeast Asian jihadist groups by increasing their coordination with one another, while helping them attract more funding and recruits. However, the declaration of an affiliate would also prompt further coordination in international efforts to counter the threat. Targeted security operations, increased intelligence cooperation, engagement with Muslim communities, the reform of terrorism legislation and economic development will all be vital tools in these efforts. By changing the conditions that have permitted or encouraged the growth of jihadist and criminal groups, Southeast Asian governments could reduce the likelihood that they will join the ISIS network.

Australia: ambiguous policies on Asian security

Australia's domestic politics continued to be characterised by instability and unpredictability. Having won a narrow victory in a leadership challenge within the Liberal Party in February 2015, then-prime minister Tony Abbott tried to silence continuing criticism of his governing style and unimpressive public-approval ratings. However, by mid-September, Abbott had spent his political capital and was defeated by his long-standing party rival, Malcolm Turnbull, in another party-leadership ballot. Turnbull, the fifth prime minister since 2007, promised to lead a stable government and end the Liberals' internal turmoil.

Yet popular enthusiasm for the new prime minister cooled much more quickly than many commentators anticipated. Hopes that Turnbull would return to a more moderate conservative political agenda quickly faded as he pandered to his party's right wing. Facing a loss of public confidence, Turnbull called for early elections to be held on 2 July 2016, in the hope of securing a clear majority for the coalition government and his leadership. The campaign proved difficult for his Liberal–National coalition, as the opposition Australian Labor Party closed what had seemed an insurmountable gap in popular support. Nonetheless, the coalition won by a narrow margin, and a new cabinet led by Turnbull was sworn in on 19 July.

However, while the Turnbull government had to invest significant energy in domestic political affairs, it nonetheless made important decisions on security and defence policy. Abbott had stressed the perceived threat from domestic terrorist attacks by Islamic extremists, but the new prime minister toned down governmental rhetoric on the theme, placing less emphasis on Australia's continuing contribution to the multinational military campaign against the Islamic State, also known as ISIS or ISIL, in the Middle East. Turnbull's government gave greater attention to cyber security, announcing in April 2016 that it would allocate A$230 million (US$175m) to implementing a new Cyber Security Strategy, which included a commitment to strengthening Australia's offensive cyber capabilities as a means of deterring cyber attacks.

New defence White Paper and future submarine

The government published a new defence White Paper in February 2016. This had a more pessimistic strategic outlook for Australia than its predecessor, due to the assessment that there was a serious challenge to the international 'rules-based order' – a term used 56 times in the document. The White Paper pointed to the Asia-Pacific as particularly vulnerable to the threat. The document highlighted serious 'points of friction' between the United States and China, pointing to the expectation that the South China Sea 'will continue to provide a source of tension that could undermine stability'. It also directly criticised China's recent actions in the region's oceans, stating that 'Australia is particularly concerned by the unprecedented pace and scale of China's land reclamation activities' in the South China Sea. The paper's strong wording on China drew criticism from Beijing, which accused Australia of having a 'Cold War mentality'.

As well as making a commitment to strengthening its military alliance with the US and to reinvigorating regional defence engagements, the White Paper laid out ambitious plans for a more capable Australian Defence Force. The 'fully costed' capability agenda, to be paid for out of a defence budget that would increase to 2% of GDP by 2020, included 12 'regionally superior' submarines, and nine 'future frigates' optimised for anti-submarine warfare. In combination with the acquisition of three *Hobart*-class air-warfare destroyers, two 26,000-tonne *Canberra*-class amphibious-assault ships and 12 offshore patrol vessels, the new submarines and frigates will provide Australia with strong naval capabilities. The White Paper also announced that the government would enhance the maritime-patrol capability of the Royal Australian Air Force (RAAF) through the procurement of 15 P-8A *Poseidon* aircraft and seven MQ-4C *Triton* unmanned aerial vehicles during the 2020s. It also made clear that Australia still intended to improve the RAAF's strike and air-combat capability by acquiring at least 72 F-35A Joint Strike Fighters from 2020 onwards.

In April 2016, the government made the long-awaited decision on the procurement of Australia's future submarines. Canberra selected the French company DCNS – which had engaged in a 15-month competitive evaluation process along with the German company TKMS and the government of Japan – to be the design partner for the long-range, diesel-electric boats that Australia sought to procure. DCNS submitted a design based on the French navy's 5,000-tonne *Barracuda*-class nuclear attack submarine. The A$50-billion (US$38bn), decades-long investment in the submarine programme will be the most expensive and technologically complex in Australia's history. It will involve significant technological innovation, particularly in redesigning the *Barracuda* class as a diesel-electric submarine.

Aside from the technological challenges of the submarine programme, Canberra also faced the prospect of a cooling in its defence relations with Tokyo. The Abbott government had started negotiations with Japan as a potential sole-source supplier for the submarine programme, and Japanese Prime Minister Shinzo Abe expended considerable political capital in persuading a reluctant domestic defence industry to support the project. Facing a domestic crisis over his leadership, Abbott then agreed to the competitive evaluation process, dragging Japan's government into an open competition for which it was ill-prepared. Worse still, Tokyo only found out through a leak to the Australian media that it had lost the bid. In response, Japanese Minister of Defense Gen Nakatani called the decision 'deeply regrettable' and asked the Australian government to explain itself. Geopolitical factors in the Asia-Pacific are likely to encourage the sides to repair their defence relationship. But, in the short term at least, trust has been lost on the Japanese side due to Canberra's mishandling of the issue.

Alliance politics and regional defence engagement

When Turnbull became prime minister, there were doubts over the strength of his government's commitment to the US alliance. This was because his emphasis on Australia's international economic relations suggested that he might instead prioritise strong links with China, the country's leading trade and investment partner. In particular, it was unclear what his position would be on the intensifying contest between

Washington and Beijing in the South China Sea. The November 2015 Asia-Pacific Economic Cooperation (APEC) summit in Manila provided a first glimpse of his approach to the issue. There, Turnbull reaffirmed that Australia saw eye to eye with the US on the importance of freedom of navigation in the South China Sea, but he refused to say whether his government would contribute to freedom of navigation operations (FONOPs) by sending warships to the area. He adopted a firmer tone at the East Asia Summit in Kuala Lumpur a few days later, describing China's action in the South China Sea as 'counterproductive'. In December 2015, responding to a flight close to Chinese-occupied features in the South China Sea by an RAAF P-3 maritime-patrol aircraft, a Chinese newspaper warned that 'it would be shame if a plane fell from the sky'.

In subsequent months, Turnbull repeated his message about China's assertiveness in the seas of the Asia-Pacific. Even during his first visit to China in April 2016, accompanied by an unprecedentedly large delegation of more than 1,000 Australian business leaders, Turnbull stressed that Beijing should uphold the rule of law. However, rhetoric aside, Canberra acted cautiously. Indeed, the Australian government insisted repeatedly that RAAF surveillance flights over the South China Sea, as part of *Operation Gateway*, should not be classified as FONOPs. Australia did not claim to have conducted any such operations, indicating that Turnbull remained concerned about upsetting relations with Beijing.

Australia's policy towards the US alliance was also ambiguous. The defence White Paper was a case in point. The document made clear the country's intention to hedge against a more assertive China with the alliance as a cornerstone of this strategy: major defence-equipment and force-structure decisions aimed at facilitating closer cooperation with the US armed forces, including in the seas of Southeast Asia. These measures included additional investment in space- and ground-based intelligence, reconnaissance and surveillance systems; enhanced cyber cooperation with the US; and efforts to ensure that the future submarine would have a 'high degree of interoperability' with US capabilities.

But the White Paper used guarded language in describing measures to strengthen the rotational presence of US forces in Australia. For instance, unlike the 2013 White Paper, the new document did not refer to Australia's interest in exploring additional naval cooperation with the US by upgrading facilities such as HMAS Stirling, Australia's Indian Ocean naval base. It also failed to mention joint funding to develop infrastructure that could accommodate a full US Marine Air–Ground Task Force of around 2,500 personnel and equipment rotating through Darwin. Instead, the White Paper noted that the task force's full rotations would only begin in 2020, four years later than originally planned. In June 2016, Australia and the US announced that they were still engaged in negotiations over cost-sharing arrangements for the new infrastructure.

The countries' alliance relationship was also complicated by the Northern Territory government's November 2015 decision, approved by the Department of Defence in Canberra, to offer the Chinese company Landbridge a 99-year lease on the port of Darwin, which will be used by the US marines rotating through the territory. To the consternation of its American ally, Canberra did not discuss the lease arrangements with US officials, despite the fact that Landbridge has direct ties to China's People's Liberation Army. In response, US President Barack Obama publicly chided Turnbull, saying 'let us know next time', when they met at APEC in November. Moreover, reactions in the US policy community indicated its uncertainty about whether the Landbridge lease was an aberration or pointed to a more fundamental shift in Australia's attitude towards the alliance. In a report on the lease published in April 2016, the US Senate Standing Committee on Economics concluded that there were 'serious concerns' about the foreign-investment framework behind the decision.

The Turnbull government's regional defence diplomacy also had a mixed record. In her first major defence-policy speech, delivered at the Australian Strategic Policy Institute in April 2016, new defence minister Marise Payne proclaimed that regional defence engagement was very much in her country's 'DNA'. However, the government made little progress in restoring Australia's critical defence relationship with Indonesia, which had been damaged by Jakarta's execution of two Australian drug smugglers in 2015. The third Australia–Indonesia Foreign and Defence Ministerial Meeting, held in December 2015, failed to generate any major bilateral defence initiatives. Moreover, by mid-2016, the Australian government had yet to make an effort to advance bilateral defence ties with Japan in the wake of the submarine decision.

Nonetheless, Canberra developed one important aspect of its bilateral defence relations in Asia. Australia and Singapore announced in May 2016 that they would establish a Comprehensive Strategic Partnership, an initiative begun by the Abbott government. The countries also signed an agreement on providing the Singapore Armed Forces with increased access to Australian military training areas, paving the way for up to 14,000 Singaporean personnel to train in Australia for as many as 18 weeks per year. To that end, Canberra and Singapore agreed jointly to develop major military training facilities at Shoalwater Bay and Townsville in northern Australia, which Singapore would fully fund at a cost of around A\$2.25bn (US\$1.7bn).

Despite this bright spot, some observers saw Payne's absence from the 15th IISS Shangri-La Dialogue in Singapore in June 2016 – after 14 consecutive years of attendance by Australian defence ministers – as not just a wasted diplomatic opportunity but also an indication that she may have wanted to avoid public contention with Beijing over the South China Sea. Less than a year into Turnbull's tenure as prime minister, his government gave the impression that it preferred to stay on the sidelines of an increasingly contested Asia-Pacific security environment.

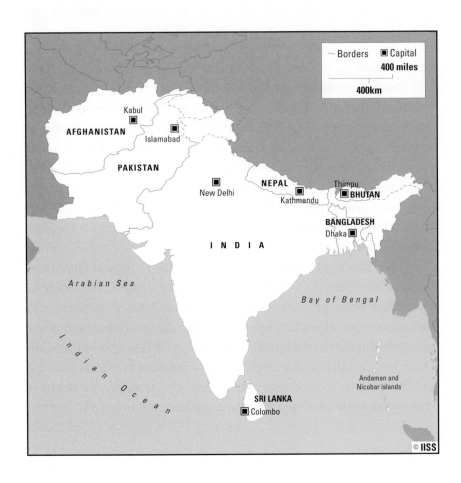

Borders ■ Capital
400 miles
400km

Kabul ■

AFGHANISTAN

Islamabad ■

PAKISTAN

New Delhi ■

NEPAL

Kathmandu ■

Thimpu
■ **BHUTAN**

BANGLADESH

Dhaka ■

I N D I A

Arabian Sea

Bay of Bengal

I n d i a n   O c e a n

Andaman and
Nicobar islands

SRI LANKA
■ Colombo

© IISS

Chapter 5

South Asia and Afghanistan

By mid-2016, Indian Prime Minister Narendra Modi had made official visits to nearly 40 countries in two years. While his efforts had the immediate effect of raising India's global profile and emphasising his commitment to diaspora communities, they centred on substantive policies designed to strengthen the country's economy. And Modi appeared to be succeeding: India's GDP grew by 7.6% in 2015–16, a rate higher than that of any other large country. Moreover, foreign direct investment – essential for modernising India's worn-out infrastructure – grew by 30%, to US$40 billion, in the same period (with more than US$420bn pledged to future projects). Relations with the United States deepened as Modi made his fourth visit to the country as prime minister in June 2016, finalising the text of a much-delayed defence-logistics agreement. The same month, India became a member of the Missile Technology Control Regime, a privilege that it had previously been denied.

India implemented its 'Act East' policy through enhanced maritime-security cooperation with Japan and the formation of a trilateral ministerial group with Tokyo and Washington. Following visits to Malaysia, Japan and China, Indian Minister of Defence Manohar Parrikar travelled to Singapore and Vietnam in June 2016. There, Parrikar addressed the IISS Shangri-La Dialogue, established a new India–Singapore defence ministers' dialogue and enhanced defence and maritime ties with Vietnam. Meanwhile, a flotilla of Indian Navy ships visited Vietnam, the Philippines, Japan and South Korea, and participated in another round of the India–US–Japan *Malabar* naval exercises off the coast of Okinawa. India also conducted in February the *International Fleet Review* exercise in the Bay of Bengal, involving 95 ships and 60 aircraft from 50 countries.

The Gulf became a new area of focus, as Modi visited both Saudi Arabia and Iran to balance India's relations with the rivals, amid growing tension in the region. India targeted Pakistan by making key pledges on counter-terrorism cooperation with the United Arab Emirates, Saudi Arabia and Qatar. The most significant pledge was that with the UAE, which concerned extraordinary cooperation on counter-extremism and counter-terrorism, providing the template for similar joint statements with Saudi Arabia and Qatar. New Delhi and Abu Dhabi also sought to increase bilateral trade by 60% over five years, and the latter announced its intent to invest US$75bn in India. Parrikar's visit to the UAE in May was linked with the arrival of Indian Navy ships in Dubai, and the vessels subsequently engaged in exercises with UAE forces. India and the UAE also established an annual policy dialogue to discuss issues related to peace and security in their regions.

India planned to invest US$500 million in the Iranian port city of Chabahar, creating a transport link to Afghanistan and Central Asia that would bypass Pakistan, enhance economic cooperation in the region and respond to China's construction of port facilities at Gwadar. To that end, New Delhi signed in May 2016 a deal on the port with Tehran and Kabul. India and Iran also set up a bilateral joint working group on defence cooperation, which would be led by the countries' top defence officials.

At the same time, Modi worked to improve the economic relationship between New Delhi and Beijing, even as Indian lawmakers grew more wary of Chinese assertiveness in South Asia. Meanwhile, there continued to be significant friction between New Delhi and Islamabad.

India's troubled relationships with Pakistan and China

India's 'neighbourhood first' policy, intended to make the most of its influence in South Asia, paid few dividends beyond Bangladesh and Bhutan. This was due to the complex domestic politics of countries in the region, their historical suspicion of India as the dominant regional power, the influence of Indian domestic and ethnic politics, and increasing Chinese engagement with the region. Equally important was the failure to meet expectations generated by Modi's initial outreach to other leaders in the South Asian Association for Regional Cooperation (SAARC), after he invited them to his May 2014 inauguration ceremony. Indeed, in the cases of Pakistan and Nepal, relations with India deteriorated.

India's major security threat remained the terrorism emanating from Pakistan, on which Modi took a tougher position than his predecessor. India deliberately intensified what it called 'retaliatory' firing across the Line of Control in the disputed region of Kashmir and the international border, with each side blaming the other for ceasefire violations, as well as the deaths of civilians and troops. New Delhi also refused to resume the stalled bilateral dialogue between the sides, which the Modi government had inherited from its predecessor, until Islamabad took action against anti-India militants based in Pakistani territory.

A meeting between the Indian and Pakistani national-security advisers scheduled for August 2015 was cancelled, with New Delhi refusing to allow the Pakistani official to meet the leaders of the Kashmiri separatist group All Parties Hurriyat Conference, or to discuss anything other than terrorism. Tensions rose on 2 January 2016, when a terrorist attack on the Indian Air Force base in Pathankot led to the deaths of seven Indian security personnel and four Pakistani militants. India blamed the Pakistan-based militant group Jaysh-e-Mohammad (JeM) for the assault, and regarded Pakistan's intelligence agency, Inter-Services Intelligence (ISI), as complicit. New Delhi sought to arrest the members of the JeM thought to be involved in the attack, including its leader, Masood Azhar. Although a senior Indian official stated in June 2016 that the investigation failed to discover evidence linking the attack to the Pakistani authorities, this was quickly contradicted by the Indian foreign ministry, which commented that Pakistani nationals had been involved.

In a departure from past practice, Islamabad accepted that the militants were Pakistani (although it did not identify a particular group as responsible) and agreed to begin an official investigation into the attack. It denied that the government or the ISI had been involved. Islamabad also detained several JeM operatives, reportedly on other charges, but not Azhar, who was believed to be in protective custody in Pakistan. The arrest of an alleged Indian spy in the Pakistani province of Balochistan in March 2016 further strained bilateral relations. Islamabad accused the man, a retired Indian naval officer, of orchestrating terrorist attacks in Pakistan, a charge denied by New Delhi.

Yet, even as India refused to resume the stalled bilateral dialogue, it maintained channels of communication with Pakistan. Modi and Pakistani Prime Minister Nawaz Sharif met on the sidelines of the July 2015 Shanghai Cooperation Organisation summit in Ufa – scheduling there the August meeting between their national-security advisers – and again on the sidelines of the UN Climate Change Conference in Paris the following November. The latter discussion led to surprise talks between the Pakistani and Indian national-security advisers and foreign secretaries on 6 December in Bangkok, where the sides attempted to restart the stalled dialogue. Modi subsequently also made an impromptu visit to Lahore on 25 December to meet with Prime Minister Sharif – an act that, believed to be perceived as provocative by elements within the Pakistani security establishment, may have led to the attack in Pathankot.

New Delhi was restrained in its response to the assault, as it had been in reaction to an attack in Gurdaspur the previous July, despite the fact that both took place outside Kashmir. Controversially, India permitted a five-member Pakistani joint investigative team, which included an ISI official, to visit parts of Pathankot Air Base in late March. Even as India awaited an invitation for a reciprocal investigative visit to Pakistan, the Indian national-security adviser continued to speak to his counterpart in Pakistan, and to the Pakistani high commissioner to India. The Indian foreign minister and foreign secretary also travelled to Pakistan for multilateral meetings in March and December 2015, and the Pakistani foreign secretary visited India in April the following year. There would be another opportunity to ease tensions in November 2016, during a meeting of SAARC – the sole region-wide organisation focusing on economic and political cooperation – in Islamabad. Assuming there were no further attacks on India by a Pakistan-based militant group in the interim, that meeting held out the possibility of sub-regional cooperation on transport, energy and other areas.

India's primary security challenge remained China's assertiveness towards the border dispute between the countries, exacerbated by

Beijing's growing trade and defence relationships with India's South Asian neighbours, as well as by an expansion of Chinese influence in the Indian Ocean. For policymakers in New Delhi, this created fears of encirclement and hardened their attitude towards Beijing, even as China continued to be India's largest trading partner, and Modi sought to establish stronger trade and investment links with Beijing.

Chinese forces made no major intrusion across the Line of Actual Control, the de facto Indian–Chinese border, in the year to mid-2016, while Modi and Chinese President Xi Jinping agreed to enhance border-defence cooperation by endeavouring to put into operation a hotline between their senior army officers. In February 2016, the countries held the inaugural India–China Maritime Affairs Dialogue in New Delhi.

Yet relations were still fraught, with Beijing blocking New Delhi's attempt to designate Azhar as a terrorist under the UN Security Council's ISIL (Da'esh) and Al-Qaida Sanctions Committee, and opposing India's membership of the Nuclear Suppliers Group. New Delhi remained suspicious of China's Belt and Road Initiative, fearing that the project sought to expand Chinese influence in South Asia at the expense of India.

Minimal returns on Indian regional policy

Modi's visits to Nepal and Sri Lanka were the first by an Indian prime minister in 17 and 28 years respectively. In Nepal, Modi offered to renegotiate a 1950 political and economic bilateral treaty, which Nepal had long regarded as inequitable. India also began to play the role of what it called a 'net security provider' to the island states of the Indian Ocean. This led New Delhi to, inter alia, begin maritime-security dialogues with Australia, China, France, Japan and the US; deploy a P-8I maritime-reconnaissance aircraft to the Seychelles for surveillance in the country's exclusive economic zone; and give a coastguard boat and a second Dornier aircraft to the Seychelles.

Sri Lankan President Maithripala Sirisena's first official foreign visit was to India in February 2016, during which he and Modi signed an agreement on strengthening civil nuclear cooperation. The deal marked an end to a period of mutual suspicion between India and Sri Lanka that had persisted under Sirisena's predecessor, Mahinda Rajapaksa. The relationship was further strengthened in May 2016, when India became the first country to assist Sri Lanka in responding to a series of floods and landslides.

Modi marked his visit to Bangladesh in June 2015 by signing an important land-boundary agreement that swapped 111 Indian enclaves in Bangladesh with 51 Bangladeshi enclaves in India. New Delhi also continued to work on strengthening its relations with Bangladesh by improving their connectivity with each other – and with Bhutan and Nepal – in areas such as energy supply. This growing rapprochement, combined with Modi's earlier remarks on the role played by India in helping Bangladesh break away from Pakistan, led to a deterioration in the relationship between Dhaka and Islamabad.

Modi visited Afghanistan in December 2015 to attend the opening of the Indian-financed and -built Afghan parliament building, and again in June 2016 to inaugurate the Salma dam – which, having been constructed by India, was renamed the Afghan–India Friendship Dam. New Delhi also supplied Kabul with offensive arms for the first time, donating four ex-Russian Mi-25 ground-attack helicopters to Afghanistan (with Moscow's consent), three of which were delivered in the year. These efforts drew India–Afghanistan relations out of a slump that had lasted more than a year, following Afghan President Ashraf Ghani's decision to reach out to Islamabad as a means of reinvigorating peace negotiations with the Afghan Taliban. The rapprochement between New Delhi and Kabul was further enhanced by the subsequent agreement on the port at Chabahar.

During Maldivian President Abdulla Yameen's visit to New Delhi in April, India and the Maldives signed six agreements, including a defence action plan that established an institutional mechanism for cooperation, which centred on discussions between the countries' top defence officials. The other accords related to the development of port facilities in the Maldives; training and capacity-building programmes for the country's security forces; increased intelligence sharing on maritime affairs; and Indian military aid to Malé, which would include maritime-surveillance capabilities. Modi and Yameen also discussed enhancing their cooperation in countering cross-border terrorism and radicalisation through increased intelligence sharing. Yet, two months earlier, India had helped pass a strong Commonwealth Ministerial Action Group resolution giving Malé a month to cease using its counter-terrorism laws to target Yameen's political opponents, and to begin a dialogue with the opposition. Amid these efforts, New Delhi remained concerned that improving relations between China and the Maldives would help the Chinese military increase its presence in the Indian Ocean.

On balance, India's regional policy paid few political dividends. Nepal's adoption in September 2015 of a new federal constitution marked the end of decades of violent instability, but also marginalised the country's ethnic Madhesis. Living largely in the Terai region, the southern belt bordering the Indian provinces of Bihar and Uttar Pradesh, the Madhesis have close ethnic and cultural ties with India. Their protests over the constitution led to a blockade of commercial trucks entering Nepal from India between September and early February, creating shortages of food, fuel and other essential commodities. With New Delhi pressing Kathmandu to address the concerns of the Madhesis, an effort intensified by local elections in Bihar in November 2015, Nepal accused India of fomenting unrest and interfering in its domestic politics. The hostility grew worse in October 2015, when K.P. Oli was elected as prime minister in Nepal on the back of rising anti-India sentiment. Although Oli's first official visit was to India in February 2016, this failed to alleviate the tension. On 6 May, the Nepalese government cancelled President Bidhya Devi Bhandari's visit to India and sacked its ambassador to the country, accusing him of disloyalty.

In contrast, during Oli's visit to China the following March, he signed ten bilateral agreements on issues that were sensitive to India, including cross-border highways, railways and power-transmission lines. China also invested more in Nepal than India in 2015.

Although Sirisena's first priority was to ensure that Sri Lankans were free from the fear prevalent under the Rajapaksa administration, he made little progress on economic and political reform. India pressed the Sri Lankan government to implement the 13th Amendment to the Constitution, which guarantees greater devolution to the Tamil-dominated northern and eastern provinces. However, the undertaking made little progress due to opposition from the right-wing Sinhalese political bloc led by Rajapaksa, Tamil intransigence and the difficulties of operating as a coalition government in the aftermath of a decades-long civil war. Political rhetoric emanating from Tamil Nadu, as it prepared for elections scheduled for May 2016, exacerbated Sinhalese Sri Lankans' fear of the far larger Tamil community in the Indian state. The Sinhalese had been suspicious of New Delhi since June 1987, when the Indian Air Force carried out a supply drop in the northern Sri Lankan town of Jaffna, a show of force designed to support Tamil rebels fighting the Sri Lankan military. This wariness generated public opposition to a proposed India–Sri Lanka Economic and Technology Cooperation Agreement, aimed at boosting bilateral trade relations and alleviating the negative local perceptions of the 1999 India–Sri Lanka Free Trade Agreement. And as problems such as the arrest of Indian fishermen by Sri Lanka went unresolved, there was growing strain on the bilateral relationship.

Moreover, Sirisena had not turned his back on Beijing. Following Prime Minister Ranil Wickremesinghe's visit to China in April 2016, Sri Lanka agreed to resume the suspended Colombo Port City project on the condition that the land for it would be provided through a long-term lease rather than a freehold. Funded with US$4bn of Chinese money, the project was designed to form a link in Beijing's Maritime Silk Road, part of the Belt and Road Initiative. Colombo also continued to seek infrastructure investment from Chinese companies – despite Sri Lanka's growing debt – at a level that India was unable to match.

China remained Bangladesh's largest trading partner, and its leading supplier of military equipment. As the relationship between Dhaka and New Delhi improved, the former hoped for the swift resolution of a dispute generating mistrust between the sides, the vexed issue of access to the Teesta river. The disagreement concerned efforts to share the waters of the river, which flows from northern glaciers through the Indian provinces of Sikkim and West Bengal and then into Bangladesh. West Bengal Chief Minister Mamata Banerjee refuses to sign a 2011 interim agreement that apportions the water equally (similar to the 1996 Ganges water-sharing pact between the countries) because she fears that the loss of water to the lower riparian would affect the northern areas of her province during dry months.

India was concerned about a wave of brutal killings targeting the Hindu minority community, secular thinkers and liberal activists in

Bangladesh, and as such welcomed Dhaka's crackdown in June 2016, which led to the arrest of more than 5,300 people in three days. As significant numbers of Bangladeshis continued to illegally enter Assam, the state's new Bharatiya Janata Party government vowed in June 2016 to seal the border, a move opposed by Dhaka.

Meanwhile, New Delhi grew more worried about the export of terrorism from Afghanistan, and the possibility that Taliban hardliners would engage in a peace process that marginalised India's role in the country. This fear was exacerbated by an assault on the Indian consulate in Mazar-e-Sharif just days after the Pathankot attack, and another on the Indian consulate in Jalalabad the following March. There was also a considerable development of China–Afghanistan relations, with Beijing pledging to provide US$327m in economic aid to Kabul by the end of 2017. China also agreed to act as an intermediary between Afghanistan and Pakistan by joining the US in the Quadrilateral Coordination Group on the Afghan peace process. General Fang Fenghui, the Chinese military's chief of staff, made a rare visit to Afghanistan in February 2016, offering to provide military aid to combat the Taliban.

Shifts in Pakistani foreign policy

As ever, the main driver of Pakistan's foreign and security policy was its rivalry with India. This consideration trumped all other factors. Islamabad responded to rapprochement between New Delhi and Washington by enhancing, and making more explicit, its partnership with Beijing. Pakistan's leaders continued to see its security and position in the world as more important than prosperity. Nonetheless, the dire need for investment in Pakistani infrastructure, particularly in the energy sector, has been a focus of the leadership's external engagement, both with Beijing – through the China–Pakistan Economic Corridor (CPEC) – and the Central Asian republics.

Two other factors were also important to Pakistan's foreign policy. The first of these was the effort to improve relations with Afghanistan and to enhance stability there, not least because of the impact of cross-border terrorism on the security of Pakistan. The second was the attempt to balance the relationship with the Gulf states, especially traditional ally Saudi Arabia, and Iran amid tension between the sides. Although important for trade, relations with the European Union and East Asia (barring China) were a lower priority.

The conduct of Pakistan's foreign and security policy was still split between the civilian and military leaderships, represented by Prime Minister Nawaz Sharif and Chief of Army Staff Raheel Sharif. The civilian–military relationship itself had been broadly stable since the two sides reached a modus vivendi after the political turmoil of 2014. Yet, within that context, there were variations in the way they interacted on issues of foreign and security policy. Given its importance, they worked in close partnership on the relationship with China, as the civilian side took the lead amid the development of CPEC. The military and civilian leaderships also effectively collaborated on their approach to Afghanistan, sharing the broad aim of improving their often deeply troubled relations with Kabul. In this, the importance of security issues to interactions between Pakistan and Afghanistan, coupled with Ghani's outreach to Raheel Sharif, gave the military and the ISI (which oversees Pakistan's relationship with the Afghan Taliban) a lead over the civilian government. There was sometimes tension between the Sharifs over India policy, as Nawaz pushed for resuming dialogue with New Delhi. However, this tension was not enough to destabilise the government as a whole.

Two other significant developments also affected the formulation of Pakistani policy. The prime minister and the army chief began meeting regularly (roughly once per week) to discuss the country's most important foreign-affairs and security issues. These discussions occurred on a small scale – with the involvement of only a few close advisers, at most – and outside the formal mechanisms of the Pakistani government (although the prime minister chairs a cabinet committee on national security, this has rarely convened during Nawaz Sharif's tenure). These informal meetings became the key forum in which the civilian and military leaderships coordinated their activities and took collective decisions. The second development was the appointment in October 2015 of Lieutenant-General (Retd) Naseer Khan Janjua as the government's full-time national-security adviser. Janjua succeeded Sartaj Aziz, who had fulfilled the role on a part-time basis, and who remained the prime minister's foreign-affairs adviser (de facto foreign minister). Having previously served as the commander of the Quetta-based XII Corps, responsible for counter-insurgency operations in Balochistan, Janjua is close to Raheel Sharif, and his appointment created a new channel of contact with India.

China

An element of the Belt and Road initiative, CPEC was crucial to Pakistan's foreign policy. The undertaking was designed to create road and rail links from western China to the Arabian Sea through the Pakistani port city of Gwadar, in Balochistan. CPEC also involved considerable Chinese investment in Pakistan's energy-generation capacity – intended to increase output by 17,000 megawatts, ending chronic electricity shortages – and enhanced collaboration in science and technology, as well as several other areas.

But the implementation of the project was controversial. The Indian government objected to the fact that the transport links ran through Gilgit-Baltistan, a part of the former princely state of Jammu and Kashmir disputed by New Delhi and Islamabad since 1947. Pakistan repeatedly accused India of using its objections to CPEC as a pretext for destabilising Balochistan. Meanwhile, Baloch nationalists also objected to the project, claiming that it would have few benefits for them, despite their claim to the province's natural resources. This led to fears that the nationalist insurgency in Balochistan would prevent CPEC from coming to fruition. In response, the Pakistan military began to raise an additional Light Commando brigade to provide security for the project. The routing of the transport links was criticised by Tehreek-e-Insaf, the opposition party led by former cricketer Imran Khan. Controlling the Khyber Pakhtunkhwa legislature, the party claimed that CPEC favoured Punjab and Lahore, both of which were ruled by Prime Minister Nawaz Sharif's Pakistan Muslim League–Nawaz.

From a Pakistani perspective, CPEC is strategically important for three reasons. Firstly, it provides much-needed investment at a time when the country is unable to acquire similar amounts on international capital markets (although the government raised money by selling bonds, the rates involved were high). CPEC therefore has the potential to transform Pakistan's economy and boost its long-term development. Secondly, the project creates a route to Central Asia that circumvents

Afghanistan. Nawaz Sharif has emphasised the importance of relations with the Central Asian republics, principally for economic reasons. While the Afghanistan–Pakistan Transit Trade Agreement could allow Pakistan to access Central Asia through Afghanistan, Kabul will only allow this if Islamabad permits Afghan cargo to travel to India through Pakistani territory – a move the Pakistani military has been unwilling to countenance. Lastly, CPEC strengthens the Pakistan–China relationship – to mutual benefit – in the long term. This is particularly vital at a time of deepening cooperation between New Delhi and Washington, and of ongoing friction in US–Pakistan relations caused by the perception that elements of the Pakistani state support terrorist groups, such as the Haqqani network.

As a consequence, Pakistan's government and military establishment are determined to implement CPEC. Internal political disputes will not derail this process. And, despite its vocal objections to the undertaking, India does not have the power to prevent CPEC from going ahead. The most significant challenge is likely to be the sheer complexity of completing so many large-scale projects simultaneously. Nonetheless, CPEC will tie Pakistan more closely to China – traditionally, the country's 'all-weather friend' (and ally against India) – even if members of the elite are more naturally inclined to look towards the US, the United Kingdom and the Gulf states.

Middle East

Having resisted strong pressure to join the Saudi-led coalition taking military action against Houthi rebels in Yemen, the Pakistanis put considerable effort into mending fences with Riyadh. Overall, Pakistan stuck to its position that it would only participate in a military intervention in defence of Saudi Arabia itself. But Pakistan's civilian and military leaders both visited Saudi Arabia to repair relations. This effort was especially important to Prime Minister Sharif due to the close personal ties his family had established with the Saudi royals while exiled in Saudi Arabia in the Musharraf era. Relations between Pakistan and the UAE (Saudi Arabia's principal partner in the intervention in Yemen) were also troubled, resulting in a significant improvement in the latter's links with India, and prompting Modi to visit Abu Dhabi in August 2015, the first such trip by an Indian prime minister in 34 years.

Yet, like India, Pakistan endeavoured to strike a balance between its relationships with the Gulf states and that with Iran. The Pakistanis warmly welcomed the Iran nuclear deal reached in July 2015. Having abided by international sanctions on Iran, leading to the suspension of work on a cross-border gas pipeline, Islamabad saw the agreement as providing an opportunity to develop commercial relations with Tehran, and to use Iranian oil to meet some of its energy shortages. Although Pakistan and Iran shared some interests, the relationship was likely to be less important to Islamabad than that with Riyadh. Moreover, it would continue to face challenges from issues such as border disputes and competition for influence in Afghanistan.

Pakistan was careful not to choose sides in the dispute between Riyadh and Tehran resulting from the Saudis' execution in January of the Shia cleric Sheikh Nimr al-Nimr. Mindful that to do so would be to risk fuelling sectarian tensions within Pakistan, Nawaz Sharif instead engaged in shuttle diplomacy, visiting Saudi Arabia and then Iran to offer Pakistan's good offices and thereby reduce tensions between the rivals. Although the initiative failed to get off the ground, it relieved some of the domestic pressure on him to act, and indicated that Pakistan felt able to pursue a more outward-looking foreign policy after many years of focusing almost exclusively on its immediate neighbourhood. Despite the deep, long-standing military-to-military relationship with Saudi Arabia and Prime Minister Sharif's personal ties to the Saudi royals, Pakistan worked hard to avoid having to choose between Riyadh and Tehran.

Afghanistan

Pakistan's relations with Afghanistan were somewhat volatile throughout the year. In summer 2015, the Pakistanis made a concerted effort to bring the Afghan Taliban into talks with Kabul, hosting a meeting between the sides in Murree on 7 July. The US and China were also represented at the talks. But a scheduled follow-up meeting was postponed amid mutual recriminations, following the announcement that Taliban leader Mullah Omar had died two years prior. Intense violence in Afghanistan in early August, including major attacks in Kabul ascribed to the Haqqani network, led to the swift deterioration in the relationship between the Pakistani and Afghan governments, and the last-minute suspension of a meeting of the Afghanistan–Pakistan Joint Economic Commission.

Much of the remainder of the year was devoted to efforts to put the relationship back onto the positive trajectory that began after Ghani came to power. Although the commission finally met in December, there was limited progress on economic issues. Nonetheless, following a meeting between Nawaz Sharif and Ghani on the margins of the UN Climate Change Conference, the latter agreed to attend the Heart of Asia summit, held in Islamabad on 9 December. On the sidelines of the conference, Afghanistan, Pakistan, China and the US came together to launch a Quadrilateral Coordination Group. Over four meetings in January and February, the group agreed on a road map to end the violence in Afghanistan, calling on the Taliban to attend a first round of peace talks in March.

This did not take place, as the insurgents refused to participate. Although the Quadrilateral Coordination Group met again in May, it seemed unlikely to make rapid progress. The absence of a peace process made it inevitable that there would be further decline in the Afghanistan–Pakistan relationship. The Afghans would continue to believe that the Pakistanis were not doing all they could to tackle the Afghan Taliban. Meanwhile, the Pakistanis would still regard Afghanistan as the source of terrorist attacks inside Pakistan, such as the armed assault on a university in Charsadda on 20 January. The death of Mullah Mohammad Akhtar Mansour, Mullah Omar's successor, in a US air attack on 21 May further reduced the prospects for peace. Given that Mansour was travelling through Balochistan on Pakistani travel documents, the US and other countries would have strengthened their view that Islamabad could do more to reduce the Afghan Taliban's scope to operate from Pakistan.

Chapter 6

Sub-Saharan Africa

The year to mid-2016 saw a reconfiguration of the security hierarchy in sub-Saharan Africa and beyond. This shift was in part driven by factors outside the control of sub-Saharan states, especially the declining price of oil, which undermined the performance of some of the region's most powerful countries, such as Angola and Nigeria, and placed strain on the Gulf states – to which several African nations had turned for assistance. Their resources were further reduced by the economic slowdown in China, a significant trade and aid partner. Nonetheless, the strategic importance of the Horn of Africa, in particular, meant that Beijing remained committed to sub-Saharan Africa, building its first overseas military base in Djibouti. Saudi Arabia also continued to strengthen its ties in the region, in support of its campaign to counter Iranian influence.

Like all nations, African states committed to the Sustainable Development Goals (SDGs), adopted in September 2015 as part of the 2030 Agenda for Sustainable Development, and implemented on 1 January 2016. The 17 goals have a security dimension based on the United Nations' position that 'sustainable development cannot be realised without peace and security; and peace and security will be at risk without sustainable development.' Covering a 15-year period, they are designed to build on the 2000–15 Millennium Development Goals (which included no security provisions), and to end poverty, tackle inequality and protect the environment. They included targets for reducing

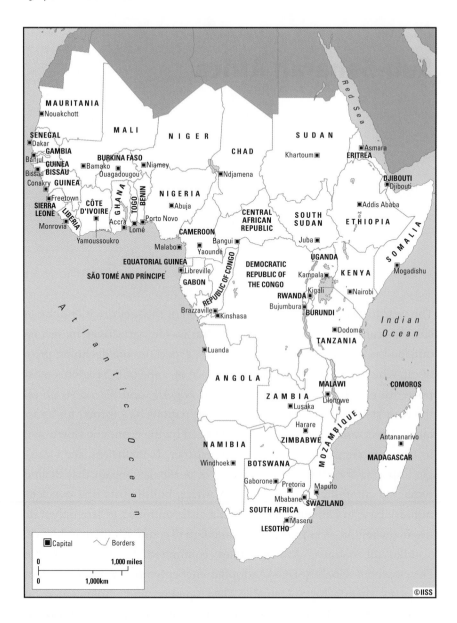

all forms of violence and associated death rates; promoting the rule of law at the national and international levels; hampering illicit financial and arms flows; developing effective, accountable and transparent institutions at all levels; and combating terrorism and other crime. However, it was unclear who was primarily responsible for promoting peace and development under the SDGs.

Meanwhile, the African Standby Force, comprised of 25,000 troops operating under the aegis of the African Union (AU), finally appeared to be making some headway – although there were still doubts about whether it had access to sufficient funding and training. Less encouragingly, international organisations and Western states continued to worry about the relationship between regional groupings such as the AU and long-serving African leaders, particularly those who sought to further extend their terms in office. Concern grew as these leaders appeared increasingly unwilling to step down – posing a threat to security in already unstable countries – and as several African states called for an end to cooperation with the International Criminal Court (ICC).

Changing relations with the international community

The adoption of the SDGs came at a time when many Western countries were rethinking their troubled bilateral relationships in the developing world, partly due to concerns about regime stability in several states. This sometimes led them to strengthen their ties to states with poor democratic records, such as Ethiopia. In the country's 24 May legislative elections, the ruling Ethiopian People's Revolutionary Democratic Front and its allies won all 547 seats in parliament, as the opposition lost even the token seat it had held since the previous vote, five years earlier.

There was little outright violence around the time of the elections, in contrast to the 2005 vote, when the opposition claimed that there had been serious voting irregularities, spurring a wave of bloodshed that met with a strong state response. Arguably, however, the authorities had little reason to resort to force, having progressively restricted Ethiopia's political space through overt attacks on opposition leaders and the implementation of restrictive legislation covering political funding, civil-society groups and the media. As part of this effort, the government regularly used controversial counter-terrorism laws against its critics in the media: according to the Committee to Protect Journalists, more than a dozen journalists critical of the authorities had received prison sentences under the legislation since 2009. In August, 17 Muslim activists were jailed for between seven and 22 years, after they were convicted of plotting to create a state subject to Islamic law in Ethiopia. All the defendants claimed to have been targeted after taking part in peaceful anti-government protests in 2011–12. In this context, there was little need for overt interference in the electoral process. While the AU observer mission described the election as 'calm, peaceful and credible', it did not explicitly state that the vote was free and fair.

Despite this apparent erosion of the democratic process, the Western response to the election was relatively muted. The European Union stated that 'true democracy' had yet to take root in Ethiopia, and, while the United States expressed concern about 'continued restrictions on civil society, media, opposition parties, and independent voices and views', shortly thereafter Barack Obama became the first sitting US president to visit the country. Western states therefore continued to balance doubts about the democratic process in Ethiopia with an awareness of the country's strategic importance as a bulwark of stability in the region. Since 2011, the US has used an air base in Arba Minch, 250 miles south of Addis Ababa, to launch drones monitoring East African terror groups with links to al-Qaeda, particularly the Somalia-based al-Shabaab. In January 2016, the US announced that it was shutting down these operations – most likely to focus on more pressing threats, such as the growing presence of Islamic State, also known as ISIS or ISIL, in Libya, and Boko Haram's expansion out of northeastern Nigeria into parts of Cameroon, Chad and Niger. Still, Ethiopia remained an important Western ally, not least because of its considerable military might. It has one of the most effective armed forces in the region, with significant combat experience and enough deployable capability to make it a leading contributor to UN and AU missions in sub-Saharan Africa.

At the other end of the scale is South Sudan, where violence and political failure are a growing source of concern. The country received substantial international support after officially gaining independence from Sudan in 2011, and this persisted for several years despite the government's poor record on reform and tackling poverty. However, international patience – already tested by the country's decline into civil conflict in late 2013 – waned still further amid the sluggishness with which the government implemented a tentative peace agreement signed in August 2015. In September, for example, the US proposed the introduction of targeted sanctions against two key players in the conflict: Paul Malong Awan, army chief of staff, and Johnson Olony, leader of a rebel militia. But China, Russia and some governments in sub-Saharan Africa opposed the move, with Angola stating that it wanted to give the warring parties more time to implement the peace deal. Nonetheless, due to the continuing inertia in the peace process, the Angolan government proposed in March that the UN Security Council impose an arms embargo on South Sudan. In part, this was in line with Angola's ongoing efforts to establish itself, under President José Eduardo dos Santos, as a regional peacemaker. The move also reflected growing international anxiety that, if it failed to form a government of national unity, South Sudan would become a failed state.

The threat of sanctions had some impact, prompting rebel leader and former vice-president Riek Machar to return to Juba in April, allowing for the new cabinet of the transitional government of national unity to be sworn in shortly afterwards. The government of national unity seeks to create a balance of power between the ruling Sudan People's Liberation Movement (SPLM), Machar's SPLM–In Opposition, the SPLM–Former Detainees and other opposition parties – as well as between the interests of Dinkas and Nuers (President Salva Kiir is Dinka, while Machar is Nuer). However, there has been almost no sign of genuine rapprochement between the sides. In May, Kiir announced that he was appointing ten presidential advisers, none of whom were members of the SPLM–IO or other opposition groups. While the peace agreement did not rule out such appointments, the SPLM–IO and opposition groups had previously condemned Kiir for making major decisions unilaterally. They were especially critical of his plans to increase South Sudan's number of administrative states from ten to 28 (claiming that this was exactly the kind of issue that the government of national unity was supposed to address).

Even without this mistrust, the government faced huge challenges, given the way in which all sides had exacerbated ethnic tension as a means to mobilise local populations. This was underscored in November 2015, when UN Secretary-General Ban Ki-moon provided the UN Security Council with a report on political, security and humanitarian developments in South Sudan. He found that the conflict had 'shattered the social fabric' of South Sudan, displacing as many as 2.3 million people (few of whom fled the country). Western states doubted that the situation would rapidly improve, as there were still outbreaks of violence in areas such as Jonglei, Unity and Upper Nile states. Moreover, several influential militia leaders, including Peter Gadet, had reiterated their commitment to the fight.

While attempting to coerce South Sudan to reform, Western countries took a more conciliatory approach towards Zimbabwe. For example, the EU signed an agreement to normalise relations with Harare and to provide funding for Zimbabwe's agricultural sector (among others), while the European Investment Bank announced in April that it would provide technical and financial support to the country's financial-services sector. Similarly, the IMF produced three generally positive assessments of the Zimbabwean Staff-Monitored Programme in October, March and May. This was despite Harare's reintroduction of exchange and import controls, and limited moves towards the re-establishment of the Zimbabwean dollar – in contravention of the fund's preferences. These moves were partially motivated by concerns about Zimbabwe's transition process, and perceptions that the 92-year-old president, Robert Mugabe, would not remain head of state for much longer (an assumption underscored by a series of health scares). As the president had failed to appoint a successor, the ruling Zimbabwe African National Union–Patriotic Front (ZANU–PF) split into two main factions, one centring on his wife, Grace, and the other on Vice-President Emmerson Mnangagwa. As the president had dominated the political scene for more than 35 years (becoming prime minister in 1980, and president in 1987), Zimbabwe was entering uncharted territory. Fearing potential unrest caused by ZANU–PF infighting, Western states were keen to support a transition process.

Threat of extended presidential terms
Although regional security groupings had a role to play in resolving situations such as that in Zimbabwe, the AU and similar organisations showed considerable solidarity with some of sub-Saharan Africa's longest-serving leaders. As a consequence, Robert Mugabe served as chairman of the AU throughout 2015. Although the position is largely symbolic – the chairperson can influence topics for debate, but other leaders and commissions also frame discussions – his appointment sent

a powerful signal about AU members' attitudes towards some of the most divisive figures in African politics.

On previous occasions, international pressure had prompted the AU to break with tradition in appointing its chairperson, who is usually the leader of the country hosting the organisation's next summit. For example, Sudanese President Omar al-Bashir should have become chairman in 2005, but the AU reselected the incumbent (Nigeria's Olusegun Obasanjo) due to international condemnation of violence in Darfur. However, AU members wholeheartedly backed the appointment of Mugabe, dismissing Western criticism that he was poorly placed to deal with the some of the problems faced by the organisation. One difficulty related to the situation in Burundi, where the incumbent president, Pierre Nkurunziza, announced in April 2015 that he would run for a third term in elections due to be held two months later – in what the opposition called a violation of the Arusha Peace and Reconciliation Agreement for Burundi. The announcement led to public protests that were violently put down, as well as an abortive military coup. Given Mugabe's long reign amid persistent allegations of electoral malpractice, his critics argued that he lacked the moral authority or commitment to lead the AU in addressing Burundi's crisis.

While the AU questioned the legitimacy of the country's elections and called for them to be postponed, the crisis proved to be a thorny issue for both the organisation and the international community. The presidential polls went ahead after a one-month delay, and according to results released on 24 July by the electoral commission, Nkurunziza secured around 69% of the vote, with the main opposition leader, Agathon Rwasa, winning just under 19% and the other six candidates the remainder. The commission put the turnout at around 73%, a figure that the opposition disputed, having earlier called for a boycott of the vote. The EU and the US responded quickly, describing the elections as lacking credibility. Brussels also drew up sanctions targeting those involved in the alleged fraud with measures such as travel bans and asset freezes.

The AU backed a mediation process led by Ugandan President Yoweri Museveni (who has been in office since 1986) but this made little progress due to disputes over the agenda, the participants and even the venue. There were growing fears that the unrest would spread across national borders, as Burundians fled to neighbouring states, including the Democratic Republic of the Congo, Rwanda, Tanzania and Uganda. In December 2015, with the UN Office of the High Commissioner for Human Rights (OHCHR) warning that there would soon be a 'complete breakdown' of law and order in Burundi, the AU Peace and Security Council took the unusual step of proposing a protection and prevention mission to the country. Deploying an uninvited peacekeeping mission with the chief aim of protecting civilians, and involving as many as 5,000 troops, would have been an unprecedented move by the AU. The organisation had decided against sending such missions to Darfur in 2005 (amid widespread human-rights abuses there) and Libya in 2011 (during the revolution against Muammar Gadhafi). However, the AU appeared to believe that the importance of the mission warranted the risk, given that the escalating violence threatened to develop into a civil war similar to Burundi's 1993–2005 conflict. Article 4 of the AU's charter gives it the right to intervene in one of its member states 'in respect of grave circumstances, namely: war crimes, genocide and crimes against humanity'. Spokespersons for the Burundian administration adopted a 'non-negotiable' position that any uninvited mission would be seen as an invasion, and that foreign troops would be 'shot down'.

African countries have traditionally been reluctant to deploy troops to a country against the wishes of its government, partly because this would set a precedent. Moreover, the AU Assembly requires a two-thirds majority to pass a motion to intervene. In January, Smail Chergui, AU commissioner for peace and security, told a press conference that the proposed deployment would be deferred until the Burundian authorities granted permission for the move. As some of Nkurunziza's counterparts in other African states were unwilling to publicly question his legitimacy, the AU also faced practical problems in funding, training and supplying the proposed mission. Appearing to strike a compromise, the organisation continued to call for the deployment of an international police force, as well as more military and human-rights observers, in Burundi. This resembled the AU's response to the crisis in Darfur a decade earlier, in which it eventually reached an agreement with Khartoum on deploying a small force with a narrow mandate.

As well as underscoring the limitations of the AU, the crisis in Burundi demonstrated that the sharp fall-off in coups (actual or attempted) since the early 2000s did not necessarily reflect a democratic upsurge in sub-Saharan Africa. Rather, some African leaders' pursuit of constitutional changes allowing them to prolong their rule has become a substantial threat to peace and security. The problem was widespread: 16 African heads of state tried to remain in power by changing national constitutions and removing presidential term limits between 2000 and 2015; ten of them were successful.

In Chad, the debate over term limits became increasingly public. Two months before presidential elections scheduled for April, Chadian union activists and civil-society organisations called for a half-day of strike action to protest against attempts by the incumbent, Idriss Déby, to stand for re-election. Déby had seized power in a coup in 1990 and been subsequently reappointed president in several disputed elections, creating rising public discontent with the length of his rule. This led to a series of 'citizen whistles', in which people were encouraged to blow whistles as a form of peaceful protest. After repeatedly trying to block the demonstrations and strikes, the authorities began in April to arrest opposition activists. Although the security services contained the protests, the president conceded that he would reintroduce term limits if he won the upcoming elections. Déby duly secured victory in the first round, gaining more than 60% of the vote. Opposition groups questioned the credibility of the elections, but the only substantial scrutiny of the vote came from observers employed by the AU – of which Déby became chairman in early 2016 (a position he was due to hold throughout the year, suggesting that the AU was confident he would win the vote). As with the elections in Ethiopia, Déby's victory met with little international criticism. Part of the reason for this was that Chadian troops continued to play a prominent role in the UN peacekeeping mission in Mali, as well as cross-border efforts to tackle Boko Haram.

Denis Sassou-Nguesso, Déby's counterpart in Congo (Brazzaville), also extended his rule. Having already held the presidency for 32 years, in two separate stints, he formally called in September 2015 for a referendum on revising the constitution, ostensibly to enable the modernisation of state institutions. The proposed measure also sought to eliminate the maximum age limit for candidates, while reducing the presidential term from seven years to five, but allowing the president to serve three consecutive terms rather than two. Under the 2002 constitution, the 72-year-old Sassou-Nguesso would have been prevented from seeking re-election in 2016 by both age and term limits. Days later, a march organised by opposition groups to protest against the constitutional revisions drew between 3,000 and 25,000 people (as estimated by the police and opposition groups respectively), an unusually large number by Congolese standards. Like other heads of state in the region, Sassou-Nguesso wished to avoid a repeat of events in Burkina Faso in 2014, when mass protests against this type of constitutional change developed into an uprising that toppled the president. As a result, Sassou-Nguesso took a strong line against these demonstrations and, in October, four people were killed when the police fired live ammunition into crowds protesting in the capital and Pointe-Noire.

In the event, state officials reported that 72% of the country's 1.8m registered voters participated in the referendum, with 92% of them backing the proposed revisions. Given that opposition groups had called on their supporters to boycott the referendum, the turnout figures appeared to be particularly unreliable. Sassou-Nguesso similarly dominated the March 2016 presidential elections, officially securing 67% of the vote in the first round. However, for all the administration's suppression of its opponents, sporadic protests continued, not least because the opposition lacked alternate channels through which to exert pressure on the regime. Although they resulted in armed clashes in Brazzaville in April, the demonstrations were unlikely to present a serious threat to the regime. Nonetheless, they added to the growing instability in Central Africa. Cameroon received substantial numbers of refugees fleeing Boko Haram, while there was persistent violence in the Central African Republic – even while the February 2016 elections in the country led to the formation of its first democratically elected government in years.

There was also political instability in the Democratic Republic of the Congo, where President Joseph Kabila faced mounting opposition to his attempts to remain in office past constitutional limits. In May the Constitutional Court ruled that he could stay in power beyond 2016 if elections scheduled for November were delayed. Such delays appeared likely, given that the local electoral commission conceded in a January technical note that the process of updating the electoral roll (one of a series of prerequisites for the elections laid down by the president) was expected to take 13–16 months. At the same time, the government became increasingly repressive. In January 2016, the authorities suppressed events organised by the opposition to commemorate protests held a year earlier, in which the security services killed more than 40 demonstrators. According to the UN, reported human-rights violations rose by 64%, to 3,850, between 2014 and 2015. Nearly half of these crimes were committed by government officials, and around 7% were directly linked to the electoral process. The situation deteriorated further in May, after the government issued an arrest warrant for presidential candidate Moise Katumbi (who had been injured in clashes with police), and Olivier Kamitatu, a former planning minister – who alleged that opposition groups might charge President Kabila with treason if it could be proved that he had deliberately undermined the electoral process. In view of this, the international community expressed concern at the prospect of serious instability in the Democratic Republic of the Congo, which threatened to fall deeper into conflict.

Africa rising?

The year to mid-2016 saw steady revision of the narrative of a rising Africa, as there emerged a series of threats to sub-Saharan Africa's post-2007 trajectory of rapid economic growth. This was partially due to fears about the size of the middle class, as well as the falling price of the commodities on which many of the region's economies relied. For example, Nestlé, the world's largest food and drinks company, announced in June 2015 that it would cut 15% of its workforce across 21 African states because it had overestimated the rise of the middle class. Debate over the size of this grouping persisted. Initial optimism surrounded research such as a 2011 survey by the African Development Bank, which calculated that there were 330m members of Africa's middle class. However, a report published in 2014 by Standard Bank suggested that the total was closer to 15m people in 11 countries – adding that Kenya, with a population of 44m, had only 800,000 middle-class households. An October 2015 survey by Credit Suisse took a similar stance. The company's 2015 Global Wealth Databook stated that, measuring assets and wealth accumulation rather than criteria related to income or consumption, Africa's middle class might be 'almost seventeen times smaller than had been previously thought'. Moreover, this segment of the population is highly concentrated, with almost one-quarter living in South Africa, and approximately 1m in Nigeria.

This is particularly problematic because both states, as well as other traditional major players, met with substantial economic, political and security challenges. In South Africa, real GDP grew by just 1.3% in 2015, its lowest rate in six years. Constraints on the economy included a severe drought (related to an El Niño event), ongoing problems with power supplies, the slowdown in China – which reduced demand for some minerals – and ongoing strike action across a range of sectors. These difficulties showed little sign of improvement. In May, the South African Reserve Bank cut its 2016 growth forecast from 0.8% to 0.6%, which had an impact on state spending. The 2016–17 budget, presented in February, had already implemented tax increases and spending cuts, and Minister of Defence Nosiviwe Mapisa-Nqakula warned that the security sector was facing budget cuts of R5.4 billion (US$370m) over the following three years. The cuts, she argued, would result in low salaries, an ageing force, troop numbers insufficient to sustain operations and a larger skills gap. Indeed, she suggested that the South African National Defence Force (SANDF) might be forced to suspend its activities in the medium term.

The ongoing cuts also seemed to undermine South Africa's 2014 Defence Review – passed by parliament in mid-2015 after almost four years of consultation – which foresees a crucial role for the country in regional peacekeeping and crisis-response operations. As it stood, 1,400 South African troops served in the Force Intervention Brigade in the eastern Democratic Republic of the Congo in 2015 and 2016, and another 850 were deployed to Sudan. South Africa also pledged to contribute to the AU's rapid-response force. However, the defence review envisages an expansion of the SANDF's responsibilities in peace missions to include more humanitarian roles, while stressing that the force is 'too poorly equipped and funded to execute the widening spectrum of tasks to the desired level'. While the SANDF, one of Africa's most powerful militaries, was unlikely to be shut down, further spending cuts threatened to have a significant impact domestically and in the broader region.

One of the SANDF's principal missions remained maritime security: South Africa has an exclusive economic zone of more than 1.5m square kilometres, and this area could almost treble in size if its claim to recognise the extension of the continental shelf, submitted under the UN Convention on the Law of the Sea, is authorised. South Africa's maritime-constabulary commitments cover an even larger area, as the country is a signatory to the Djibouti Code of Conduct, under which it is partly responsible for anti-piracy efforts in the western Indian Ocean and the Gulf of Aden. States in the region had reservations about whether South Africa would pursue national rather than regional interests in this role, and whether the country had the resources needed to fulfil the mission. According to local reports, there was no South African naval vessel on station for *Operation Copper*, an anti-piracy mission, between mid-December 2015 and late February 2016. The SANDF increasingly struggles to balance external missions such as *Operation Copper* with internal ones such as *Operation Corona* (which deals with border protection, as well as illegal immigration and the trafficking of contraband) and *Operation Fiela* (designed to maintain law and order in the wake of xenophobic attacks against foreign nationals from across Africa). These efforts are being further complicated by participation in peacekeeping activities, as well as the Southern African Development Community (SADC) Brigade, which forms part of the African Standby Force. While the SANDF has broadly fulfilled its commitments, the 2014 Defence Review, passed by parliament in mid-2015, warned of a 'critical state of decline' in the force. Proposed defence cuts threaten to exacerbate the problem.

Nigeria's armed forces were also preoccupied with domestic concerns, as large parts of the country were affected by the Boko Haram insurgency, as well as outbreaks of violence stemming from ethno-nationalist and sectarian tensions. Although it contributes around 3,000 soldiers to UN peacekeeping operations and has Africa's largest economy, Nigeria did not play a commensurate role in regional security. Muhammadu Buhari, the former major general elected president in March 2015, had some success in the year to mid-2016. He moved the Nigerian army's headquarters to Maiduguri, in the northeast of the country, where Boko

Haram had taken hold of vast swathes of territory. The military's top commanders were replaced, while the president strengthened Nigeria's relationship with partner countries in the Multinational Joint Task Force: Benin, Cameroon, Chad and Niger. The Nigerian government retook much of the territory held by Boko Haram. And relations between Abuja and Washington improved, despite the fact that the US had tended to focus its assistance efforts in the battle against Boko Haram on countries such as Cameroon, Chad and Niger. The Obama administration stated in May 2016 that it was preparing to sell up to 12 light attack aircraft to Nigeria as part of its counter-insurgency campaign in the region. But the US Congress had yet to approve the deal, which drew intense criticism from some lawmakers. They cited a May report by Amnesty International that stated that 149 detainees, some of them children, had died in 2016 in the Nigerian military's Giwa barracks, in Maiduguri.

Despite losing territory, Boko Haram remained lethal, killing 22 people in a suicide bombing at a mosque in Maiduguri in March. By mid-2016, almost 1,000 Nigerians had died in terrorist attacks since Buhari took office. Whereas the military had some success in the northeast, it made much less progress in tackling the insurgency in the oil-rich Niger Delta, in the south of the country. Long unstable because of the perception that it did not enjoy the benefits of the oil industry, the region saw the emergence of a new ethnic militia, the Niger Delta Avengers (NDA). Despite the heavy military presence in the area, the group mounted complex attacks on oil platforms and pipelines, leading to a sharp decline in oil production – from more than 2.2m barrels/day in October 2015 to around 1.5m b/d in June 2016 – that had a severe impact on state resources. These developments were particularly worrying because they threatened to create a destabilising downward spiral, given that participation in militant groups has been partly fuelled by a lack of economic opportunities.

The authorities were even more concerned about the NDA's public support of those campaigning for an independent 'Republic of Biafra' in the southeast. Biafra's 1967 declaration that it would secede from Nigeria led to a three-year civil war in the country. As there are large numbers of weapons in the Delta, collaboration between such groups – and with smaller organisations such as the Niger Delta Suicide Squad – presents a serious security risk. These considerations shape the domestic focus of security policy and the drive to improve coordination with neighbours such as Chad and Cameroon. The approach is in line with the 'concentric' foreign-policy objectives that Buhari outlined prior to his election, when he stated that Nigeria's primary focus should be its neighbours, followed by West Africa, the wider continent and, finally, the rest of the world. Meanwhile, Nigeria's porous borders continued to create problems, as the authorities rejected external assistance out of a determination to appear in control. And alleged human-rights abuses by the Nigerian security services caused further damage to the security environment.

Angola's ambitions and reach were also contained by weakness in the price of oil, the country's major source of revenue. The authorities cut planned defence spending by around 25%, to around US$5.5bn, in 2015 – although there were indications that actual spending declined even more, affecting not only procurement but also ongoing operations. The trend was unlikely to continue for long, given the authorities' reliance on the military and the security services, and their growing anxiety about the possibility of civil unrest. Indeed, the Angolan government quickly reiterated its plans to boost annual defence spending to US$13bn by 2019. Within these limited confines, President dos Santos sought to position Angola as an African power and peacemaker with a global profile. As part of this, he headed the Kimberley Process, an international body set up to counter the trade in conflict diamonds, throughout 2015. Similarly, Angola chairs the International Conference of the Great Lakes Region, an intergovernmental organisation that includes 11 other states: Burundi, Central African Republic, Congo (Brazzaville), the Democratic Republic of the Congo, Kenya, Rwanda, South Sudan, Sudan, Tanzania, Uganda and Zambia. According to Angolan Foreign Minister Georges Chikoti, his country aims to use its 'war experience to promote peace [in Africa] and other parts of the globe'. Yet despite its military strength, Angola emphasises negotiation and advice over military activity. While the country participates in the SADC Standby Force, it has played only a limited role in conflicts, preferring to engage in activities such as training Congolese troops. This is partly due to Angola's experiences with civil war and its unwillingness to intervene in other countries' affairs, as well as the effects of weak oil prices.

China's broad influence

The relative decline in China's economy should not be overstated, as the country experienced real GDP growth of around 6.9% in 2015 – substantially more than that of Western states. Nonetheless, this was the lowest figure since 1990, and it followed a decade in which annual growth averaged 10%. However, neither this slowdown nor the changing global environment appeared to have a substantial impact on strategic links between Beijing and African governments, as underscored by the Forum on China–Africa Co-operation (FOCAC) held in South Africa in December 2015 (the sixth such gathering, and the first to be held in Southern Africa). During the summit, Chinese President Xi Jinping announced that there were ten major areas of cooperation between China and Africa, most of them socio-economic. They included industry, agriculture, infrastructure, environment, trade facilitation, poverty alleviation and public health – as well as regional peace and security. In pursuit of these aims, China pledged US$60bn over a three-year implementation period. At previous FOCAC summits (held every three years since 2000, with the venue alternating between China and Africa), Beijing tended to double its previous funding pledges. Thus, the commitments rose from US$5bn in 2006 to US$10bn in 2009 and US$20bn in 2012. Yet in 2015 funding was trebled.

The composition of the funding was also different, and reflected a maturing relationship between the sides. In 2006 around 60% of Chinese funding pledges took the form of concessional loans, and the remainder were buyer's credit. In 2009 and 2012, all the funding came in the form of concessional loans. Of the funding pledged at the 2015 meeting, concessional loans and buyer's credit accounted for US$35bn, grants and zero-interest loans US$5bn, and commercial financing US$20bn. And, in contrast to previous meetings, Beijing defined the funding as 'investment'. The change in terminology also reflected a shift in the relationship, with the Chinese side publicly stating its desire to move beyond the natural resources that had hitherto dominated the trade partnership. Thus, speaking at FOCAC 2015, Xi referred to natural resources only in the context of sub-Saharan Africa's 'abundant economic endowment', and instead focused on ways to develop other exports.

This is despite the fact that natural resources continued to dominate the continent's Chinese trade profile. According to Chinese data, crude oil, iron ore, diamonds and agricultural products together accounted for more than 55% of Chinese imports from Africa between January and September 2015. At the same time, the total value of imports from Africa was relatively low, due to Chinese economic slowdown, as well as the sharp reduction in the international oil price. Angola, Congo (Brazzaville), Equatorial Guinea, South Africa and Zambia collectively supplied more than 70% of Chinese imports from the continent, but in all cases the totals fell significantly. Imports from Angola dropped from US$31.1bn in 2014 to US$15.98bn in 2015, while those from South Africa declined from US$44.7bn to US$15bn during the same period. It was not just trade that diminished. Data published by the Chinese Ministry of Commerce shows that China's direct investment in the continent fell by more than 40% between the first half of 2013 and the same period the following year. Moreover, Chinese officials stated that there was likely to be a further decline in 2015, due to slower global growth and events such as the Ebola outbreak in West Africa.

Beijing's previous focus on commodities caused tension in some African states, not least because Chinese trade and investment tended to create fewer jobs than locals hoped. This is partly because the extraction of natural resources usually has relatively small employment potential. But it is also due to the fact that Chinese firms chose to use Chinese labour in infrastructure projects. Moreover, the Chinese merchants who arrived in Africa with the projects were sometimes charged with undercutting local suppliers. For example, in January 2016, anti-government protests in the Congolese capital, Kinshasa, developed into attacks on Chinese migrants and Chinese-owned shops. Thus, as part of FOCAC 2015, Beijing emphasised human development and capacity, setting up 30,000 government scholarships, as well as local vocational-education centres designed to train 200,000 technical personnel.

Another part of Beijing's broader engagement with Africa – which doubled as an attempt to protect Chinese assets in the region – was its increased focus on security. At FOCAC 2015, China pledged around US$100m over five years to support the African Standby Force (ASF), a 25,000-strong multinational force operating under the aegis of the

AU. The idea of the ASF was first proposed in 1997, and the AU has been developing the force since May 2003 with the aim of reducing African countries' reliance on extra-regional actors for conflict resolution. However, the force has a patchy record, partly because of funding issues: while the AU is expected to contribute 25% of its funding, the ASF relies on UN, EU and bilateral support for the remainder. The AU has also been constrained by poor coordination and a lack of political will among its member states; slow decision-making; a dearth of equipment, personnel and training; weak logistics and airlift capacity; and insufficient intelligence capabilities.

At least some of these issues have been addressed. For instance, the AU signed in October 2015 an agreement for locating the ASF's logistical base in the Cameroonian city of Douala, and shortly thereafter the force held a major training exercise, *Operation Amani Africa* II. Contributors to the exercise – in which troops sought to take back territory seized by rebels in a fictional state (set up in the SANDF's training centre in the Northern Cape) – included Algeria, Burundi, the Democratic Republic of the Congo, Egypt, Ethiopia, Gambia, Ghana, Kenya, Lesotho, Malawi, Mozambique, Namibia, Nigeria, Rwanda, South Africa, Swaziland, Uganda, Zambia and Zimbabwe. Reports on the exercise were broadly positive, with the AU suggesting that there had been a substantial improvement in the tactical and operational performance of its military units, as well as an improvement in coordination between the force's military, police and civilian components. Still, there were concerns over the comparatively poor performance of its police and civilian components, given that civilian-led peacebuilding formed part of the ASF mandate.

The force was due to become fully operational in July 2016, at which point the AU claims it will be able to deploy as many as 12,500 trained and equipped military, police and civilian personnel ready for action, anywhere in Africa, within 14 days of a commitment being made to act on an identified crisis. The ASF plans to be able to deploy a rapid-reaction force and as many as 5,000 personnel within 90 days, and to have the capacity to sustain itself for 30 days. But, while African troops have substantial experience in supporting UN peacekeeping missions, deploying in support of operations in almost a dozen countries over the past decade, few of these have involved African-led forces. The ASF faces another challenge in managing potential ethnic rivalries between peacekeepers and civilians in the areas in which they operate.

Jaco Theunissen, the military spokesman for *Amani Africa* II, insisted that an African force will have a greater understanding of the local environment, making for better peacekeeping. Again, though, there remain doubts about the commitment to democracy of regional groupings such as the AU, the SADC and the Economic Community of West African States.

China took its strategic investment in sub-Saharan Africa one step further in November 2015, announcing that it had signed a ten-year leasing agreement with Djibouti to set up a military base there – its first overseas. Beijing described the facility as designed to support existing peacekeeping missions and anti-piracy patrols, such as those conducted in Djiboutian and Somali waters in the Gulf of Aden since 2008. It has also hinted, however, that the base will be used as a logistics hub, facilitating intelligence-gathering in support of counter-terrorism operations in the Middle East and Central Africa. Djibouti is an obvious choice for such a base, given its political stability and its proximity to Eritrea, Somalia, South Sudan, Sudan and Yemen. France, Japan and the US already have military presences in Djibouti, suggesting that China could compete for influence with them there. Yet, the US – with Camp Lemonnier in Djibouti its largest permanent base in Africa, housing around 4,000 personnel – is focusing elsewhere. In late 2015, the US Africa Command announced a strategic outlook that focused on 'neutralising' al-Qaeda affiliate al-Shabaab (albeit while placing less emphasis on the broader fight against al-Qaeda than the previous outlook), as well as containing groups such as Boko Haram and the Libyan branch of ISIS.

New interest from Gulf Arab states

Riyadh also set its sights on Djibouti. Djiboutian Ambassador to Saudi Arabia Dya-Eddin Bamakhrama stated in March 2016 that the countries would soon sign an agreement to establish a Saudi military facility in Djibouti. Their bilateral relations had been developing since January, when Djibouti joined Saudi Arabia and its allies in cutting diplomatic ties with Iran. The attraction for Saudi Arabia stemmed from its campaign against the Houthis in Yemen. Indeed, Bamakhrama highlighted the fact that the base would be able to accommodate the basing requirements of the Saudi air force, and would be less susceptible to interference by Houthi or Iranian forces than a facility on the Arabian Peninsula. These developments marked a restoration of relations following an April 2015 diplomatic row between Djibouti and the United Arab Emirates, a key Saudi ally.

As tension between the UAE and Djibouti persisted, Saudi Arabia had stepped up its efforts to improve relations with countries on or near the Horn of Africa, especially Eritrea and Sudan. On 21 October, the UN Monitoring Group on Somalia and Eritrea published a report claiming that Eritrea had allowed the anti-Houthi coalition to use its territory, as part of a 'new strategic military relationship with Saudi Arabia and the UAE'. Eritrea had long had a troubled relationship with Western states, due to its alleged involvement in human-rights abuses and other crimes. The UN report also alleged that the Saudi and Emirati governments were paying Eritrea for this assistance, potentially violating a 2009 UN resolution and arms embargo designed to prevent the country from destabilising the region. This cooperation appeared to go beyond logistical concerns, as a former high-ranking Eritrean official reportedly said that 400 Eritrean soldiers were embedded with Emirati forces fighting in Yemen.

In early 2015, there were allegations that Eritrea was supporting the Houthi rebels and Iran on the other side of the conflict. But the regime of Isaias Afewerki had shown a propensity to switch allegiances to ensure survival, and it announced in December 2015 that it was ready to 'support the [anti-Houthi] initiative without reservations and to extend its contribution' to the Saudi-led coalition.

Riyadh and its allies also developed their ties with Sudan. The country has long been considered an ally of Tehran, which has provided diplomatic and military support to Khartoum. But, by mid-2015, the relationship had begun to decline. Following a surprise visit to Khartoum by Saudi Foreign Minister Adel al-Jubeir on 22 February 2016, Sudan's media reported that the country would receive the military aid that Riyadh originally intended to send to Lebanon (but cancelled following a diplomatic spat), claiming that this assistance could be worth up to US$5bn. This figure was almost certainly exaggerated, not least because the proposed financial support to Lebanon had been worth US$4bn, and it was possible that Sudan would not receive all of the funds. Yet the government in Khartoum was under severe financial pressure due to the fall in oil-transit fees, a key source of revenue, caused by the civil conflict in South Sudan. In this environment, the prospect of Saudi aid and investment provided an incentive for cooperation. Sudan was thought to have around 850 troops fighting against the Houthis in Yemen, and to have provided aircraft to the campaign. And, in February 2016, Sudan's forces reportedly took part in a joint military-training operation in Saudi Arabia, along with those of 20 other countries.

Opposition to the ICC

In contrast to their pursuit of self-reliance in peacekeeping and similar operations, African governments made little effort to establish a regional justice system. Moreover, they were increasingly critical of international legal structures designed to try those accused of war crimes and crimes against humanity, particularly the ICC. This was partly because, as the AU and several African politicians had pointed out, almost all the charges brought by the court in its 11-year history concerned black Africans (the ICC's response was that many of the cases were referred to it by African governments). This trend persisted in the year to mid-2016, as the trial of former Ivorian President Laurent Gbagbo and Charles Blé Goudé, an Ivorian youth leader, began; Jean-Pierre Bemba Gombo, former vice-president of the Democratic Republic of the Congo, was found guilty of war crimes and crimes against humanity committed in the Central African Republic; the ICC prosecutor announced the opening of a preliminary examination of the situation in Burundi; and the case against Kenya's deputy president, William Ruto, and Joshua Arap Sang, a Kenyan radio presenter, was suspended.

The Kenyan case, and that against Sudanese President Bashir, proved particularly controversial. The first warrant for Bashir's arrest was issued in March 2009, and the second in July 2010. During the same period, the AU issued a declaration supporting Bashir – on the grounds that his indictment could derail the Darfur peace process – and then stated that it would not cooperate with the ICC to arrest him. The AU subsequently declared that all sitting heads of state were immune from prosecution. The tensions between African governments and the ICC – and even African governments and national justice systems – came into focus in summer 2015, when Bashir attended the AU summit in South Africa. As an ICC signatory, the country was legally obliged to detain him. Indeed, these obligations are included in the South African constitution. However, the government refused either to arrest him or to comply with a court order (obtained by the Southern African Litigation Centre) to stop him from leaving South Africa. The move led to complaints from the UN International Court of Justice, and arguably undermined South Africa's hopes of winning a permanent seat on the UN Security Council. Yet the episode did not prevent other African states from allowing Bashir to visit, and in May 2016 he attended the re-inauguration of Ugandan President Museveni. Uganda was originally a proponent of the ICC, and was the first country to refer a case to the court (that of Joseph Kony, a commander in the Lord's Resistance Army whom the ICC subsequently convicted of war crimes and crimes against humanity committed in northern Uganda). But, in his inauguration speech, Museveni described the ICC as 'a bunch of useless people', prompting the US and European delegates at the event to walk out in protest.

The rejection of international – or Western-imposed, as the AU sees it – justice systems failed to result in a greater commitment to African alternatives. One such structure already exists: the African Court on Human and Peoples' Rights (ACHPR), which the AU established in 2004. The court has a broad remit, since it centres on the African Charter on Human and Peoples' Rights, which includes social rights (such as the right to education) as well as political rights. However, while 30 states are members of the court, only eight have ratified the declaration that allows private individuals or non-governmental organisations to bring their complaints to the ACHPR. Equally, although the AU's members adopted the so-called Malabo Protocol in 2014 – which expands the court's mandate to include international criminal law, enabling it to try war crimes and crimes against humanity – the measure has yet to be ratified by any AU member state. Even if there is progress in this area, the ACHPR, in line with AU proclamations, has mechanisms to prevent the prosecution of sitting heads of state or high-level officials. This threatens to reinforce a perception among many African civil-society groups, as well as the international community, that the AU is unwilling to defend human rights or promote accountability.

Strategic Geography 2016

II
China's Belt and Road Initiative

IV
TPP, TTIP and the impact on global trade

VI
Russia under sanctions

VIII
Change in Latin America

X
Competing claims in the South China Sea

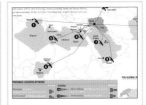

XII
The evolving threat of ISIS

XIV
Migration and nationalism in Europe

XVI
Chronic instability in the DRC

China's Belt and Road Initiative

In early 2015, China laid out the plan for implementing its Belt and Road Initiative (BRI). The undertaking comprises the Silk Road Economic Belt, made up of land routes connecting China with Central Asia and Europe, and a Maritime Silk Road, composed of sea routes running through South and Southeast Asia. Six economic corridors are proposed for its central framework. The initiat has four interconnected objectives: improve regional infrastructure; increase regional economic-policy coordination; eliminate barriers to trade; and encourage cultural ties between states. It involves more than 60 countries, covers 4.4 billion of the world's population and accounts for over 33% of global wealth.

The Belt and Road Initiative has the potential to create new markets capable of absorbing China's excess industrial capacity, improve the country's access to energy supplies and encourage economic development in its interior and western provinces. Beijing hopes to increase Chinese trade with the countries involved to more than US$2.5 trillion by the mid-2020s.

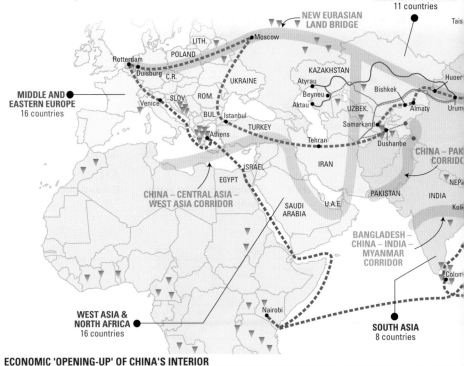

ECONOMIC 'OPENING-UP' OF CHINA'S INTERIOR

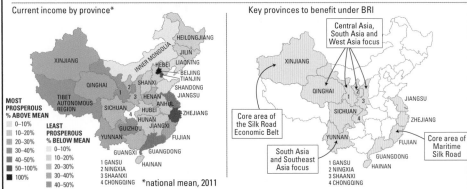

Sources: Foreign & Commonwealth Office; China Investment Research; PWC; *Financial Times*; UN; World Bank; IISS; AIIB; the State Council of the People's Republic of China

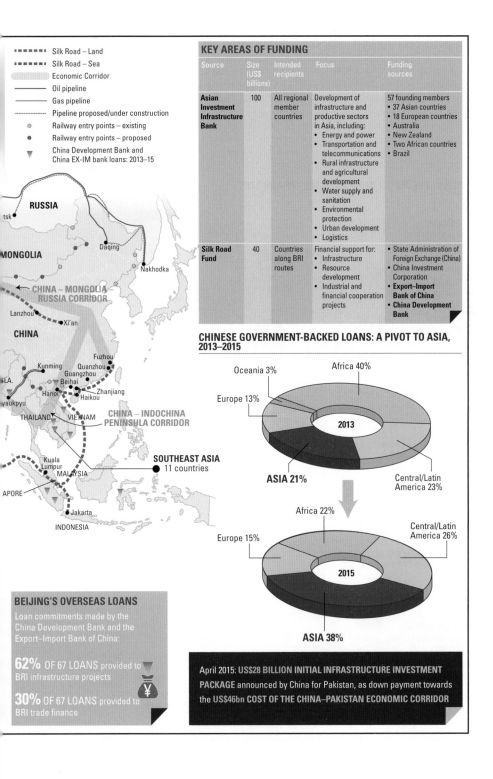

KEY AREAS OF FUNDING

Source	Size (US$ billions)	Intended recipients	Focus	Funding sources
Asian Investment Infrastructure Bank	100	All regional member countries	Development of infrastructure and productive sectors in Asia, including: • Energy and power • Transportation and telecommunications • Rural infrastructure and agricultural development • Water supply and sanitation • Environmental protection • Urban development • Logistics	57 founding members • 37 Asian countries • 18 European countries • Australia • New Zealand • Two African countries • Brazil
Silk Road Fund	40	Countries along BRI routes	Financial support for: • Infrastructure • Resource development • Industrial and financial cooperation projects	• State Administration of Foreign Exchange (China) • China Investment Corporation • **Export–Import Bank of China** • **China Development Bank**

Legend:
- ▪▪▪▪▪▪ Silk Road – Land
- ▪▪▪▪▪▪ Silk Road – Sea
- Economic Corridor
- Oil pipeline
- Gas pipeline
- Pipeline proposed/under construction
- ◎ Railway entry points – existing
- ● Railway entry points – proposed
- ▼ China Development Bank and China EX-IM bank loans: 2013–15

RUSSIA
tsk
Daqing
MONGOLIA
Nakhodka
CHINA – MONGOLIA – RUSSIA CORRIDOR
Lanzhou
Xi'an
CHINA
Fuzhou
Kunming   Quanzhou
Guangzhou
Beihai
LA.
Hanoi   Haikou   Zhanjiang
yaukpyu
THAILAND   VIETNAM   CHINA – INDOCHINA PENINSULA CORRIDOR
Kuala Lumpur   SOUTHEAST ASIA
MALAYSIA   ● 11 countries
APORE
Jakarta
INDONESIA

CHINESE GOVERNMENT-BACKED LOANS: A PIVOT TO ASIA, 2013–2015

2013
- Oceania 3%
- Africa 40%
- Europe 13%
- Central/Latin America 23%
- **ASIA 21%**

2015
- Africa 22%
- Central/Latin America 26%
- Europe 15%
- **ASIA 38%**

BEIJING'S OVERSEAS LOANS

Loan commitments made by the China Development Bank and the Export–Import Bank of China:

62% OF 67 LOANS provided to BRI infrastructure projects

30% OF 67 LOANS provided to BRI trade finance

April 2015: US$28 BILLION INITIAL INFRASTRUCTURE INVESTMENT PACKAGE announced by China for Pakistan, as down payment towards the US$46bn COST OF THE CHINA–PAKISTAN ECONOMIC CORRIDOR

TPP, TTIP and the impact on global trade

The United States was at the centre of two major trade negotiations in the year to mid-2016. The first of these, the Trans-Pacific Partnership (TPP), involves 11 other Pacific Rim states, and was signed in February 2016. The other, to establish the Transatlantic Trade and Investment Partnership (TTIP) between the US and the European Union, began in 2013 and is scheduled to conclude by the end of 2016. However, those talks have encountered hostility on both sides of the Atlantic from groups who oppose globalisation and believe that it favours companies more than workers. The TPP forms part of the US 'rebalance' to the Asia-Pacific, and is intended to create competitive advantages for the US and its allies – relative to China – in the Pacific Rim. Meanwhile, TTIP is intended to set global product standards before China can do so, and to strengthen the alliance between the US and EU states.

TTIP FACTS/PROJECTIONS
PARTIES: EU and US; led by US
CURRENT STATUS: under negotiation
COMBINED GDP: US$16.23 trillion
GAIN IN TOTAL EU EXPORTS: +6% (2027)
GAIN IN TOTAL US EXPORTS: +8% (by 2027)
GEOGRAPHICAL SCALE: 832.2 million people
EU ECONOMIC GAIN: +US$120 billion (by 2027)
US ECONOMIC GAIN: +US$95 billion (by 2027)

SELECT PROJECTED IMPACTS OF THE TPP AND TTIP

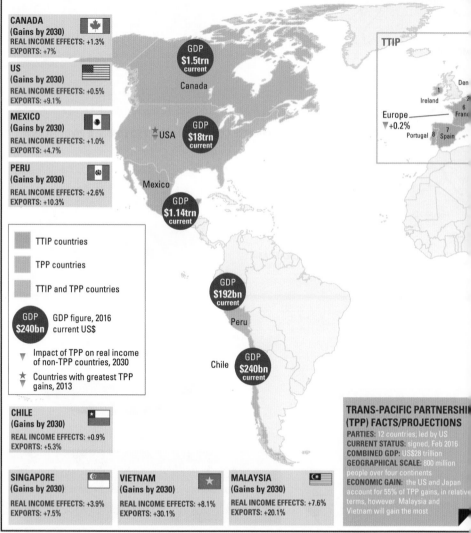

CANADA
(Gains by 2030)
REAL INCOME EFFECTS: +1.3%
EXPORTS: +7%

US
(Gains by 2030)
REAL INCOME EFFECTS: +0.5%
EXPORTS: +9.1%

MEXICO
(Gains by 2030)
REAL INCOME EFFECTS: +1.0%
EXPORTS: +4.7%

PERU
(Gains by 2030)
REAL INCOME EFFECTS: +2.6%
EXPORTS: +10.3%

TTIP countries

TPP countries

TTIP and TPP countries

GDP $240bn — GDP figure, 2016 current US$

▼ Impact of TPP on real income of non-TPP countries, 2030

★ Countries with greatest TPP gains, 2013

Canada — GDP $1.5trn current

USA — GDP $18trn current

Mexico — GDP $1.14trn current

Peru — GDP $192bn current

Chile — GDP $240bn current

TTIP
Europe ▼ +0.2%
Den
1 Ireland
6 France
7 Portugal 8 Spain

CHILE
(Gains by 2030)
REAL INCOME EFFECTS: +0.9%
EXPORTS: +5.3%

SINGAPORE
(Gains by 2030)
REAL INCOME EFFECTS: +3.9%
EXPORTS: +7.5%

VIETNAM
(Gains by 2030)
REAL INCOME EFFECTS: +8.1%
EXPORTS: +30.1%

MALAYSIA
(Gains by 2030)
REAL INCOME EFFECTS: +7.6%
EXPORTS: +20.1%

TRANS-PACIFIC PARTNERSHIP (TPP) FACTS/PROJECTIONS
PARTIES: 12 countries; led by US
CURRENT STATUS: signed, Feb 2016
COMBINED GDP: US$28 trillion
GEOGRAPHICAL SCALE: 800 million people over four continents
ECONOMIC GAIN: the US and Japan account for 55% of TPP gains, in relative terms, however, Malaysia and Vietnam will gain the most

Sources: Peterson Institute of International Economics; The World Trade Institute; European Commission; European Parliament; *Guardian; Independent*; BBC; *Diplomat*; World Bank

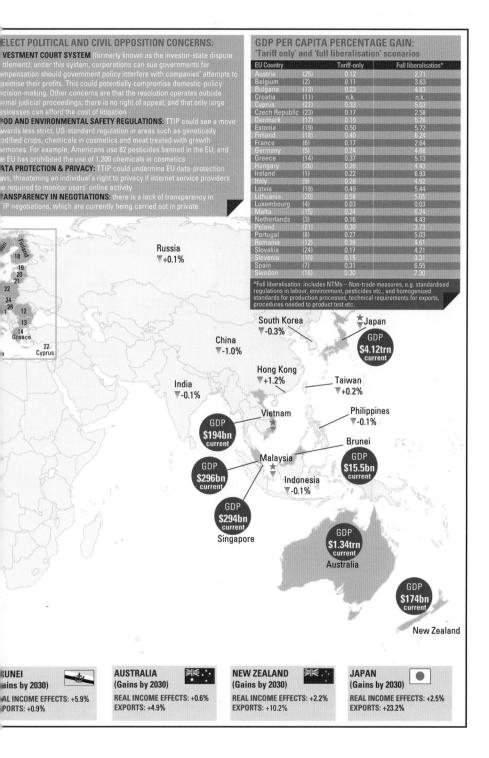

ELECT POLITICAL AND CIVIL OPPOSITION CONCERNS:

VESTMENT COURT SYSTEM (formerly known as the investor-state dispute ttlement): under this system, corporations can sue governments for mpensation should government policy interfere with companies' attempts to ximise their profits. This could potentially compromise domestic-policy cision-making. Other concerns are that the resolution operates outside rmal judicial proceedings; there is no right of appeal; and that only large sinesses can afford the cost of litigation

OD AND ENVIRONMENTAL SAFETY REGULATIONS: TTIP could see a move wards less strict, US-standard regulation in areas such as genetically odified crops, chemicals in cosmetics and meat treated with growth rmones. For example, Americans use 82 pesticides banned in the EU; and e EU has prohibited the use of 1,200 chemicals in cosmetics

ATA PROTECTION & PRIVACY: TTIP could undermine EU data-protection ws, threatening an individual's right to privacy if internet service providers e required to monitor users' online activity

ANSPARENCY IN NEGOTIATIONS: there is a lack of transparency in IP negotiations, which are currently being carried out in private

GDP PER CAPITA PERCENTAGE GAIN:
'Tariff only' and 'full liberalisation' scenarios

EU Country		Tariff-only	Full liberalisation*
Austria	(25)	0.12	2.71
Belgium	(2)	0.11	3.63
Bulgaria	(13)	0.23	4.83
Croatia	(11)	n.k.	n.k.
Cyprus	(27)	0.33	5.03
Czech Republic	(23)	0.17	2.58
Denmark	(17)	0.19	5.28
Estonia	(19)	0.50	5.72
Finland	(18)	0.40	6.24
France	(6)	0.17	2.64
Germany	(5)	0.24	4.68
Greece	(14)	0.37	5.13
Hungary	(26)	0.26	4.43
Ireland	(1)	0.22	6.93
Italy	(9)	0.28	4.92
Latvia	(19)	0.49	5.44
Lithuania	(20)	0.58	5.05
Luxembourg	(4)	0.03	0.03
Malta	(15)	0.24	6.24
Netherlands	(3)	0.16	4.43
Poland	(21)	0.30	3.73
Portugal	(8)	0.27	5.03
Romania	(12)	0.38	4.61
Slovakia	(24)	0.17	4.21
Slovenia	(10)	0.15	3.31
Spain	(7)	0.31	6.55
Sweden	(16)	0.30	7.30

*Full liberalisation: includes NTMs – Non-trade measures, e.g. standardised regulations in labour, environment, pesticides etc., and homogenised standards for production processes, technical requirements for exports, procedures needed to product test etc.

Finland
18
19
20
21
22
24
26
1 12
13
14
Greece
27
Cyprus

Russia
▼+0.1%

South Korea
▼-0.3%

★Japan

GDP
$4.12trn
current

China
▼-1.0%

Hong Kong
▼+1.2%

Taiwan
▼+0.2%

India
▼-0.1%

Philippines
▼-0.1%

GDP
$194bn
current

Vietnam
★

Brunei

GDP
$15.5bn
current

GDP
$296bn
current

Malaysia
★

Indonesia
▼-0.1%

GDP
$294bn
current

Singapore

GDP
$1.34trn
current
Australia

GDP
$174bn
current

New Zealand

UNEI
(ains by 2030)

AL INCOME EFFECTS: +5.9%
PORTS: +0.9%

AUSTRALIA
(Gains by 2030)

REAL INCOME EFFECTS: +0.6%
EXPORTS: +4.9%

NEW ZEALAND
(Gains by 2030)

REAL INCOME EFFECTS: +2.2%
EXPORTS: +10.2%

JAPAN
(Gains by 2030)

REAL INCOME EFFECTS: +2.5%
EXPORTS: +23.2%

Russia under sanctions

Russia's economy fell into recession in 2015, as low prices for its oil and other commodities combined with US and EU sanctions. Real GDP contracted by 3.7%. The rouble traded at around 60–80 to the dollar in the year to mid-2016, compared to 30–35 to the dollar prior to the Ukraine crisis. Wages and pensions failed to keep pace with surging inflation, and by February 2016 workers were owed around US$57 million in wage arrears. They were also forced to contend with shortened working hours and increasing lay-offs, which triggered labour protests in some provinces. Yet President Vladimir Putin's approval rating remained high.

Constrained by a significant fall in revenue, the Russian government cut expenditure and financed the deficit by drawing down the Reserve Fund – the balance of which fell from US$88.3 billion in mid-2014 to US$38.2bn in mid-2016. The Russian Ministry of Finance projected that, on the basis of an oil price of US$40 per barrel, the Reserve Fund would be exhausted in 2017, and the government compelled to draw on the National Wealth Fund to finance the budget deficit in 2017–19.

Meanwhile, relations between NATO states and Moscow deteriorated further, as the sides stepped up their military exercises and deployments near Russia's western border. Fighting persisted in Ukraine's Donbas region, and little progress was made in implementing the 'Minsk II' agreement between Kiev and Russian-backed separatists.

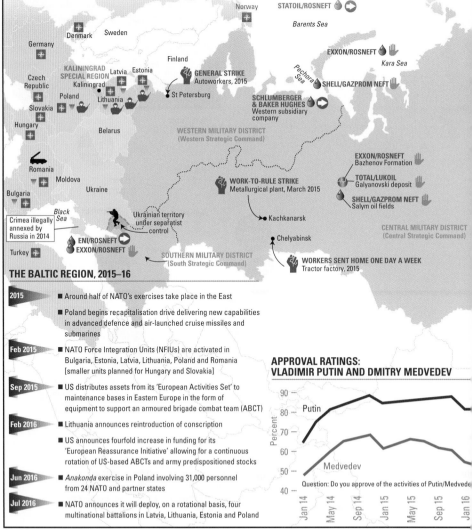

THE BALTIC REGION, 2015–16

2015
- Around half of NATO's exercises take place in the East
- Poland begins recapitalisation drive delivering new capabilities in advanced defence and air-launched cruise missiles and submarines

Feb 2015
- NATO Force Integration Units (NFIUs) are activated in Bulgaria, Estonia, Latvia, Lithuania, Poland and Romania [smaller units planned for Hungary and Slovakia]

Sep 2015
- US distributes assets from its 'European Activities Set' to maintenance bases in Eastern Europe in the form of equipment to support an armoured brigade combat team (ABCT)

Feb 2016
- Lithuania announces reintroduction of conscription
- US announces fourfold increase in funding for its 'European Reassurance Initiative' allowing for a continuous rotation of US-based ABCTs and army predispositioned stocks

Jun 2016
- *Anakonda* exercise in Poland involving 31,000 personnel from 24 NATO and partner states

Jul 2016
- NATO announces it will deploy, on a rotational basis, four multinational battalions in Latvia, Lithuania, Estonia and Poland

APPROVAL RATINGS: VLADIMIR PUTIN AND DMITRY MEDVEDEV

Putin

Medvedev

Percent
90
80
70
60
50
40

Question: Do you approve of the activities of Putin/Medvede

Jan 14 May 14 Sep 14 Jan 15 May 15 Sep 15 Jan 16

Sources: NATO; Al-Jazeera; Royal Dutch Shell; Greenpeace; Telegraph; Financial Times; New York Times; Reuters; Guardian; Trading Economics; World Bank; Yuri Levada Analytic Cent Estonian Foreign Policy Institute; The Oxford Institute of Energy Studies; UpNorth; IISS

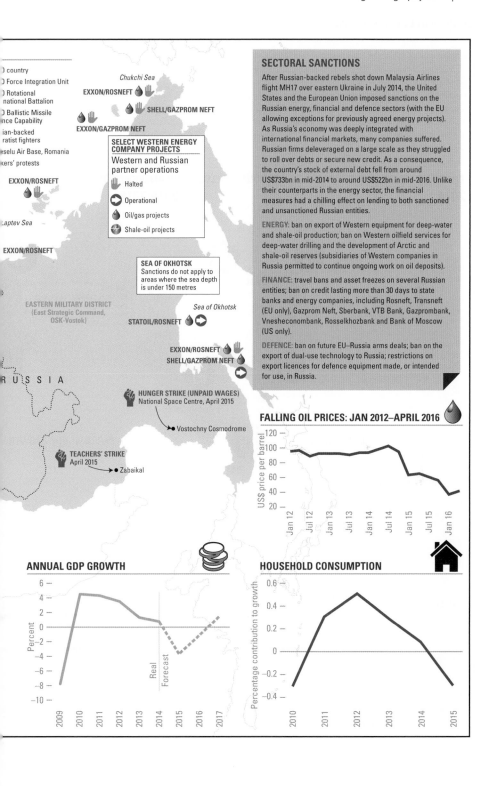

) country
) Force Integration Unit
) Rotational
national Battalion
) Ballistic Missile
nce Capability
ian-backed
ratist fighters
selu Air Base, Romania
kers' protests

EXXON/ROSNEFT

Laptev Sea

EXXON/ROSNEFT

Chukchi Sea

EXXON/ROSNEFT

SHELL/GAZPROM NEFT

EXXON/GAZPROM NEFT

SELECT WESTERN ENERGY COMPANY PROJECTS
Western and Russian partner operations

Halted

Operational

Oil/gas projects

Shale-oil projects

SEA OF OKHOTSK
Sanctions do not apply to areas where the sea depth is under 150 metres

EASTERN MILITARY DISTRICT
(East Strategic Command, OSK-Vostok)

Sea of Okhotsk

STATOIL/ROSNEFT

EXXON/ROSNEFT
SHELL/GAZPROM NEFT

R U S S I A

HUNGER STRIKE (UNPAID WAGES)
National Space Centre, April 2015

● Vostochny Cosmodrome

TEACHERS' STRIKE
April 2015
➤● Zabaikal

SECTORAL SANCTIONS

After Russian-backed rebels shot down Malaysia Airlines flight MH17 over eastern Ukraine in July 2014, the United States and the European Union imposed sanctions on the Russian energy, financial and defence sectors (with the EU allowing exceptions for previously agreed energy projects). As Russia's economy was deeply integrated with international financial markets, many companies suffered. Russian firms deleveraged on a large scale as they struggled to roll over debts or secure new credit. As a consequence, the country's stock of external debt fell from around US$733bn in mid-2014 to around US$522bn in mid-2016. Unlike their counterparts in the energy sector, the financial measures had a chilling effect on lending to both sanctioned and unsanctioned Russian entities.

ENERGY: ban on export of Western equipment for deep-water and shale-oil production; ban on Western oilfield services for deep-water drilling and the development of Arctic and shale-oil reserves (subsidiaries of Western companies in Russia permitted to continue ongoing work on oil deposits).

FINANCE: travel bans and asset freezes on several Russian entities; ban on credit lasting more than 30 days to state banks and energy companies, including Rosneft, Transneft (EU only), Gazprom Neft, Sberbank, VTB Bank, Gazprombank, Vnesheconombank, Rosselkhozbank and Bank of Moscow (US only).

DEFENCE: ban on future EU–Russia arms deals; ban on the export of dual-use technology to Russia; restrictions on export licences for defence equipment made, or intended for use, in Russia.

FALLING OIL PRICES: JAN 2012–APRIL 2016

US$ price per barrel

120 —
100 —
80 —
60 —
40 —
20 —

Jan 12 Jul 12 Jan 13 Jul 13 Jan 14 Jul 14 Jan 15 Jul 15 Jan 16

ANNUAL GDP GROWTH

Percent

6 —
4 —
2 —
0
-2 —
-4 —
-6 —
-8 —
-10 —

Real Forecast

2009 2010 2011 2012 2013 2014 2015 2016 2017

HOUSEHOLD CONSUMPTION

Percentage contribution to growth

0.6 —
0.4 —
0.2 —
0
-0.2 —
-0.4 —

2010 2011 2012 2013 2014 2015

Change in Latin America

A broad wave of public discontent swept across Latin America in the year to mid-2016, bringing to power centrist or right-leaning parties while their left-wing rivals fell into disarray. As a series of corruption scandals incensed voters and fuelled anti-establishment movements, civil society grew ever more cohesive. Yet the region's economies were increasingly constrained by weak global growth, a decline in commodity prices and economic slowdown in China. There was an especially sharp drop in the price of the fuels, metals and food products on which Latin America relied. As a consequence, governments were forced to reduce spending and curtail ambitious projects. They did so while attempting to appeal to a middle class that had grown rapidly in the preceding decade, and that had come to believe the era of burgeoning wealth would last indefinitely.

CHANGING POLITICAL AND ECONOMIC CONDITIONS IN SELECT LATIN AMERICAN COUNTRIES

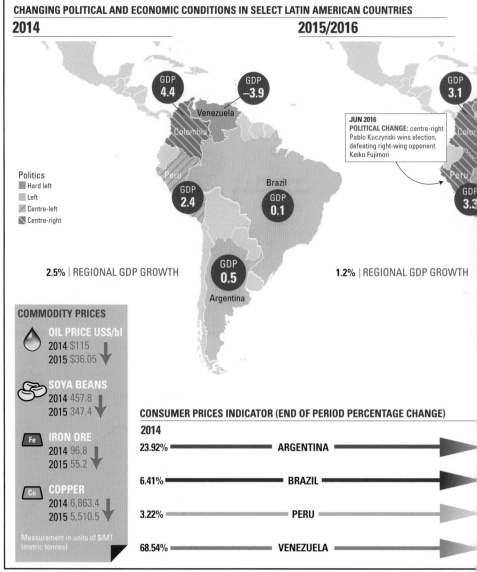

2014

2015/2016

GDP 4.4

GDP −3.9

Venezuela

Colombia

GDP 3.1

JUN 2016
POLITICAL CHANGE: centre-right Pablo Kuczynski wins election, defeating right-wing opponent Keiko Fujimori

Colom

Peru

GDP 2.4

Brazil

GDP 0.1

Peru

GDP 3.3

Politics
- Hard left
- Left
- Centre-left
- Centre-right

2.5% | REGIONAL GDP GROWTH

1.2% | REGIONAL GDP GROWTH

GDP 0.5

Argentina

COMMODITY PRICES

OIL PRICE US$/bl
2014 $115
2015 $36.05

SOYA BEANS
2014 457.8
2015 347.4

IRON ORE Fe
2014 96.8
2015 55.2

COPPER Cu
2014 6,863.4
2015 5,510.5

Measurement in units of $/MT (metric tonnes)

CONSUMER PRICES INDICATOR (END OF PERIOD PERCENTAGE CHANGE)

2014

23.92% ARGENTINA

6.41% BRAZIL

3.22% PERU

68.54% VENEZUELA

Sources: IMF; The Economist; Guardian; Wall Street Journal; ILO; OEC; Inter-American Development Bank; BBC; Telegraph; Reuters; IISS

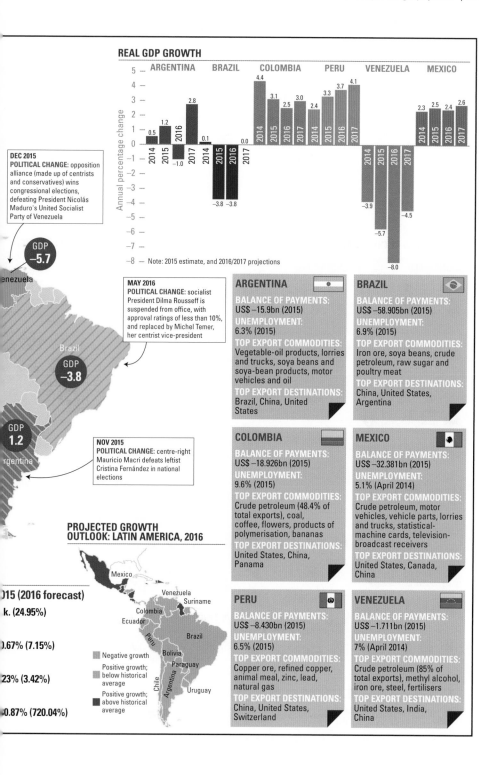

REAL GDP GROWTH

ARGENTINA BRAZIL COLOMBIA PERU VENEZUELA MEXICO

Annual percentage change

ARGENTINA: 2014: 0.5, 2015: 1.2, 2016: -1.0, 2017: 0.1
BRAZIL: 2014: 0.0, 2015: -3.8, 2016: -3.8, 2017: 2.8
COLOMBIA: 2014: 4.4, 2015: 3.1, 2016: 2.5, 2017: 3.0
PERU: 2014: 2.4, 2015: 3.3, 2016: 3.7, 2017: 4.1
VENEZUELA: 2014: -3.9, 2015: -5.7, 2016: -8.0, 2017: -4.5
MEXICO: 2014: 2.3, 2015: 2.5, 2016: 2.4, 2017: 2.6

−8 — Note: 2015 estimate, and 2016/2017 projections

DEC 2015
POLITICAL CHANGE: opposition alliance (made up of centrists and conservatives) wins congressional elections, defeating President Nicolás Maduro's United Socialist Party of Venezuela

GDP
−5.7
Venezuela

Brazil
GDP
−3.8

GDP
1.2
Argentina

MAY 2016
POLITICAL CHANGE: socialist President Dilma Rousseff is suspended from office, with approval ratings of less than 10%, and replaced by Michel Temer, her centrist vice-president

NOV 2015
POLITICAL CHANGE: centre-right Mauricio Macri defeats leftist Cristina Fernández in national elections

PROJECTED GROWTH OUTLOOK: LATIN AMERICA, 2016

Mexico
Venezuela
Suriname
Colombia
Ecuador
Peru
Brazil
Bolivia
Paraguay
Chile
Argentina
Uruguay

Negative growth

Positive growth; below historical average

Positive growth; above historical average

015 (2016 forecast)
k. (24.95%)

.67% (7.15%)

23% (3.42%)

0.87% (720.04%)

ARGENTINA
BALANCE OF PAYMENTS:
US$ −15.9bn (2015)
UNEMPLOYMENT:
6.3% (2015)
TOP EXPORT COMMODITIES:
Vegetable-oil products, lorries and trucks, soya beans and soya-bean products, motor vehicles and oil
TOP EXPORT DESTINATIONS:
Brazil, China, United States

BRAZIL
BALANCE OF PAYMENTS:
US$ −58.905bn (2015)
UNEMPLOYMENT:
6.9% (2015)
TOP EXPORT COMMODITIES:
Iron ore, soya beans, crude petroleum, raw sugar and poultry meat
TOP EXPORT DESTINATIONS:
China, United States, Argentina

COLOMBIA
BALANCE OF PAYMENTS:
US$ −18.926bn (2015)
UNEMPLOYMENT:
9.6% (2015)
TOP EXPORT COMMODITIES:
Crude petroleum (48.4% of total exports), coal, coffee, flowers, products of polymerisation, bananas
TOP EXPORT DESTINATIONS:
United States, China, Panama

MEXICO
BALANCE OF PAYMENTS:
US$ −32.381bn (2015)
UNEMPLOYMENT:
5.1% (April 2014)
TOP EXPORT COMMODITIES:
Crude petroleum, motor vehicles, vehicle parts, lorries and trucks, statistical-machine cards, television-broadcast receivers
TOP EXPORT DESTINATIONS:
United States, Canada, China

PERU
BALANCE OF PAYMENTS:
US$ −8.430bn (2015)
UNEMPLOYMENT:
6.5% (2015)
TOP EXPORT COMMODITIES:
Copper ore, refined copper, animal meal, zinc, lead, natural gas
TOP EXPORT DESTINATIONS:
China, United States, Switzerland

VENEZUELA
BALANCE OF PAYMENTS:
US$ −1.711bn (2015)
UNEMPLOYMENT:
7% (April 2014)
TOP EXPORT COMMODITIES:
Crude petroleum (85% of total exports), methyl alcohol, iron ore, steel, fertilisers
TOP EXPORT DESTINATIONS:
United States, India, China

Competing claims in the South China Sea

In 2014 China started to construct artificial islands on seven small rocks and low-tide elevations in the Spratly Islands near to features occupied by the Philippines and Vietnam. The following year, the country began a rapid acceleration in building infrastructure on the islands. In just 18 months, the land area of China's claimed features grew by 12 square kilometres. In contrast, the land area of features in the South China Sea claimed by other states – Malaysia, the Philippines, Taiwan and Vietnam – increased by 0.4 sq km in 45 years.

China's artificial islands and 'nine-dash line' claim, covering almost all of the South China Sea, became the subject of a case brought by the Philippines before the Permanent Court of Arbitration in The Hague – which acts as the arbitral tribunal referred to in the United Nations Convention on the Law of the Sea (UNCLOS). Manila argued that, under UNCLOS, China's low-tide elevations are not entitled to a maritime zone, while its rocks qualify for only a 12-nautical-mile territorial sea and airspace (rather than an exclusive economic zone).

Refusing to participate in proceedings, Beijing described Manila's claim as illegal under international law, stating that it has 'indisputable sovereignty' over the territory within the nine-dash line. On 12 July 2016 the court ruled overwhelmingly in favour of the Philippines. The ruling will likely increase international diplomatic pressure on China to scale back its expansion in the area.

KEY FEATURES IN THE SPRATLY ISLANDS: REPORTED INFRASTRUCTURE AND EQUIPMENT (as of mid-2016)

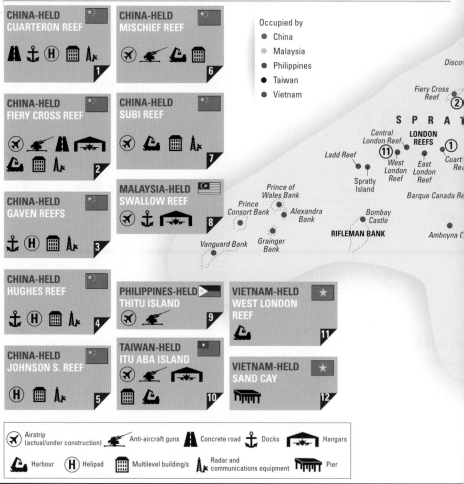

Sources: IISS; BBC; UNCLOS; Reuters; *The Economist*; CNN; *Financial Times*; Asia Maritime Transparency Initiative

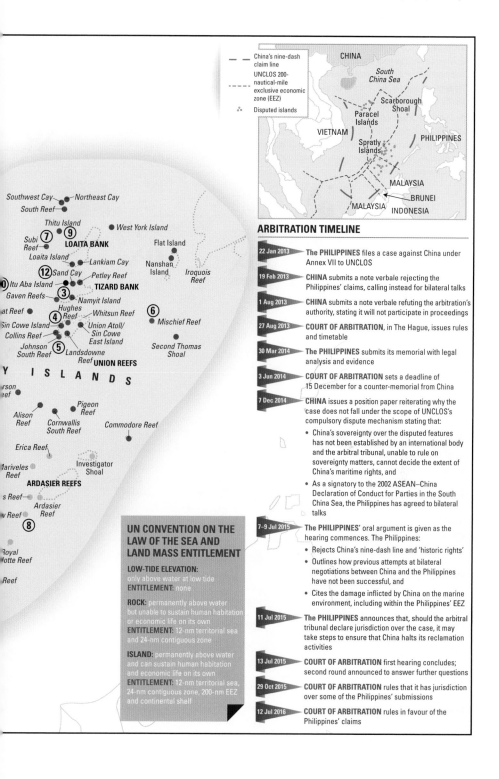

China's nine-dash claim line

UNCLOS 200-nautical-mile exclusive economic zone (EEZ)

Disputed islands

CHINA

South China Sea

Scarborough Shoal

Paracel Islands

VIETNAM

Spratly Islands

PHILIPPINES

MALAYSIA

BRUNEI

MALAYSIA

INDONESIA

Southwest Cay — Northeast Cay
South Reef

Thitu Island — West York Island
Subi Reef ⑦ ⑨ LOAITA BANK
Loaita Island — Lankiam Cay
⑫ Sand Cay — Petley Reef
⑩ Itu Aba Island — TIZARD BANK
Gaven Reefs — Namyit Island
③
Hughes Whitsun Reef ⑥
...at Reef ● ④ Reef
Sin Cowe Island — Union Atoll/ Mischief Reef
Collins Reef — Sin Cowe East Island
Johnson ⑤ Landsdowne
South Reef — Reef UNION REEFS
Second Thomas Shoal

Flat Island
Nanshan Island — Iroquois Reef

Y I S L A N D S

...rson ...eef
Pigeon Reef
Alison Reef — Cornwallis South Reef
Commodore Reef

Erica Reef
Investigator Shoal
...ariveles Reef
ARDASIER REEFS

s Reef
Ardasier Reef
w Reef — Reef
⑧

Royal ...otte Reef

...Reef

ARBITRATION TIMELINE

22 Jan 2013 — The **PHILIPPINES** files a case against China under Annex VII to UNCLOS

19 Feb 2013 — **CHINA** submits a note verbale rejecting the Philippines' claims, calling instead for bilateral talks

1 Aug 2013 — **CHINA** submits a note verbale refuting the arbitration's authority, stating it will not participate in proceedings

27 Aug 2013 — **COURT OF ARBITRATION**, in The Hague, issues rules and timetable

30 Mar 2014 — The **PHILIPPINES** submits its memorial with legal analysis and evidence

3 Jun 2014 — **COURT OF ARBITRATION** sets a deadline of 15 December for a counter-memorial from China

7 Dec 2014 — **CHINA** issues a position paper reiterating why the case does not fall under the scope of UNCLOS's compulsory dispute mechanism stating that:

- China's sovereignty over the disputed features has not been established by an international body and the arbitral tribunal, unable to rule on sovereignty matters, cannot decide the extent of China's maritime rights, and
- As a signatory to the 2002 ASEAN–China Declaration of Conduct for Parties in the South China Sea, the Philippines has agreed to bilateral talks

7–9 Jul 2015 — The **PHILIPPINES'** oral argument is given as the hearing commences. The Philippines:

- Rejects China's nine-dash line and 'historic rights'
- Outlines how previous attempts at bilateral negotiations between China and the Philippines have not been successful, and
- Cites the damage inflicted by China on the marine environment, including within the Philippines' EEZ

11 Jul 2015 — The **PHILIPPINES** announces that, should the arbitral tribunal declare jurisdiction over the case, it may take steps to ensure that China halts its reclamation activities

13 Jul 2015 — **COURT OF ARBITRATION** first hearing concludes; second round announced to answer further questions

29 Oct 2015 — **COURT OF ARBITRATION** rules that it has jurisdiction over some of the Philippines' submissions

12 Jul 2016 — **COURT OF ARBITRATION** rules in favour of the Philippines' claims

UN CONVENTION ON THE LAW OF THE SEA AND LAND MASS ENTITLEMENT

LOW-TIDE ELEVATION:
only above water at low tide
ENTITLEMENT: none

ROCK: permanently above water but unable to sustain human habitation or economic life on its own
ENTITLEMENT: 12-nm territorial sea and 24-nm contiguous zone

ISLAND: permanently above water and can sustain human habitation and economic life on its own
ENTITLEMENT: 12-nm territorial sea, 24-nm contiguous zone, 200-nm EEZ and continental shelf

The evolving threat of ISIS

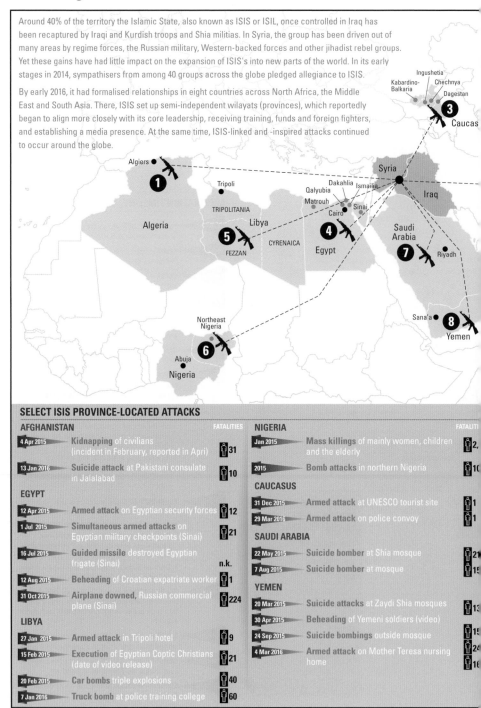

Around 40% of the territory the Islamic State, also known as ISIS or ISIL, once controlled in Iraq has been recaptured by Iraqi and Kurdish troops and Shia militias. In Syria, the group has been driven out of many areas by regime forces, the Russian military, Western-backed forces and other jihadist rebel groups. Yet these gains have had little impact on the expansion of ISIS's into new parts of the world. In its early stages in 2014, sympathisers from among 40 groups across the globe pledged allegiance to ISIS.

By early 2016, it had formalised relationships in eight countries across North Africa, the Middle East and South Asia. There, ISIS set up semi-independent wilayats (provinces), which reportedly began to align more closely with its core leadership, receiving training, funds and foreign fighters, and establishing a media presence. At the same time, ISIS-linked and -inspired attacks continued to occur around the globe.

Map labels: Ingushetia, Kabardino-Balkaria, Chechnya, Dagestan, ❸ Caucas, Algiers ❶, Tripoli, Dakahlia, Ismailia, Syria, Qalyubia, Matrouh, TRIPOLITANIA, Cairo, Sinai, Iraq, Algeria, Libya ❺, ❹, Saudi Arabia, CYRENAICA, Egypt ❼, Riyadh, FEZZAN, Northeast Nigeria, Sana'a ❽, Yemen, Abuja ❻, Nigeria

SELECT ISIS PROVINCE-LOCATED ATTACKS

AFGHANISTAN

FATALITIES

Date	Attack	Fatalities
4 Apr 2015	Kidnapping of civilians (incident in February, reported in Apri)	31
13 Jan 2016	Suicide attack at Pakistani consulate in Jalalabad	10

EGYPT

Date	Attack	Fatalities
12 Apr 2015	Armed attack on Egyptian security forces	12
1 Jul 2015	Simultaneous armed attacks on Egyptian military checkpoints (Sinai)	21
16 Jul 2015	Guided missile destroyed Egyptian frigate (Sinai)	n.k.
12 Aug 2015	Beheading of Croatian expatriate worker	1
31 Oct 2015	Airplane downed, Russian commercial plane (Sinai)	224

LIBYA

Date	Attack	Fatalities
27 Jan 2015	Armed attack in Tripoli hotel	9
15 Feb 2015	Execution of Egyptian Coptic Christians (date of video release)	21
20 Feb 2015	Car bombs triple explosions	40
7 Jan 2016	Truck bomb at police training college	60

NIGERIA

FATALITI

Date	Attack	Fatalities
Jan 2015	Mass killings of mainly women, children and the elderly	2,
2015	Bomb attacks in northern Nigeria	10

CAUCASUS

Date	Attack	Fatalities
31 Dec 2015	Armed attack at UNESCO tourist site	1
29 Mar 2016	Armed attack on police convoy	1

SAUDI ARABIA

Date	Attack	Fatalities
22 May 2015	Suicide bomber at Shia mosque	21
7 Aug 2015	Suicide bomber at mosque	15

YEMEN

Date	Attack	Fatalities
20 Mar 2015	Suicide attacks at Zaydi Shia mosques	13
30 Apr 2015	Beheading of Yemeni soldiers (video)	
24 Sep 2015	Suicide bombings outside mosque	15
4 Mar 2016	Armed attack on Mother Teresa nursing home	26 / 16

Sources: IISS; *Washington Post*; The Wilson Center; *Guardian*; IntelCenter; Soufan Group; BBC; *New York Times*

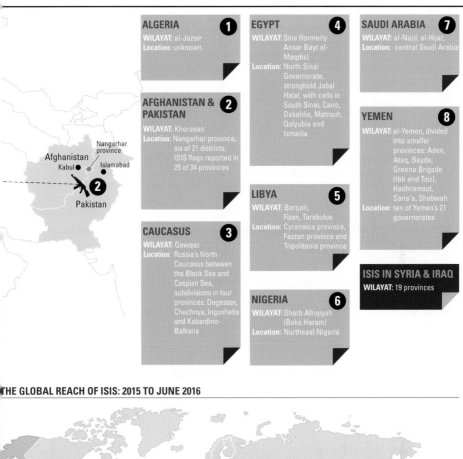

ALGERIA ①
WILAYAT: al-Jazair
Location: unknown

AFGHANISTAN & PAKISTAN ②
WILAYAT: Khorasan
Location: Nangarhar province, six of 21 districts, ISIS flags reported in 25 of 34 provinces

CAUCASUS ③
WILAYAT: Qawqaz
Location: Russia's North Caucasus between the Black Sea and Caspian Sea, subdivisions in four provinces: Dagestan, Chechnya, Ingushetia and Kabardino-Balkaria

EGYPT ④
WILAYAT: Sina (formerly Ansar Bayt al-Maqdis)
Location: North Sinai Governorate, stronghold Jabal Halal, with cells in South Sinai, Cairo, Dakahlia, Matrouh, Qalyubia and Ismailia

LIBYA ⑤
WILAYAT: Barqah, Fizan, Tarabulus
Location: Cyrenaica province, Fezzan province and Tripolitania province

NIGERIA ⑥
WILAYAT: Gharb Afriqiyah (Boko Haram)
Location: Northeast Nigeria

SAUDI ARABIA ⑦
WILAYAT: al-Najd, al-Hijaz,
Location: central Saudi Arabia

YEMEN ⑧
WILAYAT: al-Yemen, divided into smaller provinces: Aden, Ataq, Bayda, Greene Brigade (Ibb and Taiz), Hadhramaut, Sana'a, Shabwah
Location: ten of Yemen's 21 governorates

ISIS IN SYRIA & IRAQ
WILAYAT: 19 provinces

Nangarhar province
Afghanistan
Kabul
Islamabad
Pakistan

THE GLOBAL REACH OF ISIS: 2015 TO JUNE 2016

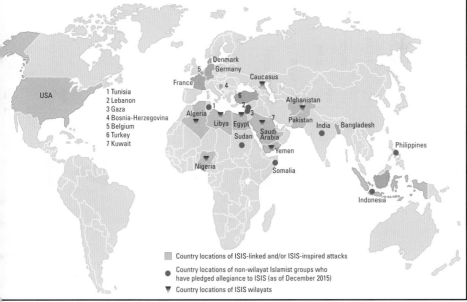

1 Tunisia
2 Lebanon
3 Gaza
4 Bosnia-Herzegovina
5 Belgium
6 Turkey
7 Kuwait

USA
Denmark
Germany
France
Caucasus
Afghanistan
Algeria
Libya Egypt
Sudan Saudi Arabia
Pakistan
India Bangladesh
Yemen
Philippines
Nigeria
Somalia
Indonesia

▢ Country locations of ISIS-linked and/or ISIS-inspired attacks

● Country locations of non-wilayat Islamist groups who have pledged allegiance to ISIS (as of December 2015)

▼ Country locations of ISIS wilayats

Migration and nationalism in Europe

Since 2014, there has been an unprecedented rise in the number of migrants entering the Schengen Area. More than 1.2 million first-time asylum seekers arrived there in 2015. This pattern continued into 2016, with INTERPOL reporting in May that 800,000 migrants in Libya were waiting to cross into Europe. Almost one in three first-time registered asylum seekers travelling to Europe were Syrian, while Afghans and Iraqis made up the second- and third-largest groups among these people respectively.

German Chancellor Angela Merkel initially implemented an 'open-door policy' on Syrian refugees, and Germany received 35% of all irregular migrants to the European Union in 2015. The policy increasingly led to political division within Germany and undermined support for her party, the Christian Democratic Union.

Iceland

More widely, the future of the Schengen Area's open-border arrangements was brought into question, exposing disagreements on the issue among European countries, particularly between east and west. At the same time, countries within the area experienced a sharp rise in support for far-right nationalist parties.

RISE OF FAR-RIGHT NATIONALIST PARTIES IN EUROPE: results from recent national elections

AUSTRIA **49.7%** Freedom Party	FRANCE **14%** National Front	HUNGARY **21%** Jobbik	SLOVAKIA **8%** Our Slovakia
DENMARK **21%** Danish People's Party	GERMANY **4.7%** Alternative for Germany	ITALY **4%** Northern League	SWEDEN **13%** Sweden Democrats
FINLAND **18%** Finns Party	GREECE **7%** Golden Dawn	NETHERLANDS **10%** Freedom Party	SWITZERLAND **29%** Swiss People's Party

Irela

TOP TEN HIGHEST MIGRANT INTAKE SCHENGEN COUNTRIES, 2015

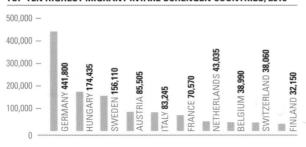

- GERMANY 441,800
- HUNGARY 174,435
- SWEDEN 156,110
- AUSTRIA 85,505
- ITALY 83,245
- FRANCE 70,570
- NETHERLANDS 43,035
- BELGIUM 38,990
- SWITZERLAND 38,060
- FINLAND 32,150

(Y-axis: 0, 100,000, 200,000, 300,000, 400,000, 500,000)

SHORT-TERM COST TO GERMANY

93.6 BILLION EUROS BY 2020

Finance ministry's calculations based on 600,000 arrivals in 2016, 400,000 in 2017 and 300,000 in the following years

Portugal

2015

Jun

HUNGARY:
First border fence built, sealing entry for migrants entering from Serbia

Aug

GERMANY:
Angela Merkel extends an 'open-door' policy to Syrians

BULGARIA:
Seals southern border with Turkey

ESTONIA:
Announces plan to build a 70-mile-long, eight-foot-high wall, starting 2018

Sep

HUNGARY:
Train stations in Budapest sealed off, preventing migrants from travelling onwards

SLOVAKIA:
Announces closure of border with Hungary

GERMANY:
Opens borders to ease the situation in Hungary and Austria; 1,000s head to Munich

EU:
Interior ministers' majority vote approves the relocation of 120,000 refugees across EU states

Oct

HUNGARY:
Imposes controls on border with Slovenia

Nov

MACEDONIA & SLOVENIA:
Erect border fences

AUSTRIA:
Erects fence on border with Slovenia

Sources: European Commission; UN; *Independent*; Cologne Institute of Economic Research; BAMF; *Guardian*; BBC; *Telegraph*; CNN; Reuters; IISS; Politbarometers

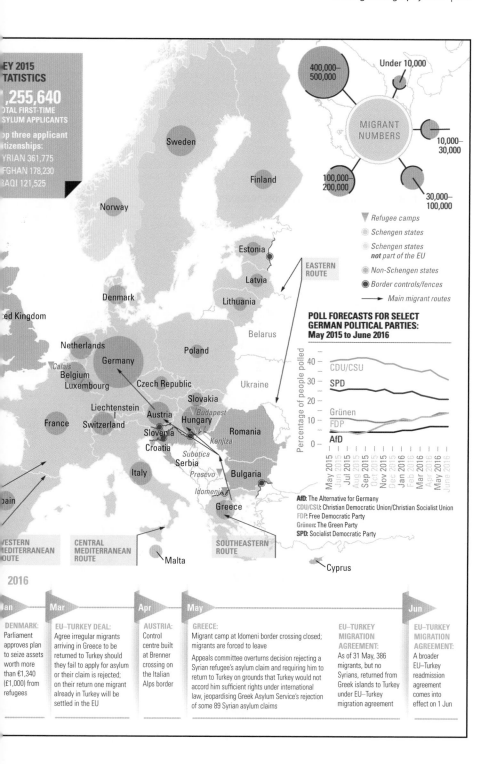

EY 2015 TATISTICS

,255,640
TAL FIRST-TIME
SYLUM APPLICANTS

p three applicant
tizenships:
YRIAN 361,775
FGHAN 178,230
AQI 121,525

Sweden

Finland

Norway

Estonia

Latvia

Lithuania

Denmark

ed Kingdom

Belarus

Netherlands

Germany

Poland

Belgium
Luxembourg

Czech Republic

Ukraine

Calais

Liechtenstein

Slovakia

France

Switzerland

Austria

Budapest

Hungary

Romania

Slovenia

Kanjiza

Croatia

Subotica

Serbia

Italy

Presevo

Bulgaria

Idomeni

ain

Greece

Malta

Cyprus

MIGRANT NUMBERS

400,000–500,000

Under 10,000

10,000–30,000

100,000–200,000

30,000–100,000

▼ Refugee camps
◉ Schengen states
◉ Schengen states *not* part of the EU
◉ Non-Schengen states
◉ Border controls/fences
→ Main migrant routes

EASTERN ROUTE

POLL FORECASTS FOR SELECT GERMAN POLITICAL PARTIES: May 2015 to June 2016

Percentage of people polled

40
30 — SPD
CDU/CSU
20
10 — Grünen
FDP
0 — AfD

May 2015
Jun 2015
Jul 2015
Aug 2015
Sep 2015
Oct 2015
Nov 2015
Dec 2015
Jan 2016
Feb 2016
Mar 2016
Apr 2016
May 2016
June 2016

AfD: The Alternative for Germany
CDU/CSU: Christian Democratic Union/Christian Socialist Union
FDP: Free Democratic Party
Grünen: The Green Party
SPD: Socialist Democratic Party

WESTERN MEDITERRANEAN ROUTE

CENTRAL MEDITERRANEAN ROUTE

SOUTHEASTERN ROUTE

2016

an	Mar	Apr	May		Jun

DENMARK:
Parliament approves plan to seize assets worth more than €1,340 (£1,000) from refugees

EU–TURKEY DEAL:
Agree irregular migrants arriving in Greece to be returned to Turkey should they fail to apply for asylum or their claim is rejected; on their return one migrant already in Turkey will be settled in the EU

AUSTRIA:
Control centre built at Brenner crossing on the Italian Alps border

GREECE:
Migrant camp at Idomeni border crossing closed; migrants are forced to leave

Appeals committee overturns decision rejecting a Syrian refugee's asylum claim and requiring him to return to Turkey on grounds that Turkey would not accord him sufficient rights under international law, jeopardising Greek Asylum Service's rejection of some 89 Syrian asylum claims

EU–TURKEY MIGRATION AGREEMENT:
As of 31 May, 386 migrants, but no Syrians, returned from Greek islands to Turkey under EU–Turkey migration agreement

EU–TURKEY MIGRATION AGREEMENT:
A broader EU–Turkey readmission agreement comes into effect on 1 Jun

Chronic instability in the DRC

Scheduled to go to the polls in November 2016, the Democratic Republic of the Congo (DRC) is yet to complete a peaceful transfer of power. And, having served two terms, President Joseph Kabila is barred from re-election by constitutional amendments made in 2006. Yet he shows no sign of stepping down. His opponents have accused him of postponing the upcoming vote and of violently repressing political and civil-society opposition groups.

Despite a rapidly growing economy and a wealth of natural resources, the DRC has one of the highest poverty rates in the world. The country has experienced persistent conflict for more than 20 years. More than 70 warring factions, largely concentrated in the east, are competing to control territory and resources while subjecting civilians to severe human-rights abuses. An estimated 1.8 million people have been internally displaced, 90% of them by violence.

IDP NUMBERS, MINERALS AND UN MISSION PRESENCE: 2015

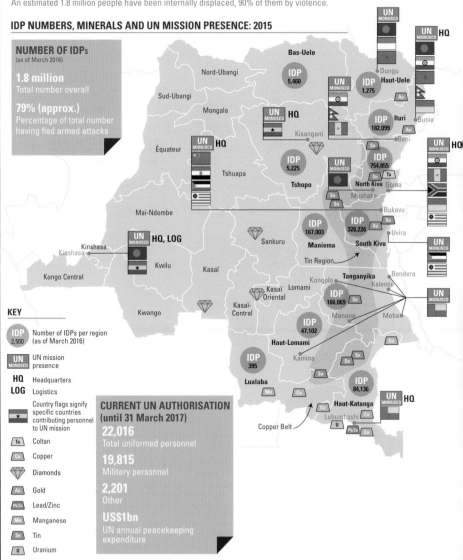

NUMBER OF IDPs
(as of March 2016)

1.8 million
Total number overall

79% (approx.)
Percentage of total number
having fled armed attacks

KEY

IDP 2,500	Number of IDPs per region (as of March 2016)
UN MONUSCO	UN mission presence
HQ	Headquarters
LOG	Logistics
★	Country flags signify specific countries contributing personnel to UN mission
Ta	Coltan
Cu	Copper
◆	Diamonds
Au	Gold
Pb/Zn	Lead/Zinc
Mn	Manganese
Sn	Tin
U	Uranium

CURRENT UN AUTHORISATION
(until 31 March 2017)

22,016
Total uniformed personnel

19,815
Military personnel

2,201
Other

US$1bn
UN annual peacekeeping
expenditure

Sources: UNOCHA; United Nations; BBC; IPIS; IISS; World Bank; Congo Research Group; Amnesty International; *The Economist*; Al-Jazeera; Reuters; Bloomberg

ELECT ARMED GROUPS IN RTH KIVU AND SOUTH KIVU

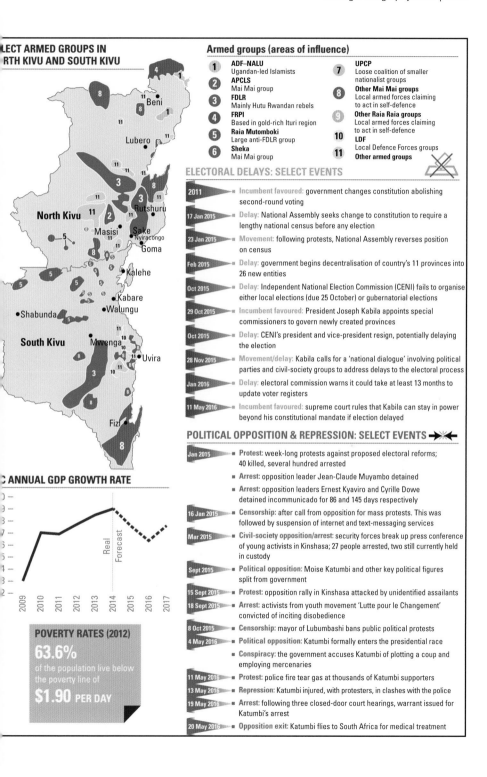

ANNUAL GDP GROWTH RATE

Real
Forecast

2009 2010 2011 2012 2013 2014 2015 2016 2017

POVERTY RATES (2012)

63.6%
of the population live below the poverty line of
$1.90 PER DAY

Armed groups (areas of influence)

1 ADF–NALU
Ugandan-led Islamists

2 APCLS
Mai Mai group

3 FDLR
Mainly Hutu Rwandan rebels

4 FRPI
Based in gold-rich Ituri region

5 Raia Mutomboki
Large anti-FDLR group

6 Sheka
Mai Mai group

7 UPCP
Loose coalition of smaller nationalist groups

8 Other Mai Mai groups
Local armed forces claiming to act in self-defence

9 Other Raia Raia groups
Local armed forces claiming to act in self-defence

10 LDF
Local Defence Forces groups

11 Other armed groups

ELECTORAL DELAYS: SELECT EVENTS

2011 — Incumbent favoured: government changes constitution abolishing second-round voting

17 Jan 2015 — Delay: National Assembly seeks change to constitution to require a lengthy national census before any election

23 Jan 2015 — Movement: following protests, National Assembly reverses position on census

Feb 2015 — Delay: government begins decentralisation of country's 11 provinces into 26 new entities

Oct 2015 — Delay: Independent National Election Commission (CENI) fails to organise either local elections (due 25 October) or gubernatorial elections

29 Oct 2015 — Incumbent favoured: President Joseph Kabila appoints special commissioners to govern newly created provinces

Oct 2015 — Delay: CENI's president and vice-president resign, potentially delaying the election

28 Nov 2015 — Movement/delay: Kabila calls for a 'national dialogue' involving political parties and civil-society groups to address delays to the electoral process

Jan 2016 — Delay: electoral commission warns it could take at least 13 months to update voter registers

11 May 2016 — Incumbent favoured: supreme court rules that Kabila can stay in power beyond his constitutional mandate if election delayed

POLITICAL OPPOSITION & REPRESSION: SELECT EVENTS

Jan 2015 — Protest: week-long protests against proposed electoral reforms; 40 killed, several hundred arrested

Arrest: opposition leader Jean-Claude Muyambo detained

Arrest: opposition leaders Ernest Kyaviro and Cyrille Dowe detained incommunicado for 86 and 145 days respectively

16 Jan 2015 — Censorship: after call from opposition for mass protests. This was followed by suspension of internet and text-messaging services

Mar 2015 — Civil-society opposition/arrest: security forces break up press conference of young activists in Kinshasa; 27 people arrested, two still currently held in custody

Sept 2015 — Political opposition: Moise Katumbi and other key political figures split from government

15 Sept 2015 — Protest: opposition rally in Kinshasa attacked by unidentified assailants

18 Sept 2015 — Arrest: activists from youth movement 'Lutte pour le Changement' convicted of inciting disobedience

8 Oct 2015 — Censorship: mayor of Lubumbashi bans public political protests

4 May 2016 — Political opposition: Katumbi formally enters the presidential race

Conspiracy: the government accuses Katumbi of plotting a coup and employing mercenaries

11 May 2016 — Protest: police fire tear gas at thousands of Katumbi supporters

13 May 2016 — Repression: Katumbi injured, with protesters, in clashes with the police

19 May 2016 — Arrest: following three closed-door court hearings, warrant issued for Katumbi's arrest

20 May 2016 — Opposition exit: Katumbi flies to South Africa for medical treatment

Chapter 7

Middle East and North Africa

In the year to mid-2016, much of the Middle East continued to be affected by state-driven and jihadist violence, political turmoil and worsening economic and social conditions. A sense of drift and despair pervaded the region, as hoped-for de-escalation on various battlefields failed to materialise and no genuine effort at political reform was made. Instead, repression grew and public space was tightened, with regimes everywhere strengthening their hold on power.

The wars in Syria, Iraq, Yemen and Libya led to no decisive victories nor political settlements, while their humanitarian toll and security repercussions increased. Progressively losing territory in Iraq and Syria, the Islamic State, also known as ISIS or ISIL, gradually reverted to its role as an insurgent group, and mounted attacks outside the Middle East.

Simultaneously, rivalry between Saudi Arabia and Iran took centre stage. The Saudi monarchy sought to build a Sunni front to contain Iranian influence, but hedging, mistrust and competing priorities among Riyadh's allies and partners frustrated the effort.

Importantly, the Russian intervention in Syria opened a new chapter in the internationalisation of Middle Eastern crises. This and the accompanying retrenchment by the US, ahead of the country's 2016 presidential elections, raised the prospect of greater brinkmanship and hedging.

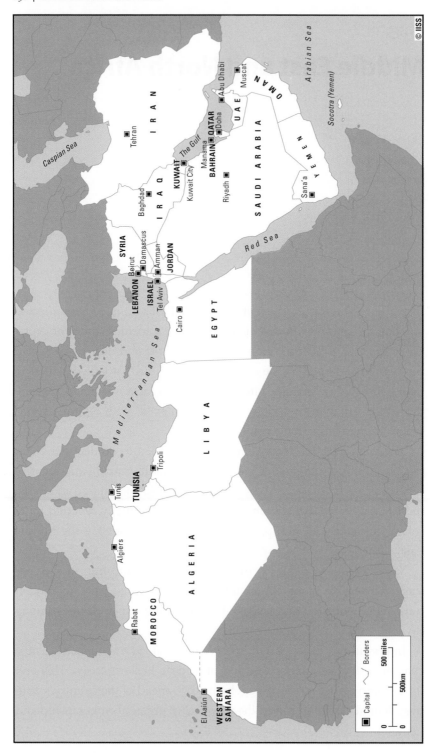

Syria

As Syria remained the fulcrum of regional competition in the Middle East, it also emerged as a potential flashpoint for conflict between international powers. Once believed to be containable, the Syrian conflict fully demonstrated its destabilising effects.

The Russian intervention in Syria that started in autumn 2015 profoundly shaped the war, as well as the diplomacy designed to end it. The intervention also affected the region's perceptions of the United States and Russia, and sparked an international debate about the regional order. The weakening of the regime of Syrian President Bashar al-Assad in the first half of 2015 at the hand of a rebel coalition that included the Syrian affiliate of al-Qaeda, Jabhat al-Nusra, as well as hardline Islamist and mainstream factions, prompted Russia to build up its forces and intervene in concert with Iran. Moscow's deployment of significant air capabilities (including bombers and fixed- and rotary-wing aircraft for close air support) combined with a surge of Iranian fighters and Shia jihadists from Iraq, Lebanon and South Asia to restore Assad's fortunes.

The first phase of the intervention lasted until February 2016, and overwhelmingly focused on the mainstream and Islamist elements of the rebellion in western and northern Syria, creating significant setbacks for the rebels, particularly around Aleppo, Latakia and Damascus. Russian advisers helped reorganise and direct Syrian-government and allied forces on the battlefield. Russia waited until the second stage of the intervention to target the jihadist groups – notably, ISIS – whose growth provided the ostensible justification for the intervention. Russian support allowed pro-Assad forces to retake in March the historic city of Palmyra, which ISIS had controlled for around a year.

The deployment of advanced air-defence systems and aircraft gave Russia dominant control over western Syria. This increased the cost for the United States or other countries of potentially imposing a no-fly zone there, and allowed Moscow to intimidate and enforce new rules on neighbouring countries. Turkey's shoot-down of a Russian fighter jet that briefly crossed into its airspace spurred Moscow to punish Ankara through economic sanctions, diplomatic bullying and the targeting of Turkish-supported rebels. Russia allowed Israel to conduct air operations over southern Syria to identify and destroy Iranian and Hizbullah targets, including weapons shipments. The Russian intervention also created further dilemmas and risks for the US, whose air force conducted an anti-ISIS operation in eastern Syria. As a consequence, Washington became concerned about whether and how to de-conflict with Moscow without engaging in active collaboration. While the US resisted any form of cooperation, Russia attempted to entangle it under the cover of joint operations against ISIS or Jabhat al-Nusra, or to monitor truces.

The battlefield grew even more complex with Kurdish expansion in eastern and northern Syria, to the detriment of not only ISIS but also Islamist and mainstream rebels. Leading a coalition named the Syrian Democratic Forces, the Kurdish Democratic Union Party (PYD), the main Kurdish faction, became a central element of Washington's anti-ISIS strategy, especially for sealing off the border with Turkey and conquering the town of Manbij and eventually the city of Raqqa. But this strategy antagonised Arab Syrians, as well as Turkey, which faced a reinvigorated Kurdish insurgency at home. Russia also became a partner for the Kurds, especially as Russian–Turkish tensions increased.

Moscow seemed in control of the agenda, at least momentarily. Its military operation, unforeseen and underestimated by the US, delivered tangible results for Assad within months and put Russia at the heart of Middle Eastern politics. Indeed, a series of Middle Eastern leaders made frantic trips to Moscow in the wake of the intervention. These included US allies such as the Jordanian monarch, Gulf Arab heads of state and the Israeli prime minister. For them, Russia's ruthlessness and determination contrasted with the perceived passivity and miscalculations of the US administration. However, their primary goal was to hedge and seek a temporary accommodation, rather than to shift away from the US.

Uncertain diplomacy

Momentum for diplomacy in Syria grew out of the escalation and internationalisation of the conflict, which had repercussions for Europe. These primarily took the form of massive numbers of refugees entering EU states from summer 2015 onwards, and large-scale attacks on French and Belgian soil mounted by returning ISIS fighters and young people who had been radicalised locally.

Starting in November 2015, the US and Russia led an international effort to de-escalate the fighting and broker a political settlement between the warring parties. They formed the International Syria Support Group (ISSG), the first such construct to include Iran, despite the reservations of Gulf Arab states. In December, the UN Security Council adopted Resolution 2254, which laid out a road map for talks. In response, and with Saudi guidance, the Syrian opposition formed the High Negotiations Committee to take part in UN-mediated negotiations. The committee was the most inclusive opposition body to date, as it comprised a wide range of political factions and received conditional support from hardline Islamist groups such as Ahrar al-Sham and Jaysh al-Islam. However, it excluded the PYD.

The diplomatic effort was continually threatened by fighting, particularly in Aleppo, where the regime attempted to fully encircle rebel-held areas. In response, the US and Russia brokered in late February an agreement on a nationwide cessation of hostilities, which excluded ISIS and Jabhat al-Nusra. Most Syrian rebels grudgingly accepted the deal, but it had a weak monitoring mechanism and no means for enforcement. The ceasefire led to a marked, if problematic, reduction in violence: the Assad regime and Russia continued to conduct select operations, while the rebel groups overwhelmingly respected the agreement. For Jabhat al-Nusra, the ceasefire proved both a challenge and an opportunity. Lower levels of violence undercut support for the group, but the regime's ceasefire violations and the lack of political progress in Geneva validated its position in the eyes of rebel sympathisers. Jabhat al-Nusra therefore mounted attacks against regime targets and sought to implicate rebel groups abiding by the ceasefire.

The diplomacy was predicated on the ability of Russia and the US to pressure their respective allies into a significant de-escalation and negotiate in good faith. Staffan de Mistura, the UN special envoy for Syria, nominally led the talks, supported by ISSG officials. He attempted to jump-start direct discussions between regime and opposition delegations. While they made headway on important matters, the key issue of Assad's fate remained unresolved. The regime resisted any talk of removing him or weakening the powers of the president, while the opposition insisted on his early resignation during the transitional period. The negotiators proposed several ideas – such as the appointment of vice-presidents with executive authority on a sectarian basis, and the establishment of a new constitution prior to a transition – but none gained traction. The ceasefire was undermined by a lack of progress on political talks and arrangements for urgently needed humanitarian access. Indeed, despite fleeting international pressure, sieges imposed by the regime continued to cause large-scale starvation and misery, with the aim of displacing, or forcing the capitulation of, large numbers of civilians.

The talks reflected the imbalance between Moscow and Washington. Russia shaped the diplomacy largely because of its greater involvement in Syria, while the US, fixated on defeating ISIS, appeared to have little leverage. While imperfect, the alignment of interests between Assad, Moscow and Tehran allowed the regime to harden its position in Geneva. It was unclear whether Russia would be, as the US hoped, willing or able to adjust this position. The divergence between Moscow and its ally, notably over Assad's maximalist military objectives, led Russian officials to regularly voice their frustration with him, but there was no sign that the relationship would break down. Russia's ostensible support for a Syrian-led (loosely defined) transition also contrasted with Iran's unwillingness to force Assad to step down. In contrast, the US remained reluctant to shape events on the battlefield, resisting calls to provide greater quantities of weapons (especially anti-aircraft missiles), conduct direct strikes and impose no-fly zones. There was a strong sense that Washington had toned down its military and political goals, alienating its European, Arab and Turkish partners, and generating distrust among the Syrian opposition.

The diplomatic deadlock and lack of political options revived talk on the partition of Syria, informal or declared, in which Assad would continue ruling the west of the country and the Kurds would administer most of the north and east. Proponents of the plan believed that freezing the conflict would allow them to focus on combating ISIS and Jabhat al-Nusra. However, partition had little support among Syrians. Assad repeatedly stated his intention to recapture all Syrian territory. Controlling a shrinking, non-contiguous and poorly resourced territory, mainstream and Islamist rebels were likely to reject such an arrangement. Many Syrian civilians also objected to the proposal. Instead, the parties considered the idea of de-centralisation as part of a political settlement.

Iraq

In the year to mid-2016, Iraq was at the epicentre of three geopolitical trends destabilising the wider Middle East. The first of these, which originated in the aftermath of regime change in the country, was the exceptionally violent but effective form of Islamist radicalism deployed by the Islamic State, also known as ISIS or ISIL. Established there by the Jordanian Salafi jihadist Abu Musab al-Zarqawi, the group declared itself al-Qaeda in Iraq in 2004, before taking the name the Islamic State of Iraq in November 2006. It reached the peak of its power in May 2015, when it seized the city of Ramadi in Anbar Province. Yet, between July 2015 and June 2016, the group lost 50% of the territory it controlled in the country, as its fighters were pushed out of the cities of Ramadi and Falluja, also in Anbar Province, as well as Sinjar in the north.

The second, interlinked regional trend was rising political sectarianism, both from above, in the form of state-controlled rhetoric, and from below, through intercommunal hatred. The antipathy started following the US-led invasion of Iraq in 2003, when successive Iraqi elections, and the governments that resulted from them, were dominated by appeals to sectarian identity. The hatred has been exacerbated by the use of the Shia-dominated Hashd al-Shaabi (Popular Mobilisation Units). These informal militias had been raised after the fall of Mosul, Iraq's second-largest city, in June 2014, and were used to clear areas controlled by ISIS. They have been mobilised and motivated by overt sectarian rhetoric, and have been repeatedly accused by Human Rights Watch and Amnesty International of engaging in human-rights abuses, population transfers and extrajudicial murders in their fight against the jihadist group.

The final trend is the result of the continuing weakness in the price of oil. Iraq is one of the most oil-dependent countries in the world, with 95% of government expenditure paid for by the export of the product. A decline in public services, following a sharp drop in oil prices, triggered mass popular protests across the south of the country from July 2015 onwards. Tens of thousands of ordinary Iraqis came into the streets at the height of summer to protest about the lack of electricity and clean water. They blamed endemic government corruption but also the Muhasasa Ta'ifia, the ethno-sectarian quota system that has been used to form every Iraqi governing body since 2003, and that is widely regarded as encouraging graft. As a consequence, the first half of 2016 was dominated by Iraqi Prime Minister Haider al-Abadi's ineffectual attempts to meet the protesters' demands and reform his government.

The military campaign against ISIS started in August 2014, when US President Barack Obama authorised the use of American airpower in Iraq. He followed this initial deployment with *Operation Inherent Resolve*, forming a multilateral coalition to defeat the group. This combined US aircraft with what Obama described as 'tens of thousands of Iraqi and Syrian forces fighting ISIS on the ground'. In Iraq, these forces are made up of Peshmerga, the military forces of the Kurdistan Regional Government and the 60,000–100,000 men enlisted in the Hashd al-Shaabi. The problems of using Peshmerga forces became apparent when the largely Yazidi town of Sinjar was retaken on 13 November 2015. It is estimated that up to 80% of the town was destroyed during its liberation. Six military units comprising over 7,500 men were used to retake Sinjar, where they battled an estimated 2,500 ISIS fighters. Members of Syrian Kurdish militia the Democratic Union Party supplemented forces from the two main Kurdish parties, the Patriotic Union of Kurdistan and the Kurdistan Democratic Party. The animosity between these different Kurdish groups was such that they advanced on the city from different directions to avoid open conflict with one another on the battlefield.

The recapture of Ramadi and Falluja involved the even greater problems of deploying the Hashd al-Shaabi. Ramadi was retaken in December 2015, after a seven-month campaign against an estimated 1,000 ISIS fighters. This time, the Hashd al-Shaabi were deliberately excluded from the fight for the city, with the Golden Division, Iraq's elite counter-terrorism service, conducting the majority of the fighting. However, an estimated 80% of the city's buildings were damaged in the fight. Finally, Falluja was retaken in June 2016. While the Golden Division again carried out most of the fighting, Human Rights Watch reported that the Hashd al-Shaabi had abused civilians fleeing the city and conducted extrajudicial executions.

The US military command in Iraq stated that its chief campaign goal was to turn ISIS back into an insurgent force – in effect, destroying its capacity to hold territory. By mid-2016, it appeared that the campaign to retake Mosul would come to fruition in the first months of 2017 and, if successful, potentially fulfil this aim. But ISIS grew rapidly between 2011 and 2014 because it was able to recruit Iraqi Sunnis who felt persecuted by the government in Baghdad. Due to the destruction and widespread human-rights abuses that accompanied the campaign against the group, Sunni anger and alienation was undiminished, and may have even increased. If this section of the population remains alienated – and is not reintegrated into the state and society – it is only a matter of time before a new radical Islamist force, an offshoot of ISIS, emerges and starts to recruit.

The popular protests against government corruption and inefficiency that started in July 2015 quickly received the backing of Grand Ayatollah Ali al-Sistani, the senior Shia cleric in Iraq and probably the most influential person in the country. Throughout the summer, he used his Friday prayers to back the demands of the demonstrators and to severely criticise Iraq's governing elite. When faced with mass protests backed by Sistani, Abadi had little choice but to try and meet their demands. On 9 August 2015, the prime minister launched a 44-point reform plan designed to end the Muhasasa Ta'ifia, tackle corruption and reduce the size of government. Faced with such a widespread, powerful protest movement, the rest of the ruling elite had little choice but to support Abadi's initiative. Parliament unanimously passed his plan in August.

However, by the start of 2016, Abadi's reform plans had not been implemented. Moqtada al-Sadr, whose militia, Jaish al-Mahdi, was a key player in the Iraqi civil war of 2004–08, joined the protests. The move explicitly provided protection to the demonstrators, but carried an implicit threat of violence if his demands were not met. Sadr gave Abadi 45 days to appoint a new cabinet of non-sectarian, technocratic ministers to fight corruption and mismanagement. As the deadline neared, Sadr's supporters breached the outer perimeters of the once heavily defended Green Zone, pitching tents along its access roads and pledging to stay there until Abadi met their demands. It quickly became clear that the prime minister lacked the influence over senior army commanders and Interior Ministry officials to remove Sadr and his supporters. Two days later, the prime minister presented to parliament a plan for a new, smaller cabinet made up of technocratic ministers. This plan failed to gain parliamentary approval. On 30 April, Sadr once again mobilised his supporters, who stormed the parliament building and occupied parts of the Green Zone. Although the demonstrators left after 24 hours, their actions had immense symbolic ramifications. Supporters of the protest movement claimed that parliament was no longer isolated from the realities of Iraq. Sadr asserted that 'the people had announced their revolution'. However, the Sadr challenge met with opposition from other Shia factions, which saw it as a divisive power play.

The Iraqi government faced three interlinked crises, but had little ability to resolve any of them. Although the campaign against ISIS was gaining ground, the formation of the Hashd al-Shaabi changed the coercive balance of power in the country, strengthening militias committed to a sectarian agenda. These disparate and competing forces sought to assert their political power in Baghdad, demanding greater influence in government and hence blocking any communal reconciliation. Abadi governed without the capacity or political support to reform Iraqi politics in a way that would reduce corruption or meet the demands of the demonstrators who laid siege to parliament. Although the Iraqi government struck a deal with the International Monetary Fund, this promised to bring only temporary respite to the country's balance-of-payments problems, in return for enforced austerity. Thus, Iraq's long-term structural weaknesses went well beyond the price of oil and, indeed, the capability of ISIS to take and hold territory.

This accumulation of domestic woes undermined Iraq's regional influence, although the country's future remained central to Middle Eastern politics. The US and Iran subtly competed for influence in Baghdad, with Abadi seen as closer to Washington while Tehran showed a clear preference for the Hashd al-Shaabi. Relations between Ankara and Baghdad remained tense. Some Arab countries, such as Egypt, quietly reached out to the Iraqi government due to their converging aims in combating Sunni extremism. In a remarkable move, Saudi Arabia sent an ambassador to Iraq for the first time since 2003. This was interpreted as a Saudi challenge to Iranian influence.

ISIS

The Islamic State, also known as ISIS or ISIL, suffered major military setbacks in the year to mid-2016, losing territory in Iraq and Syria, while struggling to make sustainable gains amid the crowded militant landscape in Libya. At the same time, the group mounted or inspired several terrorist operations outside its borders, including in Europe and the United States. Although its state-building project is failing dismally, ISIS may retain its standing as a jihadist group even after losing all its territory.

Territorial losses in Iraq and Syria

The influence of ISIS seemingly peaked in May 2015, when it captured the Iraqi city of Ramadi. Since then, the group has lost territory, revenue, cadres and recruits. These setbacks were primarily caused by the increased – if sometimes uncoordinated – military efforts of its opponents.

By June 2016, ISIS had been largely driven out of Ramadi and Falluja by the Iraqi security forces, rebuilt with considerable foreign assistance, and the Hashd al-Shaabi (Popular Mobilisation Units), a collection of mostly Shia militias loosely connected with the government. These forces then began their advance on ISIS-held Mosul. Meanwhile, the Kurdish Peshmerga made significant gains in northern Iraq. Large parts of the Syria–Iraq border had been recaptured from ISIS, complicating the group's movements between the countries. This campaign benefited from Western military support, especially US airpower, intelligence and advisers. But the effort was impeded by political turmoil in Baghdad and sectarian violence perpetrated by Shia militias, as well as diverging goals – with the Iraqi government prioritising the liberation of Falluja rather than, as favoured by the US, Mosul.

The situation was considerably more complex in Syria, where there was competition between three separate efforts to fight ISIS. There, the US backed the Syrian Democratic Forces, a coalition that was dominated by the Kurdish People's Protection Units – the Syrian affiliate of the Turkish Kurdistan Workers' Party – and that included various Arab tribal forces and Free Syrian Army units. Backed by US airpower, the alliance made considerable gains against ISIS across northern and eastern Syria, particularly along the Syria–Turkey border, advancing within reach of Manbij and Raqqa. However, its progress was slowed by local distrust, as many Arab residents of ISIS-controlled areas saw Kurdish forces as antagonistic. Raqqa was also in the sights of Syrian regime forces. Supported by Russian airpower, Iranian soldiers and Shia militiamen, they captured Palmyra in March and began to move north, seeking to relieve pressure on Deir ez-Zor and to reach Raqqa (possibly before the Syrian Democratic Forces).

Islamist and mainstream rebel groups in northern Syria also fought against ISIS. Yet they had less support than their competitors, and faced an advance on Aleppo by regime and Russian forces, as well as Kurdish expansion. Despite receiving Turkish assistance and artillery support, they struggled to maintain their front-lines and, as a result, lost territory. Militarily, ISIS had to fight on an increasing number of fronts simultaneously, stretching its resources and manpower. Western airstrikes disrupted the group's transit routes and destroyed many of the small oil fields and refineries that had been its primary source of cash. Improved intelligence also allowed for the targeted killing of some of the group's leaders, including Abu Sayyaf, its main financier; Abu Umar al-Tunisi, a key suicide-squad commander; Haji Imam, thought to be second-in-command; and Abu Umar al-Shishani, a senior commander.

As a result, by mid-2016, ISIS had lost more than one-third of the territory it held in Syria and Iraq in May 2015. The US-led coalition estimated that it had killed as many as 26,000 ISIS fighters by late 2015. According to leaked intelligence reports, the group struggled to offset these losses through recruitment. The decreasing appeal of ISIS, reported dissatisfaction among its fighters and tighter controls along the Turkish border also helped thin its ranks. A growing number of foreign fighters attempted to desert due to maltreatment or other causes of disillusionment, while some Syrian ISIS recruits sought refuge in Turkey.

Changing rhetoric

One of the principal distinctions between ISIS and the jihadist groups that preceded it was its focus on territorial control and state-building. This accompanied a narrative, disseminated globally, of strength and self-confidence. When ISIS leaders proclaimed a caliphate in June 2014, they claimed that to do so was a religious obligation because God had imbued the group with enough *tamkin* (strength) to administer *hudud* (religious law). ISIS spokesman Abu Muhammad al-Adnani said at the time that their enemies had been defeated and overthrown, as a result of which Muslims living under the group's rule were able to live a politically dignified life. In ISIS-controlled territory, he asserted, 'God's Law is fully enforced, the gaps [threatening] the state's frontiers are closed … and people's lives and properties are secured'.

Soon after, the caliphate's borders began to contract. In May 2016, Adnani acknowledged this reality and put forward a different narrative – one that shifted from confident triumphalism to defiant resistance with a dose of fatalism. With ISIS having incurred significant territorial losses, he was unable to boast of military victories or cover up setbacks, and instead drew on rhetorical flourishes to depict the group's resilience. This resilience was measured not by the quantity of territory captured but by the believers' unquestioning faith in the ISIS project.

Adnani conceded that the US had killed many ISIS commanders, but implied that the jihadist movement could readily replace them and insisted that, for the US, 'victory is only achieved when the enemy loses'. The implication was that, as long as ISIS had the will to fight on, its territorial and other losses were not fatal to the cause. He went on to point out that ISIS had recovered from near-annihilation in Iraq in 2007–08, and argued that it could do so again. In what may have been an effort to prepare ISIS followers for the possible loss of strongholds in Iraq, Libya and Syria, he stated:

> Do you, America, consider that a loss of a city or territory constitutes defeat?!
>
> Did we actually suffer defeat when we lost cities in Iraq and we had to roam in the desert with no city and land? Do you think that we will be defeated and that you will be victorious if you captured Mosul or Sirte or Raqqa and all the [other] cities [we continue to hold], and [even] if we [are forced to] return to our prior [stateless] status?

This amounted to a fundamental shift from its position two years earlier, when ISIS called on all other jihadist groups to dissolve and submit to its authority. Adnani held that 'defeat is determined when one loses the will and the desire to fight. Only in one condition will you [the US] achieve victory and the jihadists lose: when you succeed in removing the Koran from the hearts of Muslims.'

The official publications of ISIS no longer endlessly promote the *tamkin* resulting from 'God's promise'. Instead, they stress the religious duty to fight, regardless of the circumstances. The promise of imminent victory or of joining an organisation on the rise is absent. Adnani's declaration that 'we do not wage jihad to protect, liberate or capture a territory' marks a significant change in approach. In previous years, the group's media outlets were advertising their caliphate's victories over the global forces of unbelief, as well as its capacity to provide security and prosperity to its people.

In his May message, Adnani also hinted that ISIS was having greater difficulty recruiting fighters from Europe and the US. The threat they pose has long been a preoccupation of Western intelligence services, and one that intensified after returnees from the Syrian conflict carried out attacks in Paris in November 2015 and in Brussels in March 2016. The 2016 Worldwide Threat Assessment of the US Intelligence Community highlights the extent to which ISIS dominates the jihadist landscape, finding that around 36,500 foreign fighters from outside Iraq and Syria – 6,600 of them from Western countries – have joined the group since 2012.

In his May 2016 speech, Adnani directly addressed the 'soldiers of the caliphate and its supporters in Europe and America', telling those who had been prevented from travelling to the caliphate to 'open up the door of jihad' in the West. Even minor attacks in those territories, he said, would be more desirable and valuable for ISIS than major operations carried out in Iraq and Syria. This could be viewed as a change in ISIS strategy. Yet, revealingly, Adnani added that 'it has come to our attention that some of you cannot carry out operations due to the difficulty in reaching military targets, and are therefore refraining from targeting so-called civilians ... doubting whether [from an Islamic legal perspective] such attacks would be lawful'.

This may suggest that ISIS faces two further problems. Firstly, the reduced influx of recruits to the caliphate is not only a result of tighter controls by Western states, but is also due to a loss of enthusiasm on the part of those contemplating the *hijra* (emigration) because of battlefield losses. Secondly, Adnani's comment can be interpreted as a sign that some ISIS cells or individuals in Europe and the US – perhaps returnees from Iraq and Syria – are resisting orders from the central leadership to attack civilian targets. It is likely that the group's military setbacks and rhetorical shifts are reducing its appeal to foreign recruits. Those who performed the *hijra* in 2014, when ISIS was capturing large cities in Iraq and Syria, may have believed that God was on their side; those in Western states contemplating emigration today might harbour greater reservations on that score.

Developing franchises

As it suffered setbacks in core territories, ISIS looked to other regions to expand its influence. The widely publicised, if uneven and tentative, growth of the group's franchises has helped offset the perception that it is in decline in Syria and Iraq. In late 2015 and early 2016, the growth of ISIS in Libya suggested that the group's leadership saw the country as a potential fallback option. An increasing number of Arab fighters (especially Tunisians) moved to Libya rather than Iraq and Syria, which were harder to reach. By early 2016, ISIS controlled a territory running almost 200 kilometres along Libya's coast, fielding up to 6,000 fighters there. In March, Libya-based ISIS jihadists mounted an attack in Tunisia that killed dozens of people but was eventually repelled. However, ISIS struggled to maintain its hold in Libya, due to a military campaign involving US aircraft, European special forces and various local fighting groups. By June, ISIS had been expelled from much of Benghazi and western Sabratha, and was under pressure in its stronghold in Sirte (which it had captured in early 2015).

In contrast, the group's Egyptian franchise, Sinai Province, continued to grow. Mounting a sustained insurgency that prompted military escalation by the government, Sinai Province expanded its operations into Cairo, the Delta region and other parts of Egypt. Its most effective attack took place in October 2015, when it planted a bomb that killed all 224 civilians, most of them Russian, aboard Metrojet flight 9268.

Other affiliates of ISIS also sought to develop amid troubled domestic conditions, but their fortunes, as well as their degree of coordination with the central leadership, varied considerably. The Afghan ISIS affiliate, Khorasan Province, challenged both the Taliban and the government in Kabul, creating a complex convergence of local and regional interests, with Iran supporting Taliban factions against the new jihadist menace. Saudi Arabia's security forces mobilised after ISIS bombed several, mostly Shia, mosques, and remained concerned that the jihadist group would direct further attacks against government targets.

Despite, or perhaps because of, its setbacks in Syria and Iraq, the group continued to mount, inspire or take credit for an array of terrorist attacks abroad. Its most high-profile operations were the assaults in Paris and Brussels, which were well planned and coordinated. Several of the perpetrators had received training in the caliphate, as well as guidance from the central leadership. Even while it incurred large territorial losses, ISIS amassed considerable resources in the year to mid-2016. Accordingly, the group continued to pose a major threat within and beyond the Middle East.

The Saudi–Iranian rivalry

Rapidly deteriorating relations between Iran and Saudi Arabia emerged as the central fault line in the Middle East in the year to mid-2016. Once cloaked and subtle, the rivalry infused regional and sectarian politics while taking on an increasingly direct and confrontational tone. Fed by mutual distrust and antagonism, it exacerbated every aspect of dealings between Riyadh and Tehran, leading to a complete breakdown of their relationship.

Within this geopolitical competition, both sides used sectarianism as an instrument of policy. To mobilise domestic support, they increasingly couched their arguments in confessional, zero-sum terms. In their respective narratives, Iran sought to confront Saudi-backed takfirism (a form of violent extremism in which other Muslims are accused of apostasy), while Saudi Arabia worked to contain aggressive Shia and Khomeinist expansion in the Arab world. Tellingly, this struggle played out not only in Muslim-majority countries but also in front of Western audiences.

Breakdown in relations

The volatility of the Middle East was exacerbated by the combination of a more assertive leadership in Riyadh under King Salman bin Abdulaziz and the beginnings of a tentative accommodation of Tehran by major outside powers, following the Iran nuclear deal of July 2015. Despite US attempts at reassurance, notably at the May 2015 Camp David summit and following consultations, the deal fuelled anxiety in Riyadh that the West was changing its preferred partner in the Middle East and granting greater leeway to Iran's defence-modernisation programme and provocative behaviour.

Always wary of a potential change in Western policy on Iran, the Saudi leadership felt vindicated after Tehran maintained its assertive approach to the region in the wake of the nuclear deal. In the Saudi view, the agreement's repeal of sanctions on Iran, and transfer of around US$100 billion in frozen funds to the country, would allow Tehran to modernise its military and shore up its regional allies. Iran signalled its resolve by testing ballistic missiles, in contravention of UN resolutions, and by engaging in arms transactions with Russia (which led to the delivery of elements of the S-300 long-range air-defence system in April 2016, and ongoing negotiations over new platforms). Tehran also highlighted extensive Saudi defence spending, which at a record US$82bn in 2015 was more than five times the size of Iran's budget (although Iran's low-cost asymmetric capabilities required relatively few resources). To demonstrate its prowess and showcase its alliances, Saudi Arabia hosted in February and March 2016 its largest-ever joint military exercise, *North Thunder*, which involved troops from 20 countries.

In August 2015, Saudi intelligence operatives captured Ahmed Ibrahim al-Mughassil in Beirut and transferred him to Riyadh. A Saudi national and a member of militant group Hizbullah al-Hejaz, Mughassil was believed to have overseen the 1996 bombing of the Khobar Towers on behalf of Iran. The move was also timed, some suspected, to remind Western countries of Iran's involvement in terrorism.

The relationship between Riyadh and Tehran was further shaken by a massive stampede during the annual pilgrimage to Mecca in September. The incident led to the deaths of more than 450 Iranians, the largest contingent among the more than 2,000 fatalities. Riyadh's slow, indifferent response to the disaster and unwillingness to conduct a public investigation led to protests in Iran and prompted Tehran to accuse the Saudis of a cover-up. Riyadh interpreted this Iranian indignation as an attempt to undermine its religious legitimacy as the guardian of Islam's holiest sites.

Following the attacks in Paris and Brussels carried out by supporters of the Islamic State, also known as ISIS or ISIL, in November 2015 and March 2016 respectively, a worldwide debate over the roots of extremism began. Iran placed the blame squarely on Riyadh for its support of Sunni radicals, while Saudi Arabia highlighted Iran's sponsorship of terrorism. Iranian Foreign Minister Javad Zarif and his Saudi counterpart Adel al-Jubeir exchanged direct, increasingly acrimonious accusations, sometimes in major Western media outlets. The constant quarrelling was reflected in hostile coverage by state media on both sides. For instance, the public appearances of General Qassem Suleimani, commander of Iran's elite Quds Force, on Iraqi and Syrian battlefields and in Lebanon were extolled by the Iranian media and disparaged by Gulf outlets.

Relations significantly worsened after the Saudi authorities executed in January 2016 the firebrand Saudi Shia cleric Nimr al-Nimr. In jail since 2012, Nimr had become a champion of young Shia dissidents in Saudi Arabia, and was increasingly praised by Iran and Hizbullah, although he was not aligned with either of them. Although the Saudis also executed dozens of Sunni extremists convicted of involvement in al-Qaeda operations in the previous decade, their execution of Nimr and other Shia activists received far greater international attention.

In reaction, a mob composed of hundreds of Iranian citizens as well as organised hardliners ransacked the Saudi embassy in Tehran. The event embarrassed Iranian President Hassan Rouhani, who was eager for Iran to gain respectability in the international community. But the regret that he and other Iranian politicians expressed over the attack could not prevent a diplomatic crisis. Defending the Nimr execution as a sovereign decision, Riyadh obtained statements of condemnation for the assault on the embassy from the Gulf Cooperation Council (GCC), the Arab League and the Organisation of Islamic Cooperation. Saudi Arabia, Bahrain and other states broke off relations with Iran, while some, such as the United Arab Emirates, downgraded their diplomatic presence in Tehran.

Regional competition

The Saudi–Iranian rivalry played out in a multiplying number of arenas, making for a complex game. The sides' depth of involvement differed from country to country: in Syria and Iraq, Iran had a direct military and political role that was overwhelming; and in Yemen, Saudi Arabia expanded its military operations to defeat a Houthi insurgency that received only limited Iranian support. The complicated linkages between these arenas and the role of non-state actors in the various conflicts seemed to prevent Tehran and Riyadh from striking a grand bargain.

Saudi Arabia sought to create unity in a Sunni world facing both an ideological challenge from Sunni extremists and a geopolitical threat from Iran. In December 2015, Saudi Defence Minister Mohammed bin Salman hastily announced the creation of the Islamic Military Alliance, a counter-terrorism organisation comprising 34 countries. While ostensibly aimed at ISIS, al-Qaeda and similar groups, the move was also widely interpreted as an attempt to rally key Sunni countries behind Saudi endeavours. Riyadh subsequently gathered support for, and recruited new members to, the alliance, but struggled to explain its exact functioning and operational scope. Suggestions that it would be deployed in Syria against ISIS proved to be unfounded.

Saudi Arabia's eagerness to form a Sunni front was evident in its outreach to both Egypt and Turkey, and in its more accommodating tone towards Islamist movements, especially Hamas. Despite some dissatisfaction with the regime of Abdel Fattah Al-Sisi, particularly over its quiet support for Syrian President Bashar al-Assad, King Salman sustained the strategic relationship with Cairo and worked to broker a reconciliation with Turkish President Recep Tayyip Erdogan, a vocal critic of the Egyptian government. However, these two regional heavyweights appeared unlikely to fully endorse the Saudi project and take a confrontational line against Iran.

In parallel, the Saudi–Emirati alliance proved remarkable in its strength and reach. Despite occasional disagreements, the two leaderships increasingly coordinated their security and foreign policies. Their joint intervention in Yemen, sponsorship of Egypt and convergence on Iran set the agenda for many other Arab states.

Syria continued to be the most significant source of rivalry between Riyadh and Tehran. The Saudis persisted in demanding the ouster of Assad, as well as the withdrawal of Iranian troops and Shia militias from the country. Yet Iran, which was included in the International Syria Support Group in November, rejected any discussion of removing Assad, which top Iranian officials called a 'red line'. The presence of both Saudi and Iranian representatives in meetings of the International Syria Support Group did not lead to any rapprochement between the sides. Each reluctantly and partially committed to the de-escalation plan brokered by the United States and Russia, which was implemented in February. But the increasing numbers of Iranian troops and Tehran-backed militias in Syria suggested that the temporary lull in fighting would be followed by greater violence.

In Iraq, Saudi Arabia was deeply irritated by the major role of Iranian advisers and Shia militias in battling ISIS, notably in major Sunni cities such as Ramadi and Falluja. Nonetheless, Riyadh re-established full diplomatic relations with Baghdad, ostensibly to balance Iranian influence.

Lebanon was also affected by the rivalry. There, Hizbullah continued to block the election of a president despite hopes that, following the Iranian nuclear deal, Tehran and Riyadh would encourage cooperation between their respective allies in the Lebanese government. The Shia militant group dismissed a compromise put forward by the Saudi-aligned Saad Hariri that would have led to the election of a pro-Hizbullah president. This rejection validated the Saudi view that Hizbullah, and by extension Iran, had maximalist aims.

Saudi frustration with Lebanon continuously rose, fed by Hizbullah leader Hassan Nasrallah's vehement verbal attacks against the kingdom; the publication of video footage showing Hizbullah officers training Houthi militiamen; and the evident weakness of allies such as Hariri. In February and March 2016, the situation escalated into a diplomatic row after Lebanon failed to condemn the attack on the Saudi embassy in Tehran. As a result, Riyadh suspended security assistance to Lebanon worth US$4bn, and punished Hizbullah by imposing stricter rules on money transfers. Many in Lebanon, along with Saudi Arabia's other international partners, saw the suspension of aid as counterproductive, as it undermined Saudi allies in the country and further weakened the stretched Lebanese security forces.

The Saudi–Iranian competition also influenced energy politics. The nuclear deal facilitated Iranian oil sales and Tehran accordingly ramped up production to recover market share. However, this occurred as the oil price plunged, leading to discussion among major oil producers about whether to support prices by freezing production. Saudi Arabia refused to sign off on the freeze unless Iran followed suit. This dispute contributed to the breakdown of oil talks in Doha in April.

Tense relations with the US

Riyadh's anxiety was made worse by its frosty relations with a Washington sceptical of the new, assertive Saudi foreign policy. The US only reluctantly agreed to support the Saudi-led intervention in Yemen, and showed its displeasure at Riyadh's prioritisation of competition with Iran over the fight against ISIS. Washington and Riyadh also diverged over the Syrian conflict: unlike the US, which reduced the ambition of its military and political objectives in the war, Riyadh remained adamant that Assad be ousted. Saudi Arabia even floated the idea of intervening in Syria and providing the rebels there with anti-aircraft missiles – both proposals that the US quashed.

The friction between the allies became increasingly obvious. In a widely read interview published in the *Atlantic*, US President Barack Obama described the relationship with Riyadh as 'complicated'. He also urged Iran and Saudi Arabia to 'share' the region and to agree on a form of 'cold peace'. Such suggestions were anathema to the Saudi leadership. A couple of months later, the US president attended the GCC summit in Riyadh, but the trip was devoid of substance. Saudi and other Gulf leaders were already planning for the post-Obama era.

Fuelled in part by unsubstantiated allegations of Saudi support for ISIS, the resurfacing controversy of Riyadh's alleged involvement in 9/11 further tainted the kingdom's image. Demands grew across the US political spectrum for the release of 28 pages of the 9/11 Commission's report that detailed the alleged Saudi role in the attacks. The Saudi authorities had requested this disclosure, but the US government resisted the move. Despite active lobbying by Riyadh and the Obama administration (which promised to veto it if needed), the US Senate passed in May a bill allowing victims of the attacks to file lawsuits against the Saudi government.

This was not the only issue the US Congress seized upon. Allegations that the Saudis had committed war crimes in Yemen, including deliberate attacks on civilians, led prominent senators to introduce legislation to block arms sales to Riyadh, mirroring similar moves in the European Parliament. As a consequence, the White House quietly suspended the sale of cluster bombs to Saudi Arabia. Riyadh also stood accused of having allowed the expansion of al-Qaeda in the Arabian Peninsula, and of subordinating the fight against ISIS to the battle against the Houthi insurgency in Yemen.

The growing sources of tension between the US and Saudi Arabia did not break their relationship, but emphasised its transactional, security-oriented nature. While Saudi officials hoped that the post-Obama US administration would prove more responsive to their concerns, there was a pervasive sense that the qualitative deterioration in relations could not be fully reversed. To contain the perceived political and security threat from Tehran, Riyadh prioritised independent Saudi defence planning and sustained outreach to key Sunni states, as well as deepened relations with other Western actors. This course, defined as both offensive and defensive by the kingdom, ostensibly matched escalating Iranian rhetoric and regional assertiveness.

Iran after the nuclear deal

The historic nuclear deal Tehran signed with the E3/EU+3 (China, France, Germany, Russia, the United Kingdom and the United States, plus the European Union) on 14 July 2015 was the fulcrum of Iranians' political life and expectations in the year that followed. Although the agreement appeared to be in peril by mid-2016, it had a dramatic, if ambiguous, impact on Iranian alliances. Many effects of the deal, intended or otherwise, remained imperceptible or were yet to come to fruition.

The International Atomic Energy Agency confirmed in January 2016 that Iran had fulfilled its initial obligations to limit its nuclear activities under the nuclear agreement, officially known as the Joint Comprehensive Plan of Action (JCPOA). The move allowed the US and the EU to lift their nuclear-related sanctions on Iran and to release Iranian assets collectively worth between US$55 billion and US$100bn.

Iran's major political groups – reformists, pragmatists (modern conservatives) and hardliners – initially welcomed the deal. All three were anxious about the economic cost of the sanctions and the possibility of unrest among poor Iranians. Indeed, during the negotiations, the

Iranian economy was in its worst state since the 1979 Islamic Revolution. Political elites hoped that the suspension of sanctions would stabilise, and boost support for, the regime. An economically and socially stable Iran, they calculated, would be better positioned to address the threat from the US, as well as regional enemies such as Israel, Saudi Arabia and jihadist group the Islamic State, also known as ISIS or ISIL.

However, the JCPOA eventually became a source of tension across the political spectrum. Differences arose from varying understandings of the nature, scope and practical consequences of the deal, in a process that restructured the political scene. The traditional categories of reformists, pragmatists and hardliners gave way to new coalitions that formed in support of, or opposition to, the nuclear deal. It seemed possible that the gap between these coalitions would widen in the lead-up to the 2017 presidential elections.

Rouhani's limited power

The deal's supporters consisted of reformists, pragmatists and traditional conservatives, who coalesced around President Hassan Rouhani and former presidents Akbar Hashemi Rafsanjani and Mohammad Khatami. The majority of the Iranian people, who had suffered under economic sanctions and political isolation, were believed to have supported the deal in the expectation that it would foster growth, allow for reintegration into the global economy and facilitate the normalisation of Iran's relationship with the international community. While Rouhani and his pragmatist supporters hoped that the deal would lead to his re-election in 2017, others anticipated that economic growth would facilitate the expansion of the middle class, who would become an engine of political change – and that the normalisation of Iran's foreign relations would decrease state repression and lead to democratisation.

For some of its supporters, the JCPOA was less a one-time agreement over Iran's nuclear programme than the starting point of a new era. In this sense, the deal is similar to UN Resolution 598, which helped end the 1980–88 Iran–Iraq War. Reluctantly accepted by the Islamic Republic's founder, Ayatollah Ruhollah Khomeini (who was concerned about the regime's survival), Resolution 598 led not only to a shift of political power from the Islamic radical left wing to the conservative right, but also to the moderation of Iran's domestic and foreign policy. Internally, the resolution brought about the beginning of the reconstruction era, during which Tehran adopted liberal economic policies based on privatisation, deregulation and global integration. By easing restrictive social and cultural policies, the government laid the groundwork for the election of the reformist Khatami in 1997. The resolution also ended the policy of exporting the Islamic Revolution and led to the moderation of support for Shia militant movements, opening the way for an improvement in relations with neighbouring Arab countries.

Similarly, the nuclear deal marked the end of the era of former president Mahmoud Ahmadinejad, which was characterised by its radical, populist domestic policy and antagonistic foreign policy. The deal improved Iran's relationships with other states, leading to a gradual increase in foreign investment. Starting in July 2015, hundreds of business delegations began to visit Iran, and several Western companies re-entered the Iranian market. Rouhani sought to open Iranian markets to foreign trade and investment, improve economic rationalisation and management, and promote deregulation.

Seeking rapprochement with Arab countries and the West, Rouhani viewed the JCPOA as a model of negotiation and cooperation that could be used to solve other regional and global problems. His efforts had mixed results. After hardliners attacked the Saudi Embassy in Tehran on 2 January 2016, in protest at the execution of a Saudi Shia cleric, Rouhani and Javad Zarif, the foreign minister, condemned the assault and insisted that they wanted an end to tensions with Riyadh. However, the rivalry with the kingdom only intensified. They were more successful on other matters. In January, Iran and the US concluded an exchange of prisoners. Iran released four Iranian-American citizens, one of whom was a journalist jailed on charges of espionage, while the US freed seven Iranians jailed for breaking US sanctions. In another case, after the Islamic Revolutionary Guard Corps (IRGC) Navy arrested US Navy personnel who had entered Iranian waters on 12 January 2016, Rouhani convinced Supreme Leader Ayatollah Ali Khamenei to release them. While Rouhani strongly supports the Iranian ballistic-missile programme, he successfully encouraged Khamenei and the IRGC to not publicise their missile drills and to remove the words 'Death to Israel' from the weapons, as a means to reassure the international community that the initiative had defensive objectives.

Rouhani even tried to use the JCPOA as a model for internal negotiations. He has pushed for an 'internal JCPOA' or 'Nuclear Deal 2' to foster negotiations with hardliners about domestic issues. The internal JCPOA implicitly requested negotiations with hardliners on the freedom of the three leaders of the Green Movement who have been under house arrest since 2009. But Khamenei and his supporters rejected the requests.

In the social and cultural spheres, Rouhani subtly supported limited liberation. He denounced the moral-policing plan introduced by the Iranian police, who are under the direct control the Supreme Leader, and challenged Khamenei's criticism of English-language education. Having made gains in the legislative elections of February 2016, Rouhani used his popularity to challenge his hardline critics, with a view to the upcoming presidential vote.

Nonetheless, Rouhani continued to face opposition from bodies dominated by hardliners. Iran's Guardian Council attempted to manipulate the legislative elections by disqualifying the majority of reformist candidates, including Seyyed Hassan Khomeini, the grandson of Ayatollah Khomeini. Hardliners regard Khomeini, who is 41 years old and popular among a younger generation of regime supporters, as a threat, fearing that he may run to succeed Khamenei. Despite the Guardian Council's efforts, supporters of the deal running under the banner the 'Hope List' were able to defeat hardliners in large cities such as Tehran in the legislative elections.

Nonetheless, the hardliners won more seats overall, which allowed Khamenei's allies to continue to dominate parliament and the Assembly of Experts. Ayatollah Ahmad Jannati, a hardline cleric who heads the Guardian Council, was elected as the leader of the Assembly of Experts, which is responsible for selecting the next Supreme Leader. Moreover, Ali Larijani, a conservative politician who is a close ally of Khamenei, was re-elected as speaker of parliament with 173 votes, far ahead of the 103 votes received by the reformist Mohammad Reza Aref. In short, although Rouhani and his allies formed substantial factions in both parliament and the Assembly of Experts, their power remained limited.

Strident opposition to the nuclear deal

The JCPOA's active critics and ambivalent sceptics comprised Khamenei, the IRGC, the Basij paramilitary forces and clerics in the Guardian Council. The support base of these hardliners, mainly the lower and lower-middle class, is the more conservative and religious part of society, which, while smaller than that of the deal's supporters, benefits from the Basij's organisational reach.

Hardliners reluctantly accepted the deal and the suspension of Iran's nuclear programme to reduce the possibility of regime collapse. Reluctant to take direct responsibility for the deal, Khamenei conditionally endorsed the agreement only after it was passed by the hardliner-dominated parliament and Iran's Supreme National Security Council on 21 October 2015. These groups also viewed the deal as necessary for regime survival, as it would facilitate economic recovery and reduce the threat of sanctions on military programmes. Despite this, the hardliners believed that the deal weakened Iran's strategic deterrence; some even hoped that the next US president would tear it up.

During the domestic debate about the deal, Khamenei warned about Washington's intentions concerning Iran. For him, the talks had a specific and limited purpose, and he rejected discussions on regional security. In March, he warned against US *nofoz* (penetration) of Iran's society and politics designed to overthrow the regime from within, thus justifying his efforts to block the Rouhani administration from engaging in further negotiations with Washington. The IRGC echoed Khamenei's statements, arguing that US penetration would threaten 'Islamic ideology' and weaken the regime.

Illustrating this fear of *nofoz*, the security services arrested several journalists and other civilians, including Iranian-American businessman Siamak Namazi. Meanwhile, the IRGC aired a documentary implicitly accusing Rouhani of working with the US to overthrow the Iranian government. Unlike the often pro-Western supporters of the nuclear deal, opponents of the agreement preferred a foreign policy centred on Eastern powers such as China and Russia, which have authoritarian leaderships and compete with the US. In November 2015, Khamenei warmly received Russian President Vladimir Putin on his first visit to Iran in a decade, a trip partly intended to facilitate discussion of their joint objectives in Syria.

The opponents of the deal also worried that Western powers would seek to curtail Iranian military efforts such as the missile programme. On 11 October 2015, just days before the JCPOA was to begin its implementation phase, Iran successfully tested a medium-range ballistic missile. The US and other countries protested, arguing that missile development and testing violated UN Resolution 1929. By conducting the test, the IRGC signalled that it rejected this interpretation of the measure. While hardliners marketed the expansion of the missile programme as an essential component of Iran's defence policy, moderates suspected that the IRGC was attempting to sabotage Rouhani's policy of normalising Iran's foreign relations.

The opponents of the nuclear deal also rejected Rouhani's stated desire to de-escalate and solve conflicts in the Middle East. The IRGC warned the government against negotiating on Iran's regional policy, notably in Syria, Iraq, Lebanon and Yemen. The attack on the Saudi embassy in Tehran was in part a challenge to Rouhani's push for more amicable relations with foreign governments, as was the IRGC's detention of American military personnel who had strayed into Iranian waters. Moreover, the IRGC warned that it would prevent ships from passing through the Strait of Hormuz should the US and its regional partners threaten Iran. This rhetoric was intended to undermine the deal's supporters and to signal to the world that opponents of the agreement still controlled security policy.

Hardliners also criticised the nuclear deal on economic grounds. They argued that, despite the repeal of sanctions, foreign transactions failed to grow significantly. Four months after the implementation of the deal, Iran had retrieved only US$3bn in frozen assets, according to US Secretary of State John Kerry. Khamenei and his followers blamed Washington for Iran's continuing economic problems but, in reality, much of the drag on growth resulted from the European and US private sectors' apprehension about resuming trade and financial transactions with the country, the difficulty of dealing with its outdated banking mechanisms and its inclusion on the Financial Action Task Force's blacklist.

Instead of an opening to the West, Khamenei and his supporters pushed for trade with Eastern powers (which the JCPOA facilitated, as it permitted financial transactions) and the development of a 'resistance

economy', an insulated, self-sufficient model of domestic production that reduces dependence on imports. The doctrine is at odds with
Rouhani's vision of global integration. Hardliners supported their objec-
tion to Rouhani's economic policies by citing an April 2016 report from
the Statistical Centre of Iran, which found that annual rates of inequality,
poverty and unemployment all increased in the preceding year, ending a
four-year trend of improvement in each area.

The hostility between supporters and opponents of the JCPOA
sharply intensified in the year to mid-2016. The debate no longer solely
focused on the nuclear programme, but expanded to encompass cultural, political and social matters. Opponents of the deal were able to
obstruct fundamental political transformation and reform, as they controlled most levers of power, including the media and the finance sector.
Moreover, they dominated the majority of state institutions, including
the judiciary, the IRGC, the Basij, the police and the Guardian Council.

Yemen

The Saudi-led military intervention in Yemen wore on in the year to mid-
2016, reflecting the Gulf states' unprecedented assertiveness at a time
of regional upheaval. The desire of Saudi Arabia and the United Arab
Emirates to pursue a more autonomous and ambitious foreign policy,
and to directly shape their immediate surroundings, marked a qualitative, if uncertain and risky, change in Middle Eastern politics. Both
regional powerhouses maintained their military alliance to counter the
Houthi threat in Yemen, and the perceived reach of Iran further afield.
However, despite their superior resources, Saudi Arabia and the UAE
were inhibited by the need to deal with disparate and fractious Yemeni
allies, and to support the unpopular President Abd Rabbo Mansour
Hadi, who lacked legitimacy. Orchestrating a military campaign that
could make sustainable gains and unify the positions of these Yemeni
factions proved almost impossible.

After a year of heavy but inconclusive fighting and faltering attempts
to implement a peace process, direct negotiations restarted in April
2016 under the auspices of the United Nations, bringing together the
government of Hadi, the Houthis and supporters of former president
Ali Abdullah Saleh, the Houthis' main ally. The talks made tangible

progress towards reconciliation, but there was no consensus on the structure or leadership of a post-conflict transition. In the meantime, the coalition placed greater emphasis on stabilisation and appeared to recalibrate its priorities, focusing on tackling insecurity and the spread of jihadism.

Regional ambitions

Saudi Arabia and the UAE chose to intervene in Yemen in part because they feared the growth of the Houthi insurgency and associated Iranian encroachment on the Arabian Peninsula, and perceived the US as reluctant to contain Iran. As a result, they sought to pre-empt unfavourable changes to the security landscape. While sceptical about the merits of the intervention, the US, along with the United Kingdom and France, deliberately played an assistance role in the military operations in Yemen, providing logistical, targeting and intelligence support to the coalition, as well as weapons resupply. This was meant to preserve important relationships and modestly shape the conduct of the war, but also to conduct diplomacy that could end the conflict. The coalition's breadth and diversity (including several Middle Eastern Arab and African states, as well as a range of Yemeni factions) demonstrated the global influence of Saudi Arabia and the UAE.

The conflict, essentially a power struggle between domestic forces, became another theatre for the Saudi–Iranian rivalry. Most Gulf states viewed Houthi expansionism throughout 2014–15 as a direct provocation and an Iranian-backed attempt to unravel the transition endorsed by the Gulf Cooperation Council (GCC). Careful not to upset its relations with the other GCC states and Iran, Oman remained neutral throughout the conflict and offered to mediate on several occasions.

Tehran provided political and military support to the Houthis, but did not necessarily exert control over the movement. From the outset of the conflict, there was evidence of Iranian military assistance – such as the weapons shipments that were intercepted by the coalition and its allies close to Yemeni waters. But it was unclear how much Iran valued the Houthis: while the insurgent movement drew Saudi Arabia into a costly, protracted conflict, Iran seemed unwilling or unable to qualitatively increase its support.

Starting in 2016, the Houthis began to distance themselves from Iran, if only verbally. They were prompted to do so by a mixture of disappointment with Iran's lacklustre support and a desire to escape the stigma and ostracism attendant on being viewed as an Iranian proxy. At times, Houthi officials publicly shunned Iranian assistance and denounced Tehran's 'exploitation' of the war for political gain. These statements contributed to renewed diplomatic momentum and represented a qualitative change in the Houthi posture.

Militarily, the coalition scored several victories thanks to its combined use of airpower, special forces and local militias. It seized several southern provinces in summer 2015, broke the siege of Ta'izz the following March and succeeded in destroying much of the military capability of the Houthi militias and Saleh's forces. Anti-Houthi units benefited from superior training and equipment, a steady supply of weaponry and air support, while their enemies faced an air and naval blockade.

However, given the stated objectives of the coalition and its technological and financial superiority, the intervention could hardly be described as a resounding victory. By mid-2016, the Houthis had not capitulated or even withdrawn from key cities. Moreover, despite Saudi officials' regular pronouncements that the Houthi-held Sana'a would be liberated 'within days', the difficulty and cost of such an operation – as well as negative media attention resulting from high civilian casualties – deterred such a move. Holding the capital and, by extension, the country's beleaguered institutions became the Houthis' claim to legitimacy, as well as a valuable bargaining chip.

The high-profile nature of the intervention and its association with the new leadership in Riyadh made the stakes particularly high. Accordingly, the outcome of the conflict was likely to shape the future policies of Saudi Arabia and the UAE, as well as local and international perceptions of both countries.

Turn to diplomacy

As the war dragged on, the coalition readjusted its goal, looking to force a negotiated settlement. Following several false starts in Switzerland, peace talks held in Kuwait in April 2016 reflected both sides' acknowledgement of a need for de-escalation, given that neither could achieve total victory and that much of the Yemeni population urgently required humanitarian assistance. An official ceasefire accompanied the negotiations, but both parties failed to honour it, suggesting that they lacked both control over their forces on the ground and the political readiness needed for difficult compromises.

Mediated by UN Special Envoy for Yemen Ismail Ould Cheikh Ahmed, the talks focused on a post-conflict transition. Both the Hadi government and the Houthi–Saleh camp submitted proposals concerning their forces' withdrawal from conquered territory and disarmament, as well as the release of prisoners. But there remained fundamental disagreements between and within the two coalitions over the structure of the transitional regime.

Saleh first organised a massive demonstration in Sana'a in March to demonstrate his lasting popularity and to deter any attempt to sacrifice him as part of a settlement. He also made overtures to the opposing coalition, which swiftly rejected them due to his perceived unreliability. Meanwhile, Hadi, lacking grassroots support, failed to articulate an inclusive vision for sharing power, yet appeared intent on clinging to his position. The issue of his fate impeded the resolution of the conflict, as the Houthi–Saleh delegates demanded his ouster as part of a final settlement.

Divisions within the Yemeni government further complicated the situation. In April, Hadi dismissed Prime Minister Khaled Bahah, with whom he had a long-standing rift. The latter, a moderate and competent administrator, was seen as the most likely consensus candidate for president during a transition: the Houthis had once nominated Bahah as prime minister, and he retained support in Riyadh and Abu Dhabi. Bahah was replaced by Ali Mohsen al-Ahmar, a senior military commander with Islamist and tribal connections. This nomination was seen as a gesture of defiance and escalation from Hadi, given the deep enmity between Ahmar, Saleh and the Houthis.

The coalition faced increasing international condemnation for fuelling a severe humanitarian crisis. Loose rules of engagement and flawed targeting resulted in thousands of civilian deaths as well as damage to, or destruction of, hospitals, schools and other key infrastructure. In addition to the economic distress caused by the conflict, the blockade exacerbated shortages of basic goods. This led aid agencies to warn of an imminent famine in Yemen. There were also calls in Western capitals to suspend military assistance and sales to Saudi Arabia and the UAE. Criticism of Saudi Arabia reached the UN, where the addition of the kingdom to a list of actors violating the rights of Yemeni children provoked an angry reaction from Riyadh: the Saudis made an ultimately successful threat to cut off funding to UN missions unless it was removed from the list.

Stabilisation and the jihadist threat

Chronic insecurity in areas that the coalition had ostensibly secured illustrated the difficulty of stabilising Yemen. Armed groups proliferated in Aden as militias armed by the coalition turned against the Hadi government, while others that had never recognised it, such as southern secessionists, became more forceful, planning for greater autonomy and frustrating the government's attempt to assert itself. Jihadist groups, including affiliates of the Islamic State, also known as ISIS or ISIL, and al-Qaeda in the Arabian Peninsula (AQAP), increased their presence across the south and east of the country. This instability damaged the standing of the Hadi government and the coalition.

The situation began to change in March 2016. The coalition embarked on a campaign to restore order in Aden and to oust AQAP from the southern provinces. The following month, UAE special forces allied with Yemeni factions sought to expel AQAP fighters from Mukalla, a stronghold for the jihadist group in Hadhramaut Province. The swift AQAP retreat from the city was hailed as a significant victory, but the group continued to operate in large swathes of Yemen.

The campaign took place in conjunction with Washington's ongoing programme of attacks on AQAP using unmanned aerial vehicles, which killed dozens of the group's operatives in the year. After the coalition expelled AQAP from Mukalla, the US also deployed a small group of military personnel near the city to provide intelligence support for Emirati troops in their operations against the group. It was possible that the fight against jihadism would become an area of cooperation among the warring parties.

Turkey

Throughout the year to mid-2016, the Syrian civil war not only dominated Turkey's foreign relations but became intermeshed with a range of domestic issues, including an economic slowdown and an increasingly tenuous security situation – reflected in rising terrorist activity and the decreasing confidence in the government that may have contributed to the 15 July 2016 coup attempt. In November 2011, when he was still prime minister, Turkish President Recep Tayyip Erdogan had publicly called on Syrian President Bashar al-Assad to step down, in the hope that Syria's Alawite-dominated regime would be replaced by a Sunni Muslim government inspired by the ideals of the Muslim Brotherhood. By mid-2016, Turkey's hopes were no closer to being realised. Ankara's previous laissez-faire attitude towards the Islamic State, also known as ISIS or ISIL, had given way to concern and then alarm as ISIS sympathisers staged seven mass-casualty attacks inside Turkey in little more than 12 months.

Yet Ankara was still prepared to tolerate, and sometimes even cooperate with, other extremist groups active in Syria. This approach exacerbated the Turkish government's tense relationship with Turkey's Kurdish minority, further strained its relations with Europe and the United States, and triggered a crisis in its relations with Russia. However, Turkey's proximity to Syria compelled the European Union and the US to mute public criticism of Erdogan's growing domestic repressiveness. They also did so out of fear of jeopardising his cooperation in stemming the flow of refugees into Europe, as well as in accessing Incirlik Air Base in southern Turkey – a facility important to the US-led air campaign against ISIS.

Once Erdogan had called for Assad to step down, the Syrian civil war became a test of his ability to make good on his claims that he had transformed Turkey into a regional superpower and the eastern Mediterranean into a Turkish sphere of influence. Despite protests from Europe and the US, this priority had until early 2015 sustained a policy of opening Turkey's borders to anyone working to overthrow the Assad regime. Islamic extremist organisations fighting in Syria were discreetly permitted to use Turkey as a conduit for recruits and supplies. In early 2015, intelligence reports warning that ISIS was planning attacks against foreign targets inside Turkey led to the introduction of some restrictions on the organisation's logistical, propaganda and recruitment activities inside the country, but other extremist organisations were allowed to function with little hindrance. Turkey's National Intelligence Organization maintained contacts with extremist groups active in Syria, such as al-Qaeda affiliate Jabhat al-Nusra and its ally Ahrar al-Sham. Ankara also continued to finance and provide light arms to rebel militias drawn from Syria's Turkish-speaking Turkmen minority, including several groups that were fighting alongside Jabhat al-Nusra and Ahrar al-Sham.

Meanwhile, ISIS was losing territory in Syria to the Kurdish Democratic Union Party (PYD), which received air support from the US-led international coalition against the jihadist group. In March 2015, Erdogan unilaterally ended a two-year dialogue with the PYD's ideological affiliate, the Kurdistan Workers' Party (PKK), raising concerns that the latter would resume its violent campaign seeking autonomy for Turkey's Kurds. Erdogan feared that, as it pushed back ISIS inside Syria, the PYD would create a de facto autonomous Kurdish area along a substantial proportion of the border with Turkey. In addition to potentially inspiring the PKK to escalate its campaign for the creation of a similar zone inside Turkey, the PYD's advances threatened to close the main corridor through which Ankara supplied rebel groups with lethal and non-lethal aid. On 29 June 2015, at a meeting of the National Security Council, Erdogan instructed the Turkish military to prepare plans to launch an incursion into Syria to deny the PYD territory and protect Turkey's supply routes to the rebel groups. However, in a rare display of defiance, then-chief of the general staff Necdet Ozel refused. Hulusi Akar, who succeeded Ozel after he retired at the end of August 2015, proved no more compliant. The Turkish military's worry was that without international – preferably US – support, Turkish planes would be highly vulnerable to Syria's Russian-made air-defence systems and could suffer unacceptable losses.

Kurds, Turkmens and Russians
The military did not hesitate to obey Erdogan when the war with the PKK resumed in late July 2015. Starting in 2014, during the siege of

the border town of Kobani, Kurdish nationalists accused Ankara of attempting to weaken the PYD by using ISIS as a proxy. Although Turkey was increasingly restricting transit routes in Turkey used by ISIS, these accusations intensified from mid-2015 onwards, as the group's supporters staged a series of attacks on Kurdish nationalists inside Turkey. On 5 June 2015, four people died in an ISIS bombing at a Kurdish-nationalist rally in Diyarbakir. On 20 July 2015, the group conducted a suicide bombing in the border town of Suruc that killed 32 Kurdish nationalists as they prepared to cross into Syria. On 22 July 2015, PKK supporters reacted by assassinating two Turkish policemen in the nearby town of Ceylanpinar. However, on 23 July 2015, when ISIS militants attempted to bring a wounded fighter across the border for treatment in a Turkish state hospital – as they had done in the past – Turkish troops opened fire. One militant and one Turkish soldier were killed in the incident. On 24 July 2015, Turkish warplanes fired three missiles across the border at ISIS positions inside Syria. The same day, Turkey launched the first of hundreds of airstrikes against PKK assets in northern Iraq. The PKK responded by restarting its insurgency inside Turkey.

The Suruc bombing prompted a further tightening of restrictions on ISIS activities inside Turkey, including the closure of several of its main propaganda outlets, raids on its safe houses and a crackdown on some of its recruiting networks. On 24 July, following months of pressure from Washington, Ankara agreed to open Incirlik Air Base to the US-led coalition. The first airstrikes by planes operating out of Incirlik took place on 12 August 2015. Nonetheless, further accusations of collusion between Ankara and ISIS arose on 10 October 2015, when two ISIS suicide bombers attacked a rally in Ankara, killing 102 Kurdish-nationalist sympathisers. This was the highest death toll in a single terrorist attack in Turkish history.

Throughout late 2015, PYD gains in the north, as well as advances further south by pro-Assad regime forces – backed from September onwards by Russian airstrikes – began to drive wedges between pro-Turkish rebel groups. In mid-November, regime ground units and Russian warplanes launched an offensive against Jabhat al-Nusra and Turkmen militias in the southwestern Syrian governorate of Latakia.

On 20 November 2015, as Turkmen villagers in Latakia fled to the Turkish border, violent anti-Russian protests erupted in Istanbul. On 22–23 November 2015, Russian warplanes briefly transited Turkish airspace several times, ignoring warnings from the Turkish side. On 24 November 2015, acting on new orders from Ankara, a Turkish F-16 shot down a Russian Su-24 as it attempted to cross Turkish airspace during a bombing run against rebel forces. Turkmen militiamen shot the Russian pilot as he parachuted to earth.

Moscow reacted furiously. President Vladimir Putin accused Turkey of stabbing Russia in the back. In the weeks that followed, Putin announced a ban on charter flights from Russia to Turkey, introduced visa requirements for Turks visiting Russia and actively discouraged Russians from visiting Turkey. In 2014, tourism had been Turkey's largest source of foreign currency. The approximately 4.6 million Russians who visited Turkey each year constituted the second-largest group among, or 12.1% of, the country's tourists. Moscow also banned imports of Turkish fresh fruit, poultry and vegetables, and declared that Turkish construction companies would be prevented from bidding for new contracts in Russia. Turkish officials tried to placate Russia, arguing that a single incident should not be allowed to destroy what – despite their political differences over Syria – had been a flourishing economic relationship. But Moscow was unmoved, insisting that bilateral relations could only return to normal if Turkey formally apologised, brought the killer of the Russian pilot to justice and compensated the airman's family. Erdogan refused.

On 12 January 2016 and again on 19 March 2016, ISIS suicide bombers targeted tourists in Istanbul, killing a total of 17 foreign nationals, 12 of them Germans. Starting in mid-January 2016, ISIS forces in Syria began shelling towns on the Turkish side of the border, prompting retaliatory artillery fire by Turkish army units. During the first five months of 2016, ISIS killed 20 civilians in the Turkish province of Kilis alone. On 1 May 2016, an ISIS suicide attack on a police headquarters in the southeastern city of Gaziantep killed three police officers. This was the group's first operation inside Turkey that directly targeted the Turkish state. On 28 June 2016, three ISIS sympathisers carried out a suicide attack on Istanbul Atatürk Airport, Turkey's main international hub, indiscriminately killing 42 people – 29 Turks and 13 foreign nationals – and wounding 239 more. The PKK too conducted suicide bombings in Ankara, on 17 February and 13 March 2016, and in Istanbul, on 7 June, killing 75 people in all. In the first five months of 2015, tourist arrivals in Turkey fell by a record 34.7%, and the decline accelerated during the peak summer season.

Between sectarianism and realpolitik

Ideological and sectarian differences continued to strain Turkey's relations with other countries in the Middle East. During the early stages of the Syrian civil war, Ankara worked closely with several Sunni Arab states – particularly Saudi Arabia and Qatar – in arming and organising rebel groups. In addition, the flow of funds from the members of the Gulf Cooperation Council – notably Qatar, Kuwait, Saudi Arabia and the United Arab Emirates – into Turkey provided standing support for the Istanbul stock market and created a boom in the Turkish real-estate sector. But tensions over Ankara's support for organisations affiliated with the Muslim Brotherhood – including its supporters among rebel groups in Syria – escalated in 2013, when then Egyptian president Muhammad Morsi, a member of the organisation, was overthrown in a military coup. Saudi Arabia, Kuwait and the UAE strongly supported coup leader and eventual president Abdel Fattah Al-Sisi, while Qatar and Turkey remained sympathetic to Morsi and the Muslim Brotherhood. Erdogan was particularly vocal in his support, lambasting Sisi and allowing members of the organisation who had fled Egypt to organise and establish media outlets in Turkey. On 8–9 August 2015, members of the Muslim Brotherhood held a public conference in Istanbul at which they bitterly condemned the Sisi regime.

Although Ankara and Gulf Arab capitals continued to cooperate in some areas – for instance, in jointly backing Jaysh al-Fateh, an alliance of extremist Syrian rebel groups – Ankara's support for the Muslim Brotherhood weakened Turkey's ties with Saudi Arabia in particular. Gulf money still flowed into Turkey, but Turkish companies increasingly encountered bureaucratic difficulties in Gulf Arab states. The situation began to change in late 2015 and early 2016. Popular support for the Muslim Brotherhood appeared to be declining in the region, and its members in Turkey were quietly encouraged to leave the country. In turn, there was a decline in hostility towards Turkey over its support for the organisation.

Riyadh became more interested in enlisting Ankara's help in countering a potentially resurgent Iran. Turkey was a founding member of the Sunni-dominated Islamic Military Alliance, a counter-terrorism grouping that Saudi Arabia established on 15 December 2015. Shortly after meeting in Riyadh on 29 December 2015, Erdogan and Saudi King Salman bin Abdulaziz announced their plans to establish a bilateral Strategic Cooperation Council, which would effectively allow Turkey and Saudi Arabia to hold joint cabinet meetings. In April 2016, Turkey took over the rotating two-year presidency of the Organisation of Islamic Cooperation. At the organisation's summit in Istanbul on 10–15 April 2016, Ankara and Riyadh inserted a last-minute condemnation of Iran for allegedly 'supporting terrorism' into the closing declaration. On 28 April 2016, Turkey formally opened a permanent military base in Qatar. In May 2016, Saudi forces participated in the month-long multinational *Efes* 2016 military exercises in Turkey.

There were also signs that sectarian considerations were shaping Turkish policy in Iraq. Since 2014, around 200 Turkish military personnel had been deployed to Bashiqa, in the north of the country, under an agreement with the Kurdistan Regional Government to provide training to various Sunni militias composed of Kurds, Turkmens and Arabs fighting ISIS. During the night of 4–5 December 2015, Ankara abruptly deployed a commando battalion comprising 400 soldiers and 25 M-60 A3 tanks to Bashiqa. The Turkish government publicly described the move as 'a routine rotation and reinforcement'. Baghdad angrily condemned it as a violation of Iraqi sovereignty and demanded that the additional forces be immediately withdrawn. The deployment was Turkey's response to reports of an imminent uprising against ISIS forces occupying the nearby city of Mosul, as Ankara wanted to ensure that the city would be taken by Sunni militias rather than the Shia forces affiliated with the Iraqi government. The uprising never occurred, and the Turkish reinforcements were quietly withdrawn.

While Turkey remained wary of a sustained confrontation with Iran, varying levels of economic and tactical cooperation made their tense strategic rivalry more nuanced than the competition between Tehran and Riyadh. Although Ankara shares the Saudi concern that Tehran's tentative international rehabilitation could boost Iranian influence in the region, Turkish leaders also understand that lifting sanctions on Iran potentially creates lucrative business opportunities involving the country – opportunities that they have begun to explore.

Contentious refugee deal

Shortly after Syria's civil war began, Turkey opened its borders to Syrians fleeing the conflict in the belief that Assad would be swiftly overthrown and, after returning home, they would gratefully look to Ankara for leadership. As a consequence, Turkey did not formulate a strategic plan for the long-term accommodation of the 2.7m Syrians residing in the country by mid-2016. Only 10% of them were housed in organised camps, with the rest scattered among the Turkish population. There were also large numbers of unregistered refugees, some of whom planned to travel through Turkey on their way to Europe. Others found work in the unregistered economy, driving down wages and pushing up local rates of unemployment. These developments increased social tensions between locals and refugees, which led to numerous violent clashes.

In summer 2015, the Turkish authorities began to restrict the refugees' movements, effectively confining them to areas close to the Syrian border in the relatively impoverished east of the country, where wages are low and job opportunities limited. This development, combined with an upsurge in violence in Syria, resulted in a sharp increase in the number of refugees trying to enter Europe – most of them by making the short sea crossing to Greek islands in the Aegean. Many drowned along the way.

The EU sought to encourage Erdogan to reduce the flow of refugees into Europe, toning down official criticism of his growing authoritarianism. On 18 March 2016, after months of negotiations, Turkey and the EU reached an agreement. Ankara would prevent irregular migration to the EU and readmit any migrant who crossed illegally to the Greek islands from Turkey. The EU would admit one Syrian refugee from Turkish camps for every illegal migrant Turkey took back. Brussels also agreed to provide Ankara with €6 billion in aid over two years to mitigate the financial burden of hosting refugees in Turkey, and to lift visa requirements for Turkish citizens visiting the Schengen Area – provided that Turkey met 72 existing criteria.

In closing off the Aegean route, the agreement was a success. By late June 2016, the flow of Syrian refugees arriving in the Greek islands had slowed to a trickle. But because Erdogan ultimately refused to implement one of the most critical of the 72 criteria – a relaxation of Turkey's draconian anti-terrorism laws – the proposal to lift visa requirements had not been implemented as of July 2016. And Ankara's failure to provide details on what it would do with the EU aid delayed the disbursement of the funds.

Erdogan's blind spot and a failed coup

On 28 June 2016, Turkey and Israel signed an agreement to normalise their ties. Their once healthy, if limited, relationship had disintegrated six years earlier, when Israeli commandos killed ten Turkish nationals while storming an aid flotilla that had attempted to break the blockade of Gaza. Although the agreement included Israel's formal apology and offer of compensation to the families of those killed, it also contained Turkey's tacit recognition of the blockade, which Ankara had vowed never to accept. On 29 June, after Erdogan wrote to Putin expressing his regret for Turkey's shoot-down of the Russian plane, the leaders spoke on the telephone and the Russian president proposed negotiations on reviving bilateral economic ties.

These moves were unlikely to produce immediate political or economic gains for Turkey. The rift between Turkey and Israel had not affected bilateral trade, which grew from US$3.4bn in 2010 to US$4.4bn in 2015, but it had fostered mutual distrust and disdain that will probably continue to impede close cooperation. And the nascent warming of Ankara's relationship with Moscow appeared unlikely to rescue Turkey's beleaguered tourism sector, given growing fears among tourists in general about the security situation in the country.

Erdogan's willingness to reach out to Israel and Russia suggested that he had finally recognised the need to end Turkey's international isolation. Nonetheless, he did not seem to understand that the United States and the EU had limited tolerance for his increasing authoritarianism. By mid-2016, as he continued to tighten his grip on power and suppress any form of dissent, the resulting rise in social tension and the deteriorating security situation threatened to usher in a period of severe, sustained domestic instability.

This threat crystallised when elements of the Turkish military attempted a coup on the night of 15 July 2016. The putsch was short-lived, beginning at around 10.30pm and petering out by around 3am the next morning, when a confident and self-assured Erdogan landed in the presidential jet in Istanbul. While more than 300 people died in the episode, the putschists' resources were relatively sparse, consisting of a few F-16s, helicopters and tanks, and between 1,000 and 1,500 ground forces (some of them unwitting conscripts). The putschists apparently hoped to spark support from the officer corps and much of the public on the basis of Kemal Atatürk's secular legacy. They miscalculated, encountering resolute opposition – and implicit backing for Erdogan's Islamism. But the government and pro-state media's public accusation that Fethullah Gülen – an Islamic preacher and political rival of Erdogan's who has been living in self-imposed exile in the US since 1999 – was behind the coup seemed dubious for several reasons, including his Islamist beliefs. Washington appeared unlikely to grant Turkey's request for Gülen's extradition, despite some Turkish officials' and newspapers' allegations that the US was complicit in the putsch.

Erdogan's reaction was ominously severe. The Turkish authorities issued arrest warrants charging nearly 3,000 judges and prosecutors with membership of the Gülen movement and involvement in the coup. On the same charge, resignations were demanded from all 1,571 university deans in the country. More than 6,000 members of the armed forces, including 118 of its 358 generals and admirals, were detained, and more than 61,000 civil servants summarily dismissed. Given that many of these people were critical of Gülen, Erdogan appeared to be using the coup attempt as a pretext for purging the government of anyone he deemed insufficiently loyal. Blowback remained a concern. The purges of the military could critically diminish its operational capabilities. Those of Erdogan's political opponents could strain Turkey's relations with the US and the EU. Acrimony over Gülen's extradition might affect US–Turkey strategic cooperation. And Erdogan's crackdown could lead to heightened dissent and civil strife.

Chapter 8

Russia and Eurasia

The Ukraine crisis, which began with Russia's invasion of Crimea in March 2014, continued to define the geopolitics and geo-economics of the Russia/Eurasia region in the year to mid-2016. While Ukraine was still the locus of armed conflict – albeit at lower levels than in the previous year – and the subject of diplomatic contestation, the crisis that began there deepened beyond its borders.

Most notably, the shattering of Russia–West ties resulting from the Ukraine crisis created the circumstances that led to Moscow's first military intervention outside post-Soviet Eurasia since the 1979 Soviet invasion of Afghanistan. The breakdown in relations led Russian decision-makers to believe that only the application of military power would force Washington to take account of its interests in Syria and elsewhere. Nonetheless, Russia's entry into Syria's civil war with a bombing campaign that began in late September 2015 surprised observers and officials across the world. By summer the following year, the campaign had achieved several of Moscow's objectives, especially the prevention of regime change and a reinforcement of Russia's status as a great power. However, there were also significant costs, particularly the terrorist bombing of a Russian civilian airliner over Sinai in October and Turkey's shoot-down of a Russian military jet in November, which almost immediately spoiled the previously close relationship between Ankara and Moscow.

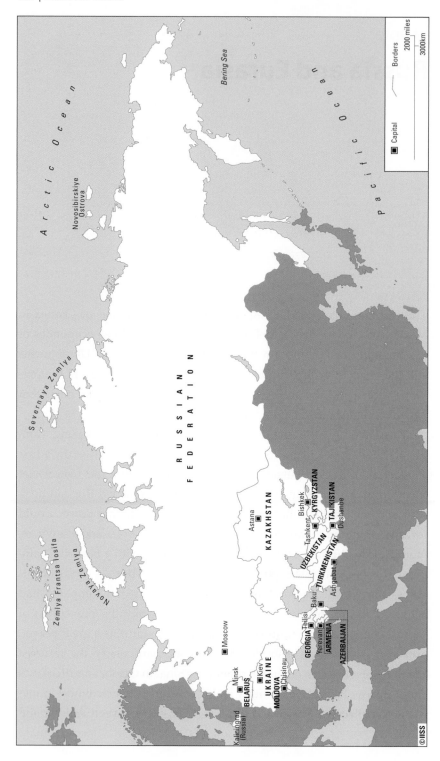

In Ukraine's Donbas region, hopes of a settlement faded as the conflict ground on. There was considerably less violence there than in the year to mid-2015, but nearly every aspect of the 'Minsk II' peace plan remained unfulfilled. The key question was whether some version of the status quo of simmering conflict would continue or Moscow would decide to escalate the war. Any attempts to resolve the broader problems in Russia–West relations depended on the Minsk process, and thus made no progress at all. Indeed, despite intensified diplomatic exchanges, the new Cold War dynamic became more entrenched in the year to mid-2016 – not least in Europe, where mutual remilitarisation threatened to undo a peace dividend that had lasted for a quarter of a century.

The Ukraine crisis has also contributed to significant economic turbulence in Eurasia through an ever-increasing web of sanctions. In addition to the exchange of sanctions between Russia and the West, Moscow and Kiev imposed various restrictive measures on one another. And the region's economies were also affected by other factors, particularly the collapse in global commodity prices. Despite all this, Kyrgyzstan joined the Eurasian Economic Union (EEU). Meanwhile, the major development in Russia–China relations was an initiative to link up the union with Beijing's Belt and Road Initiative (BRI).

Russia's intervention in Syria

By summer 2015, with the civil war in Syria into its fifth year, Russian decision-makers were growing increasingly worried about the situation in the country. The Geneva II peace process was stalled. Moreover, from Moscow's perspective, the conflict was leading to a violent overthrow of the Assad regime at the hands of proxies of the United States and its regional allies. In the view of President Vladimir Putin and those in his inner circle, such an outcome would have posed major national-security risks for Russia. Firstly, it would have been another in a string of US-led coercive regime-change campaigns. Moscow saw such diverse cases as Kosovo, Afghanistan, Iraq, Libya and even the Maidan Revolution in Ukraine as part of a single phenomenon: Washington's successful efforts to oust governments that had not done its bidding and to replace them with puppet regimes. Russia did not want to allow Syria to become the latest case; the fear, of course, was that the ultimate target of regime change was Putin's Russia. A second perceived threat was specific to Syria: Moscow did not want the country to suffer the same fate as Libya, where the overthrow of the regime had created a power vacuum that empowered Islamic extremists. After all, the Islamic State, also known as ISIS or ISIL, had declared Russia a target. While Western leaders saw Syrian President Bashar al-Assad's removal as key to addressing the extremist threat, Putin regarded the Ba'athist regime as the only credible force that could counter the extremists.

The logic of a proxy war dictated that Russia put its thumb on the scale. But few, if any, observers expected it to do so in such a dramatic fashion. Since the end of the Cold War, Moscow had never indicated that it was willing to enter the fray in the Middle East; in fact, its diplomats frequently denounced the West's interventions there. Post-Soviet Russia seemed to have neither the capabilities nor the global interests to use its military outside its neighbourhood. Yet, by summer 2015, the country had in place the capabilities for a limited mission largely confined to uncontested airspace. And Moscow had an additional strategic incentive: to break out of the diplomatic isolation that the West had attempted to impose on it following the Ukraine crisis, and to demonstrate that Russia's place at the high table of international politics could not be taken away.

Throughout August and September 2015, press and social-media reporting indicated that Russia had deployed several Su-30 fighters, Su-25 ground-attack aircraft, Su-24 and Su-34 bombers, and Il-20 spy planes, as well as a force-protection contingent. Before the operation began, Putin attempted to justify the intervention at the UN General Assembly on 28 September – his first appearance there in several years. In his remarks, Putin condemned Western policies in the Middle East, alleging that they were ultimately responsible for the upheaval there and related terrorist threats:

> Instead of bringing about reforms, aggressive intervention rashly destroyed government institutions and the local way of life. Instead of democracy and progress, there is now violence, poverty, social disasters and total disregard for human rights, including even the right to life. I cannot help asking those who created this situation: do you at least realize now what you've done? But I'm

afraid that this question will remain unanswered, because they have never abandoned their policy, which is based on arrogance, exceptionalism and impunity.

Despite this condemnation, he went on to propose a new alliance to counter extremism:

Relying on international law, we must join efforts to address the problems that all of us are facing, and create a genuinely broad international coalition against terrorism. Similar to the anti-Hitler coalition, it could unite a broad range of parties willing to stand firm against those who, just like the Nazis, sow evil and hatred of humankind.

Given the significance of the anti-Hitler coalition and Second World War generally for Russians, this was a striking offer.

Yet US President Barack Obama, Putin's primary audience, was not inclined to cooperate. In his UN General Assembly speech, Obama not only condemned the Russian intervention in Ukraine but also rejected the counter-terrorism cooperation with Assad that Putin had just proposed. The Syrian president, Obama argued, was a tyrant who 'drops barrel bombs to massacre innocent children'. Putin and Obama held a 90-minute meeting during the UN General Assembly, but its only practical outcome was an agreement to begin military-to-military discussions on avoiding accidents in the skies over Syria. Two days later, the Russian airstrikes began.

The Russian Air Force's approach to targeting purportedly centred on ISIS, but it reflected the very strategy that Obama decried at the United Nations: bolstering Assad by focusing on the rebel groups that posed the greatest threat to the regime. Some of these groups were the moderate opposition forces that had received Western and Gulf Arab financing and weapons. To many Western officials and observers, this seemed like outright endorsement of a murderous regime in the civil war under the cover of counter-terrorism. For Moscow, however, bolstering Assad was part and parcel of fighting extremism in Syria. Additionally, Russia intended to coerce the opposition, along with its Western and Gulf patrons, to abandon its ambitions for toppling the regime and instead negotiate on Moscow's terms.

Russia's 'red lines' on the negotiation process remained unchanged: Moscow would neither accept coercive regime change, nor endorse a political settlement whereby outside powers picked the winners of the civil war. This policy was often construed simply as support for Assad. Clearly, the Syrian regime was Russia's proxy and the beneficiary of Russia's bombing campaign. But Moscow was never wedded to Assad himself. Since the conclusion in June 2012 of the Geneva Communiqué that guided the peace talks, Russia had supported a political transition in Syria that would, by definition, lead to Assad's departure. Moscow reaffirmed this position in two subsequent UN Security Council resolutions, 2118 and 2254.

The Russian air campaign could strengthen the regime but, even combined with Iranian support, could not achieve total military victory. Assad's army lacked the capability to retake the entire country. As such, many Western observers predicted that Syria would become a quagmire for Russia, and argued that Western governments need not engage with Moscow; all that was required was patience in waiting for the inevitable failure. As US Secretary of Defense Ashton Carter put it in February 2016, 'I think they have a self-defeating strategy. I don't know how long it will take them to realize that.'

As a result, there was no appetite in Western capitals to respond to Moscow's overtures to enhance their cooperation in Syria. Those overtures have been a striking feature of Russia's intervention; despite decrying the policies of the US and its allies in Syria, Moscow was eager – almost to the point of desperation – for greater cooperation with Washington and its coalition partners. After the Russian bombing campaign began, the Kremlin put forth a series of proposals for engaging with the US on Syria: an offer to send an inter-agency delegation led by Prime Minister Dmitry Medvedev to Washington for talks; a bid for enhanced military negotiations; various ideas for deeper intelligence sharing; and even an offer to conduct joint airstrikes against extremist groups. Until late spring 2016, the US spurned all these entreaties. As one Pentagon official quoted in the press said, 'the Russians are seeking greater cooperation, and frankly we don't want that greater cooperation.'

At the beginning of its intervention, the confident predictions of Russia's imminent failure in Syria seemed sagacious. Weeks of bombing had led to few advances on the ground by Assad's forces. And then, on 31 October, Metrojet flight 9268 exploded over Sinai on its way from Sharm el-Sheikh to St Petersburg, killing all 224 passengers on board, the vast majority of them Russian holidaymakers. Eight hours later, Wilayat Sina (Sinai Province), the local ISIS affiliate, claimed responsibility for the destruction of the aircraft. In the aftermath of the attack, Moscow began evacuating Russian tourists from Egypt's seaside resorts, banned direct flights to Egypt and ordered all travel agencies to refund existing tour bookings and cancel future tours until the safety of Egyptian airports could be confirmed. (By mid-2016, tours and direct flights were still suspended.) Putin confirmed on 17 November the plane had been downed by a terrorist attack. Moscow retaliated with a massive air assault on Raqqa, the ISIS stronghold in Syria, employing missiles launched by strategic bombers and *Kalibr* cruise missiles launched by the Caspian Flotilla.

Less than a month later, another Russian plane fell from the skies of the Middle East. On 24 November, a Turkish F-16 shot down a Russian Su-24 that had crossed into Turkish airspace for 17 seconds, according to Ankara. However, Moscow vigorously denied that the jet violated Turkish airspace. The Turks acted less in response to this particular airspace violation; instead, several broader factors prompted the reaction. Firstly, the area targeted by the Russian Air Force near the Syria–Turkey border is populated by Turkmen, ethnic brethren of the Turks. Turkmen armed opposition groups shot one of the two Russian Su-24 crew members descending by parachute. (The other was rescued by Russian and Syrian special forces.) Secondly, several Turkish diplomatic admonishments to Russia regarding the bombing campaign and airspace violations had produced no change in behaviour. Finally, Russia's campaign had left Ankara's Syria policy – essentially, regime change – in tatters.

Whatever the reason, it was a rash escalation that prompted other NATO member states to publicly distance themselves from Turkey. The shoot-down also completely transformed Ankara's relationship with Moscow. Several weeks earlier, Putin and Turkish President Recep Tayyip Erdogan had celebrated their countries' close ties at the G20 Antalya summit; Erdogan had attended the opening ceremony of the

massive new mosque in Moscow in September 2015; and Gazprom's flag-
ship European pipeline project, Turkstream, was on track to eventually
bring gas to Europe via Turkey. All of that ended with an act that Putin
came to refer to as a 'stab in the back'. Moscow's retaliation included a
ban on Russian travel agencies selling tour packages to Turkey (Russians
made up the second-largest group of tourists in Turkey, after Germans);
an increase in military support to Kurdish militant groups in Syria; the
suspension of visa-free travel for Turkish citizens entering Russia; and an
embargo on some Turkish agricultural imports. Given the gravity of the
incident, and Erdogan's refusal to apologise for it, a far more aggressive
response might have been expected. Yet, in June 2016, the relationship
seemed to be repaired almost as quickly as it had been destroyed. After
Erdogan sent Putin a letter expressing regret for the death of the pilot,
sanctions were quickly lifted and Russian tourists immediately began
purchasing trips to Turkey. Some permanent damage had been done,
but both countries were eager to restore what had been an important and
mutually beneficial relationship.

The tide began to turn for Russia in Syria in early 2016. Backed by the
Russian air campaign, Assad's forces made significant gains in January
and February. By mid-February, the regime had gained a solid footing;
Moscow had strengthened its proxy to the point that the political process
would align with Russian interests. The diplomatic track thus intensified, leading to a joint US–Russia statement on 22 February, outlining the
terms for a 'cessation of hostilities' agreement. This was not a true ceasefire, since extremist groups were still fair game for all sides. Surprisingly
to many, Moscow largely complied with the deal. The political process
made some progress in March, but stalled following an increase in fighting between the regime and various opposition groups. While the US
and Russia again pushed the process forward with another joint statement on 9 May, the future of the talks was deeply uncertain.

On 14 March, Putin unexpectedly declared the withdrawal of 'the
main part' of Russia's forces in Syria. The announcement accompanied
the broadcast of joyous homecoming ceremonies for Russian airmen on
state television. Yet Russia had only modestly decreased its presence
on the ground. Instead, Putin was signalling that Russia did not intend
to engage in an indefinite combat mission in Syria. Moscow wanted to

achieve a stable political equilibrium in the country that could allow for survival of the state in some form; containment of the extremist threat posed by ISIS and Jabhat al-Nusra; the survival of a government that would not be hostile to Moscow; a declaration of victory for the audience at home; and a light military footprint, at most, in Syria in the long term. In other words, Russia's commitment to Assad was anything but absolute.

On balance, Moscow's intervention achieved several objectives. The bombing campaign crushed the aspirations for regime change harboured by opposition groups, some of Syria's neighbours and elements within Western governments. The campaign brought all the players to the negotiating table on Moscow's terms. It also weakened ISIS and other extremist groups. Furthermore, the intervention led to a step change in regional and global perceptions of Russia's great-power status and military capabilities. It established Russia as a key outside power in the Middle East, even though its aspirations remained modest compared with those of the US. However, the ultimate objective of the intervention was a political settlement in and around Syria, an outcome that was highly uncertain. It was therefore too early to say whether post-Soviet Russia's first major power projection was truly a success.

Conflict in Ukraine: no end in sight

The conflict in eastern Ukraine continued at a slow burn throughout the year to mid-2016, with no end in sight despite high-level international-mediation efforts. In April, the UN reported that more than 9,300 people had been killed since the start of the conflict two years earlier.

Throughout summer 2015, the level of violence remained high but never spiralled out of control. The Ukrainian military and the Russian-backed separatists of the so-called Donetsk and Luhansk 'People's Republics' (DNR and LNR respectively) agreed in September to a cease-fire that reduced the fighting. On 25 November, both sides declared a new 'silence regime', while the Ukrainian military claimed that its troops would not return fire in the event of an attack by separatists in the conflict zone. Violence remained at low levels for a month or so, although both sides almost immediately accused each other of breaking the silence regime.

Hostilities intensified early in the new year. The violence was particularly severe in the area around Donetsk city, continually threatening the fragile ceasefire. On 24 February, Ukrainian troops reportedly retook some industrial areas around Avdiivka, in Donetsk region. After the Ukrainian offensive, the separatists launched a violent counter-offensive throughout March, allegedly with the assistance of Russian regular forces. During 7–24 March, Ukrainian military intelligence reported that at least 30 Russian troops had been killed and 29 others injured in clashes with Ukrainian forces. Moreover, the Ukrainian military reported that Russian and separatist fighters had used heavy weapons. Following this spike in violence, however, the situation returned to the uneasy status quo of regular skirmishes that resulted in a few casualties per week.

Civilians living in the conflict zone were hit especially hard. The Office of the UN High Commissioner for Human Rights (OHCHR) reported a range of human-rights abuses in the area. These included allegations that DNR and LNR forces had subjected civilians to 'killings, torture and ill-treatment, illegal detention and forced labour', and similar crimes committed by the Ukrainian state-security services. According to a study released in late December by the Special Monitoring Mission (SMM) of the Organisation for Security and Co-operation in Europe (OSCE), civilians also encountered significant obstacles in tasks ranging from attending court hearings to obtaining birth and death certificates.

The Trilateral Contact Group – comprising representatives from Ukraine, Russia and the OSCE – continued to meet regularly with separatist representatives in Minsk, making only minor gains. The group agreed on plans for a verified withdrawal of heavy weapons in summer 2015, and subsequent SMM reports indicated that there was some progress in this effort. Nonetheless, these gains were largely rolled back in winter 2015 and the following spring, as the OSCE SMM regularly noted incidents that involved the redeployment of these weapons.

As the conflict drew on, the leaders and foreign ministers of Ukraine, Russia, France and Germany continued to meet and hold conference calls in the 'Normandy format', with the aim of moving ahead on a settlement under the terms of the February 2015 Minsk II agreement. Despite engaging in two summits and five ministerial meetings between June and May, the most substantive outcome of the diplomacy was an agreement to extend the deadline for implementation into 2016. The political elements of Minsk II made markedly little headway. Kiev's proposed constitutional-reform package, a partial fulfilment of one of the political elements, passed its first reading in parliament (despite violent protests that led to the deaths of three national guardsmen) on 31 August but, by mid-2016, the second reading had not been held. A major sticking point was the lack of agreement on modalities for local elections in the conflict zone. Moreover, Minsk II's amnesty provision had not been passed, Kiev's economic blockade of the breakaway regions had hardened and greater restrictions were imposed on freedom of movement across the Line of Contact.

Meanwhile, the US opened up an additional channel of communication with Russia on the Ukraine issue, in the form of talks between Victoria Nuland, assistant secretary of state for European and Eurasian affairs, and Vladislav Surkov, a close adviser to Putin in charge of relations with the Ukrainian separatists. Yet, judging by publicly available information, their meetings in January and May produced no concrete results.

The factor that will determine the immediate future of the conflict is Russia's behaviour. That behaviour, in turn, will be determined by the extent to which Moscow believes the situation on the ground is moving toward its desired outcome. In this, there are two broad possibilities. The first is the prolongment or moderate intensification of the violence: neither war nor peace, but a calibrated, simmering conflict without major escalation – much like the current status quo. In such a scenario, the fighting would absorb much of the Ukrainian government's political capital, leaving it unable to proceed with crucial economic and political reforms. Moscow would use economic and energy sanctions to ensure that the Ukrainian economy remained in disarray, and few investors would venture back into the country. Russia would also calibrate its military activities to avoid a more forceful Western response. In short, this would be a war of attrition that Moscow would eventually win. To pursue this course of action, Russia needed confidence that time was on its side and the strategic patience to wait for victory. However, the Kremlin has a track record of rash behaviour in the crisis, as seen in its invasion of Crimea only a few days after the ouster of Victor Yanukovich from the Ukrainian presidency. As such, it remained possible that Russia would engage in a major escalation of its military activity in eastern Ukraine.

This proved a successful tactic for Russia earlier in the crisis: in late August 2014 and again in late January 2015, Moscow heavily increased its support for separatists in the conflict zone, and in both cases Ukrainian President Petro Poroshenko was forced to sue for peace, resulting in the two Minsk agreements. Escalation certainly had its risks, particularly that the US and the European Union would strengthen their sanctions regimes on Russia or provide lethal military assistance to Ukrainian forces. Nonetheless, Moscow had paid little heed to these risks in the past.

The long-term outcomes of these two scenarios are similar. Should either come to pass, Ukraine would be forced to reintegrate the Donbas region on Russia's terms. In other words, Kiev would have to make concessions such as granting autonomy to the separatist regions and ending the economic blockade, with Russia withdrawing only after it was confident in the durability of the settlement. The key difference between the two scenarios is time: in the first, the endgame could take months or even years to materialise; in the second, it would happen as soon as Putin gave the order. In either case, Ukrainians would pay the price: there would be further conflict in the east; the Ukrainian economy would continue its downward spiral; and Kiev's pledges of reform and clean governance would seem increasingly empty.

For Russia, the past year has demonstrated that there is no immediate risk of 'losing' Ukraine to the West, which was the nightmare scenario that shaped its behaviour. Ukrainian politics has reverted to the business as usual of widespread corruption, back-room deals among oligarchs and little substantive reform. Meanwhile, cracks are emerging in the unity of Western policy. Germany and France lead a results-oriented camp that pushes Kiev to enact the political elements of the Minsk agreements. In contrast, the US, the United Kingdom, Lithuania and Poland have insisted that Moscow must fully implement its ceasefire and withdrawal commitments for the Ukrainian government to pursue the political process. These trends would seem to be in Russia's favour.

New Cold War continues

Due to the lack of progress on Minsk II and the ongoing conflict in Ukraine, it appeared inevitable that the West and Russia would lapse into a relationship reminiscent of the Cold War. Two years after Russia's annexation of Crimea, the situation was as grave as it had been since the heated days of the early 1980s. In addition to the struggle over Ukraine, there was a US–Russia proxy war in Syria in all but name, the lethal military exchanges between Russia and NATO member Turkey in northern Syria, and other troubling signs. As Russian Prime Minister Dmitry Medvedev put it at the Munich Security Conference in February 2016, 'we have slid into a time of a new Cold War'.

The year to mid-2016 saw a marked contrast between the regular activity in diplomatic channels and the overall deepening of tensions. Obama met Putin three times, and the two leaders spoke on the phone several times, while US Secretary of State John Kerry visited Putin in Russia twice. Kerry also had near-weekly interactions with Russian Foreign Minister Sergei Lavrov. Even CIA Director John Brennan travelled to Moscow, in March 2016. European foreign ministers also regularly visited the city. The NATO–Russia Council met in April 2016 for the first time since its suspension two years earlier, and again in July 2016.

This active diplomacy has given the lie to Western claims of having isolated Russia. However, the exchanges with senior Russian officials largely concerned either Syria or the narrow question of implementation of the Minsk agreements; no systematic efforts were made to address the broader questions of the European regional-security architecture that lie at the core of the dispute.

The Western approach is to maintain cooperation with Moscow on key global issues that require its involvement, such as Syria or the Iranian nuclear deal, while at the same time keeping up the pressure on Russia over its actions in Ukraine. The calculus is that a new Cold War can be avoided without having to negotiate with Russia about the regional order on its periphery. Even those states that might be open to such a negotiation are locked into the politics of conditionality: implementation of the Minsk agreements is seen as a prerequisite to beginning a broader dialogue with Moscow, but there seems to be little hope of achieving this outcome.

However, the mismatch between the declared policy of 'no business as usual' and the reality that *some* business is being conducted very much as usual has created tensions within the Western coalition. In February, press reports indicated that Obama had urged Japanese Prime Minister Shinzo Abe not to meet Putin in Sochi the following May; Abe rejected the request, but called the meeting an 'informal' summit to downplay its significance. When European Commission President Jean-Claude Juncker announced that he would attend the St Petersburg Economic Forum in June 2016, he faced criticism from some EU members. 'Meetings for the sake of meetings as such do not bring added value to EU–Russia relations', commented Linas Linkevicius, the Lithuanian foreign minister. The US State Department has said that no American officials will attend the forum, and has discouraged US businesses from doing so.

Meanwhile, the tensions between Russia and the West manifested beyond Ukraine and Syria. In February, Moscow announced that it would cease its cooperation with Washington on Afghanistan, a theatre in which the US and Russia had worked together since 2001. Russia also boycotted the US-led Nuclear Security Summit in April, severely limiting the event's impact. The most consequential development in the relationship has been the deepening of military tensions between Russia and NATO. While the sides managed Turkey's shoot-down of the Russian jet without a major overall deterioration in relations, the escalatory dynamic in Europe has intensified in terms of both incidents and policies.

This is particularly noticeable in Russia's continual testing of NATO through a series of provocations, ranging from Russian military jets' efforts to probe air defences to increased submarine activity in the North Atlantic. In October, US Navy jets intercepted two Tu-142 maritime-reconnaissance and anti-submarine-warfare aircraft flying near the aircraft carrier USS *Ronald Reagan* in the Pacific, and, in January, an Su-27 flew within seven metres of an American RC-135 reconnaissance aircraft over the Black Sea. In April, Russian jets buzzed a US surface ship, the USS *Donald Cook*, and conducted a barrel roll over an RC-135 in the Baltic Sea.

Washington has responded to this challenge. The US will spend an additional US$789 million in the 2016 fiscal year, and US$3.4 billion in the 2017 fiscal year, to expand its presence along the NATO–Russia front-line, including through periodic rotations of armoured and air-borne brigades to Poland and the Baltic states. Germany and the UK also have troops on regular rotation in the Baltic states, and the Alliance has expanded its programme of military exercises. For example, the *Allied Shield* activities conducted in June 2015 involved four distinct exercises in several Eastern European member states, and more than 15,000 personnel from 19 allies and three partner states. In June 2016, 24 NATO members and partners sent approximately 31,000 troops to Poland to participate in *Anakonda* 2016.

This effort is intended to reassure NATO allies and to deter Russia. But it has also convinced Moscow that NATO is merely accelerating the long-running process of moving its military infrastructure closer to Russia's borders. In response, Russia has announced a build-up in its Western Military District. In May, Russian Defence Minister Sergei Shoigu announced that the military would form two new divisions in the Western Military District and one in the Southern Military District by the end of 2016. The nuclear sabre-rattling of the Cold War seems to be returning, albeit in new incarnations. In November, the state-owned Channel One displayed images of a Russian general studying plans for a project codenamed *Status*-6, a doomsday retaliation weapon designed to irradiate large areas of coastline, rendering them uninhabitable.

While that effort seemed somewhat quixotic, a more serious potential flashpoint concerned ballistic-missile defence (in fact, Russia's fly-bys past the USS *Donald Cook* could have been related to the ship's *Aegis* missile-defence capability). In early May, NATO completed the second phase of its Phased, Adaptive Approach to ballistic-missile defence by putting into operation an interceptor and radar site at Deveselu, in Romania. Putin made several pointed comments in the following weeks, stating on 27 May that

> we have been persistently repeating the same thing, like a mantra ... Nobody listens to us, nobody is willing to have talks with us, we do not hear anything but platitudes, and those platitudes mainly boil down to the fact that this is not directed against Russia and does not threaten Russia's security. Let me remind you that initially there was talk about thwarting a threat from Iran, it was all about the Iranian nuclear programme. Where is the Iranian nuclear programme

now? It no longer exists … while the US anti-missile deployment area is being created and was commissioned in Romania … How can this not be a threat to us? It is a clear threat to our nuclear forces … That is the reason we have to respond now, and if yesterday some areas in Romania did not know what it is like to be a target, today we will have to take action to ensure our security. Let me repeat, these are response measures, a response only.

He also reiterated the charge that the interceptor launchers in Romania, the Mk 41 vertical-launch system, could easily be repro-grammed to launch *Tomahawk* cruise missiles, which would constitute a breach of the Intermediate-Range Nuclear Forces Treaty. Finally, he warned that once the third phase of NATO ballistic-missile defence goes live in Poland in 2018, Russia will target Poland too.

Regional economic turbulence

There were wide-ranging consequences to the economic discord in Russia and Eurasia resulting from low oil prices, an increasingly complex web of sanctions and weak governance. The troubling situation fostered expectations of even greater change to come. While there was little change in the US and EU sanctions on Russia, Kiev and Moscow imposed new restrictions on each other. Meanwhile, the EEU experi-enced growing pains as it admitted new members. Many Eurasian states – both producers and consumers – felt the pain of the collapse in global commodity prices.

The EU voted in December 2015 to extend its sanctions on Russia for another six months, and it seemed likely that the bloc would renew them once more the following July. The US sanctions regime also remained largely unchanged, although the Treasury Department added several Russian individuals and entities to the list. Both US and EU officials con-firmed that the most severe restrictive measures – the so-called sectoral sanctions implemented in July 2014 – would be lifted if Moscow and Kiev were to fully implement the Minsk II agreement. Moscow vowed in May 2016 to renew its counter-sanctions – a ban on the import of food-stuffs and other agricultural goods – for another 18 months. According to August 2015 estimates by the International Monetary Fund, the Western sanctions and Russian counter-sanctions could reduce Russia's

GDP by 1–1.5 percentage points in the short term, potentially leading to a medium-term cumulative loss of 9% of GDP.

Russia and Ukraine also engaged in a bilateral sanctions war. In November 2015, Ukrainian Prime Minister Arseniy Yatsenyuk announced that he had ordered Ukrainian airspace to be completely closed to Russian commercial aircraft – both those landing and in transit. Russia retaliated soon thereafter, a step that put an end to direct air links between the countries, affecting up to 70,000 passengers per month. In December 2015, trilateral talks involving Moscow, Kiev and the European Commission on Ukraine's Deep and Comprehensive Free Trade Area Agreement (DCFTA) with the EU broke down after having failed to produce a deal. Therefore, when the DCFTA went into effect on 1 January 2016, Russia suspended bilateral trade preferences accorded to Ukraine under the provisions of the free-trade agreement of the Commonwealth of Independent States. Moscow also placed an embargo on Ukrainian agricultural goods similar to its counter-sanctions on the West. In response, Kiev banned a variety of Russian imports, including meat, fish, vegetables, fruit, dairy products and alcohol. Both governments also imposed other sanctions. For example, for several weeks in February, there was a ban on lorry transit between Russia and Ukraine, and, in December 2015, Ukraine cut off Crimea's electricity supply.

Russia's economy was buffeted by low commodity prices, along with the lack of structural reform and Western sanctions. The current downturn was the most protracted in Russia's post-Soviet history. GDP growth was negative for more than six quarters, compared to three in the 1998 crisis and four in the global financial crisis that began in 2008. The Russian economy was expected to contract by between 1.5% and 2% in 2016 (after experiencing a 3.7% drop in 2015), and to grow by under 1% in 2017. Russian households suffered more severe effects than in previous crises, as the poverty rate rose from 11.2% to 13.4%, and real wages decreased by 9.5%, in 2015.

The GDPs of the other hydrocarbon-exporting countries in the region were also hit by the drop in oil prices. Azerbaijan suffered the worst effects – the IMF projected a 3% decline in GDP in 2016. Kazakhstan's GDP was projected to stagnate. Both countries steeply devalued their currencies and experienced double-digit inflation. The situation became so dire in Azerbaijan that the government began bailout talks with the International Monetary Fund, the World Bank and the European Bank for Reconstruction and Development in January. The talks were ongoing as of June 2016.

Commodity-poor states Armenia, Georgia, Kyrgyzstan and Tajikistan were more insulated from the oil-price drop but experienced other difficulties. Armenia, Kyrgyzstan and Tajikistan in particular are highly dependent on remittances from labourers working in Russia (approximately 42% of Tajikistan's GDP came from this source in 2014). As a result of the economic downturn in Russia, this crucial source of income almost disappeared. For example, remittances from Tajikistani migrant workers fell by 67%, from US$3.8bn in 2014 to US$1.28bn in 2015. Central Asian countries' exports to the Russian market also suffered.

Meanwhile, Ukraine faced an unprecedented economic decline. According to the World Bank, the country's GDP contracted by approximately 12% in 2015, while inflation remained at more than 40%. The organisation forecasted that the economy could grow by 1% in 2016 in a best-case scenario that involved peace and progress on reform. Yet that would not end Ukrainians' woes, after they experienced zero growth in 2013, and a 6.8% drop in 2014.

Moldova faced continued fallout from the 2014 banking scandal that cost it US$1bn, around 15% of its GDP. Throughout 2015, large anti-corruption protests wracked the country. In October, Vlad Filat, a member of parliament and former prime minister, was stripped of his immunity and detained in connection with the theft that precipitated the crisis. At the same time, Prime Minister Valeriu Strelet received a vote of no confidence amid cracks within his pro-European coalition. In January 2016, the parliamentary majority proposed Vlad Plahotniuc – a leading oligarch known as the 'grey cardinal' of Moldovan politics – as the new prime minister, although many Moldovans once again took to the streets to protest against his candidacy. Ultimately, parliament selected Pavel Filip, who faced the unenviable task of quelling the unrest in the shadow of Plahotniuc, regarded as the true power broker.

Despite the regional economic downturn, the EEU acquired a new member, Kyrgyzstan, which joined the organisation in August 2015. Heavily dependent on remittances from Russia, Kyrgyzstan was drawn to the EEU by the promise of its open labour market – after the country's accession, migrants were no longer required to obtain work permits in fellow member countries. However, with the harmonisation of external tariffs, Kyrgyzstan could no longer profit from the re-export of Chinese goods to Russia, previously a lucrative business. Additionally, Moscow established a US$1bn Russian–Kyrgyz Development Fund to help Kyrgyzstan address the economic impact of the policy changes required by its accession to the EEU.

Kazakhstan, a founding member of the EEU, joined the World Trade Organisation (WTO) in October 2015. Rather than conforming its WTO accession commitments to the EEU's regulations and tariffs, Kazakhstan negotiated a range of exemptions from the union's rules to accommodate the demands of WTO accession. These exemptions challenged the basic concept of a single EEU market.

Broader regional economic issues also presented problems for the EEU. In August, Kazakhstan decided to float its currency, which had been steeply devalued earlier in 2015. The decision was supported by many in Kazakhstan as a means to combat the inflow of cheap Russian goods, but reportedly caused additional friction within the EEU because the country did not inform other members in advance.

The economic downturn thus posed a major challenge to the EEU, particularly as it came in the union's first year. While the organisation's supranational institutions were operational and likely to have passed the point at which they could be quickly unravelled, regional integration was difficult when states' economies were being affected in different ways, resulting in divergent policies on key economic matters. The EU's regional integration efforts – its DCFTAs with Ukraine, Moldova and Georgia – were in an equally parlous condition. Without the prospect of improved governance or increased prosperity, neither the public nor the elite in those countries was likely to support full implementation of these highly complex and potentially disruptive accords.

The long-term political consequences of the regional downturn remained unclear. With little prospect of easy growth on the horizon, governments were more likely to consider much-needed and long-touted structural reforms. However, political considerations mitigated against such steps, as they might threaten the fortunes of entrenched interests or the livelihood of key demographic groups, especially pensioners. The recession had a deep effect on households across Eurasia, and some economically driven protests – not least those related to unpaid wages – were likely to occur. That said, there seemed little prospect that such issues alone would produce mass political revolts; after all, the population had experienced far worse circumstances in the preceding 25 years. In the meantime, popular support for political incumbents will have to be sustained by factors other than increased prosperity. That may push vulnerable regimes to take destabilising actions as a means to distract their populations from economic problems. This could be seen, for instance, in Azerbaijan's escalation of its conflict with Armenia, which led in April 2016 to a flare-up in violence in Nagorno-Karabakh.

Russia–China relations: enhanced cooperation despite economic headwinds

Cooperation between Moscow and Beijing continued to intensify, as it had since the Russian invasion of Crimea. Russia has been disabused of some of its initial, sky-high expectations, particularly that China could serve as a stand-in for Europe and the US. Beijing has proceeded cautiously, preferring a more incremental approach, and demonstrating no interest in making partnership with Russia the centrepiece of its foreign policy.

In the year to mid-2016, bilateral military-to-military cooperation intensified. The Russian and Chinese navies conducted in August 2015 the largest joint exercise in their history. Over the course of one week, they simulated anti-submarine combat, air-defence operations and amphibious assaults in the Sea of Japan, off the coast of Vladivostok. In May 2016, the sides conducted a joint computer-simulated missile-defence exercise at an undisclosed Russian military-research facility. Chinese media outlets explicitly linked this drill to Washington's planned deployment of missile-defence platforms in South Korea, although the official statements of both sides emphasised that the drills were not aimed at any third party. Russian troops also marched in the military parade during China's September 2015 Second World War remembrance ceremonies.

Several of Russia's leading hydrocarbon companies also secured major financing deals with Chinese firms, especially state-owned banks.

In December, the state-owned China Petroleum & Chemical Corporation (also known as Sinopec) received approval to purchase a 10% stake in the Russian petrochemical company Sibur (valued at US$1.3bn), with the option to buy an additional 10% in the following three years. In March, Gazprom secured a five-year, €2bn loan from the Bank of China with a view to investing in its large-scale infrastructure projects. In April, the Export–Import Bank of China and the China Development Bank agreed to provide loans of €9.34bn (US$10.6bn) and 9.76bn renminbi (US$1.5bn) respectively to finance the Yamal LNG project, led by the private Russian energy firm Novatek – one of the first companies to be sanctioned by the EU and the US. That project already had heavy Chinese investment, with a 20% stake owned by China National Petroleum Corporation and another 9.9% owned by the Silk Road Fund, a sovereign-wealth investment fund. Beyond their size, these loans were notable because they did not involve US dollars, but rather euros and renminbi – presumably to minimise the risk of sanctions, as well as to reduce the centrality of the dollar to bilateral trade.

The most significant Sino-Russian economic development of the year was the establishment of a framework for cooperation between the EEU and the BRI. Russia traditionally took a suspicious view of all other major powers' economic initiatives for post-Soviet Eurasia. Its initial reaction to the BRI was consistent with this tradition: caution, concern about the implications for Russian interests and anxiety about potential encroachment. However, unlike the West, the Chinese understood that Russia would undermine other powers' initiatives in the post-Soviet region if it felt threatened by them. So Beijing agreed to a significant political gesture, first proposed by Moscow during a summit in the Russian capital in May 2015: a framework would be negotiated to coordinate BRI projects in EEU member states centrally through the Eurasian Economic Commission, the executive policymaking arm of the EEU.

Following the May 2015 joint statement, the details of EEU–BRI coordination were being discussed in a bilateral forum chaired by deputy foreign ministers, as well as at the Eurasian Economic Commission and among EEU member states. By mid-2016, the coordination mechanism had been raised to the level of deputy prime ministers, and the parties identified more than 60 projects to be considered. Moreover, EEU member states also agreed to begin negotiating an agreement on a trade- and economic-cooperation framework with China at a summit held on 31 May in Astana.

For the purposes of understanding the trajectory of Russia–China relations, the details of the BRI, the extent to which it is a real or virtual project and the precise mechanisms of its cooperation with the EEU are of secondary importance. Far more crucial is the fact that through the EEU–BRI dialogue Russia and China created a model for effectively managing their relationship. The development was particularly strik- ing given that observers had long predicted a clash between Moscow and Beijing in Central Asia. Based on the available evidence, Russia and China appeared to belie these predictions, and to transform a potential source of tension into a means of cooperation and mutual reassurance.

Chapter 9

Europe

The future of the European Union was thrown deeper into question in the year to mid-2016. After years of arguments over financing Greece, the sudden arrival in Europe of more than a million refugees caused new divisions between member states. Then came the most significant shock of all: the United Kingdom's referendum vote to quit the 28-nation Union after 43 years of membership.

The UK would be the first state to leave the EU since it was founded, as the European Economic Community, in 1957. The departure of the country with Europe's largest defence budget, second-richest economy and third-largest population would be an enormous setback for the European project that had begun in the aftermath of the Second World War.

The vote for Britain's exit (dubbed 'Brexit') was a surprise, even to those who campaigned for it. British Prime Minister David Cameron, who had staked his career on a vote to remain in the EU, immediately announced his resignation. The country faced negotiations on its future relationship with Europe while in a period of political and economic instability. If carried out, the act of leaving the EU would force the re-legislation of a significant proportion of UK laws and regulations, as well as a complete reshaping of Britain's trade and economic relationships. Scotland's government began to examine its options for holding a referendum on secession from the UK, and there was also uncertainty about

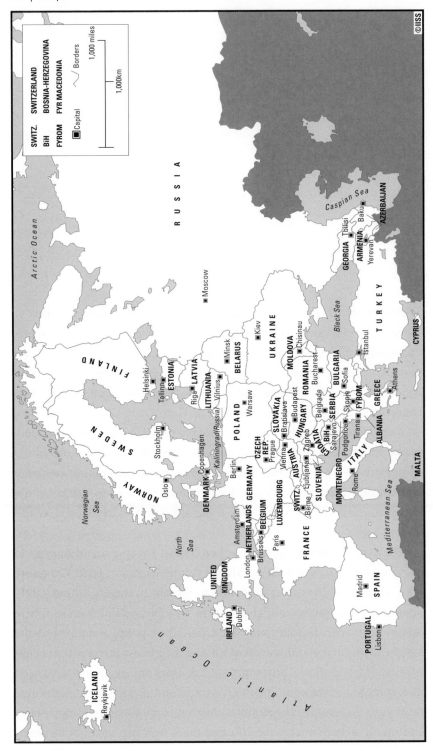

SWITZ. SWITZERLAND
BiH BOSNIA-HERZEGOVINA
FYROM FYR MACEDONIA

■ Capital
⌇ Borders

1,000km
1,000 miles

©IISS

the impact of Brexit on Northern Ireland. Meanwhile, Brussels too faced difficult questions: while the UK's membership was always tempered by a strong element of euroscepticism, the vote catalysed fears that British voters might not be alone in viewing EU institutions as distant and opaque, and even as actively working against them. This could make the Union a target for other populist and nationalist movements wishing to exploit voters' grievances.

Fearing such a boost to eurosceptic sentiment in their own countries, many European leaders urged a quick divorce from the UK so as to limit the period of uncertainty and minimise long-term damage to the EU. They hastened to rebut any argument that Britain could earn a special deal through the result of the referendum – ruling out any agreement in which the country could limit the free movement of people while retaining access to the single market. They called on the UK to swiftly invoke Article 50 of the Lisbon Treaty, which triggers the process for leaving the EU and stipulates negotiations to define the terms of the exit.

Regardless of what politicians across Europe were saying in initial reactions to the referendum vote, the unprecedented situation appeared to leave enormous room for manoeuvre on both sides, setting the stage for several years of uncertainty. The hiatus would cause problems for German and French leaders, who were facing national elections in 2017. In the meantime, the EU and its members were likely to come under pressure to improve the transparency and accountability of European institutions. In sum, it was possible that the ground would shift significantly in the years before the UK reached a final settlement with the Union.

However, to achieve a relatively benign outcome, leaders needed to overcome the mutual mistrust that was undermining European unity more broadly. Fractious disputes dominated the year to mid-2016, as governments tried to cope with multiple challenges. The principal new factor was the influx of migrants from Syria, Afghanistan, Iraq and other countries, many of whom risked their lives by journeying to Europe from North Africa and Turkey aboard hazardous boats. Thousands died in the attempt. Hundreds of thousands of people landed in Greece or Italy, putting huge pressure on both countries. 'If this is your idea of Europe, you can keep it', snapped Italian Prime Minister Matteo Renzi in the early days of the crisis, as EU leaders rejected a small-scale quota scheme to share the resettlement of some refugees.

His words seemed to reflect an atmosphere unsuited to tackling the persistent dangers Europe faced: Islamist terrorism, Russian aggression and Middle East turmoil. The scale of the threat from jihadist group the Islamic State, also known as ISIS or ISIL, was only too evident, as its adherents carried out a series of attacks. The largest of these in Europe took place on 13 November 2015, when a group of ISIS supporters killed 130 people with bombs and gunfire at a concert venue, a stadium, restaurants and bars in Paris. This was the deadliest attack on the continent since the Madrid bombings of 2004. On 22 March 2016, ISIS followers murdered 32 people at an airport and a metro station in Brussels.

These events, as well as the continuing stand-off in the conflict in eastern Ukraine, underlined the need for European solidarity and cooperation. But instead, throughout the year, the continent was embroiled in internal arguments. It was not only the substance of the disagreements that provided cause for concern about the EU's future, but also their tone. During the 2015 confrontation between the Greek government of Alexis Tsipras and creditors led by Germany, he repeatedly mentioned Greece's long-standing claims for reparations for Nazi occupation during the Second World War. Street posters in Athens showed German Chancellor Angela Merkel wearing a military uniform emblazoned with a swastika, and newspaper cartoons depicted the EU's hated negotiators in Nazi uniforms.

Intra-European tensions grew as refugees who had landed in the south travelled to Northern Europe in search of better living standards and job opportunities. Their journey across borders put great pressure on transit countries such as Hungary, Slovenia, Croatia and Austria, as well as on the most desired destinations, Germany and Sweden. After Merkel had dramatically opened German borders to Syrian refugees in August 2015, Hungary's Prime Minister Viktor Orbán accused Berlin of 'moral imperialism'.

The ideals upon which the EU had been built seemed increasingly in question. Arguments about refugees, as well as the attacks by ISIS adherents who had apparently moved freely across national borders, brought into focus an important theme of this scepticism: concern about immigration. In the UK, the campaign to leave the EU successfully played on anti-immigration feeling. It painted the EU as an anti-democratic establishment in which unelected bureaucrats presided over a sclerotic, dying European economy. Similar messages came from Marine Le Pen, leader of France's right-wing, populist National Front. In Austria, a far-right candidate for the country's non-executive presidency was defeated by a margin of only 0.6% in an election that, following a legal challenge from his party, was due to be re-run in October 2016.

Pope Francis, the Argentinian head of the Catholic Church, noted 'there is the growing impression that Europe is weary, ageing, no longer fertile and vital, that the great ideals that inspired Europe seem to have lost their appeal.' Accepting the Charlemagne Prize for contributions to European understanding, he asked, 'what has happened to you, the Europe of humanism, the champion of human rights, democracy and freedom?'.

Britain's vote to leave the EU

The decision by British voters to leave the EU, taken in a referendum held on 23 June 2016, did not originate in a national groundswell of anti-European feeling. For many years, opinion polls had consistently shown that EU membership was not one of voters' major concerns. However, there had always been a strong undercurrent of euroscepticism, ranging from left-wing politicians' view of European institutions as anti-democratic and capitalist in the 1970s, to the right-wing portrayal, from the 1990s onwards, of the EU as a super-state encroaching on the sovereignty of the Westminster Parliament. Britain's general lack of enthusiasm for Europe could be seen in the semi-detached status that it had secured, staying outside the common currency and the border-free Schengen zone.

Europe had long been a toxic issue within the Conservative Party, dividing the government of John Major between 1990 and 1997. When the Conservatives regained power in 2010, it again came to the fore, mainly because David Cameron, who was centrist and pragmatic, lacked support on the right of the party. He was vulnerable for two reasons: firstly, he had failed to win an outright majority and was forced to form a coalition with the Liberal Democrats; and, secondly, he was faced with the rise of the UK Independence Party (UKIP), whose explicit and vocal agenda was to leave the EU. To maintain party unity and prevent defections to UKIP, Cameron made a series of concessions to the right wing, culminating in his promise in January 2013 to hold a referendum on EU membership within five years.

After unexpectedly winning an outright Conservative majority in the 2015 elections, Cameron had little choice but to hold the promised referendum. He made a twofold gamble. He would ask European leaders to make concessions on Britain's EU status that he could take back to the electorate with a strong recommendation to back continued membership. Then, he would win the referendum, preserve the UK's place in Europe and end the dispute within his party. This proved a misjudgement in several ways.

Cameron reached an agreement with EU leaders to make minor alterations to Britain's status. The largest concession related to the ability to limit payments of welfare benefits to new migrants from elsewhere in the EU. Yet the Leave campaign easily dismissed the changes as having failed to address what they saw as the key issues: the return of British sovereignty, and the capacity to control immigration.

Several members of Cameron's cabinet joined the Leave campaign, of which the de facto leader was former mayor of London Boris Johnson. His choice was widely viewed as a calculated move that would enable him to challenge Cameron for the party leadership. Michael Gove, the justice secretary, who had long been committed to leaving the EU, was also prominent in the campaign. They succeeded in painting a positive picture of an independent Britain, freed from what they saw as the EU's straitjacket, which would 'take back control' of its destiny and could strike trade deals with fast-growing economies. The Union, they said, was moribund, and the common currency a failure.

Immigration was the underlying theme, apparently tipping the balance of the vote. The Leave campaign castigated Cameron for his failure to fulfil an undertaking to limit immigration to tens of thousands of people per year – an unwise pledge that was beyond his powers to meet. Net migration had surged over the preceding decade, and reached a record 333,000 in 2015. One in eight of the UK's 64m people were born elsewhere. Although 5m of these 8m people were born outside the EU, the largest increase in recent years had been from eastern EU members. By 2014, Poles made up by far the largest non-British nationality group among UK residents, accounting for 853,000 people, and Romanians the fifth-largest, with 175,000 (after people from India, Ireland and Pakistan). Nigel Farage, the abrasive leader of UKIP, had long dwelt on the issue, and one of the main slogans of the Leave campaign was 'control our borders'. Johnson and Gove promised to institute an Australian-style points system, under which prospective migrants would be vetted for skills and employment potential – a scheme impossible under the EU principle of free movement. In fact, the expanding UK economy clearly needed a flow of migrants, with 2m non-British EU nationals already in the workforce. But this point could not easily be advanced by a government that had promised to slash immigration.

The Remain campaign, led by Cameron, saw the economic benefits of the EU as its trump card. Membership of the world's largest free-trade area, and the EU's clout in dealing with other trade partners, should indeed have been a telling factor. EU membership had increased investment and created jobs in the UK, boosting the country's prosperity. However, George Osborne, the finance minister, chose to cast this argument in a negative fashion, warning of the potential economic damage of a vote to leave. This was dismissed as 'Project Fear', and as showing an unpatriotic lack of confidence in Britain's potential. The chorus that weighed in behind Osborne – which included the IMF, the Organisation for Economic Co-operation and Development, the Bank of England and numerous economists, businesses, banks and think tanks – was rejected as a global conspiracy of the elite. 'People in this country have had enough of experts,' said Gove.

This illustrated the dangers of holding a referendum. Inevitably, the vote came to be about far more than whether the UK should be a member of the EU. Firstly, the Remain campaign's emphasis on the economy failed to resonate with many people in England's former industrial heartlands, who did not feel that they were taking part in economic recovery. They experienced low wages and job insecurity, in which they saw immigration as playing a part. Thus, Leave campaigners in the Conservative Party, many of them government ministers, managed to cast themselves as champions of ordinary people who had been let down by the establishment. Secondly, this same feeling of economic insecurity weakened traditional Labour voters' support for Remain, leading many to back what had for the previous 30 years been a right-wing cause. In normal times, the Labour Party would have been expected to deliver millions of votes in favour of staying in the EU. But Jeremy Corbyn, the old-style socialist who led the party, had voted against EU membership in a referendum in 1975. A surprise choice for the leadership after his predecessor, Ed Miliband, was humiliated in the 2015 election, Corbyn campaigned for Remain, but in a muted and qualified manner for which he was heavily criticised by Labour members of Parliament. The referendum campaign thus reflected divisions within both the main parties, creating a confusing picture for voters, not least because politicians indulged in lies and hyperbole to press their cases. Thirdly, the campaign exacerbated to an unhealthy degree the divisions within British society: between rich and poor; older people who tended to favour leaving and younger people who voted Remain; large cities (led by pro-European London) and the rest of England; as well as England, which voted to leave, and Scotland and Northern Ireland, which elected to stay. The vote caused tension within families and communities. Emotions ran high. And, one week before the vote, pro-European Labour MP Jo Cox was killed in the street in her northern English constituency. Appearing in court, the man accused of her murder gave his name as 'death to traitors, freedom for Britain'.

Throughout the campaign, opinion polls indicated a tight vote, and some showed a majority favouring Leave. Nevertheless, the London political establishment was shocked by the outcome, in which 17.4m people (51.9%) voted for Leave compared to 16.1m (48.1%) for Remain. Turnout was strong, at 72.2%. The result was narrow but clear. Constitutionally, its status was murky, since only Parliament could take the decisions necessary to enact it, and MPs were overwhelmingly pro-Remain. But any government working openly to circumvent the vote would do so at its peril. Still, it was unclear how the new Conservative government would proceed. Theresa May, the long-serving home secretary (interior minister) who succeeded Cameron as prime minister, had sided with the Remain campaign, but accepted after the vote that 'Brexit means Brexit'.

While the policy of the new government could not be anticipated, a view was emerging in London that the UK should be in no hurry to activate Article 50 of the Lisbon Treaty. Invoking it, so the argument went, would hand the initiative to other EU members, who would seek to set exit terms unfavourable to the UK. Amid a flurry of meetings between EU leaders to discuss their response to the British referendum, Merkel dismissed Johnson's assertion that the UK could retain access to the single market while controlling immigration. 'Whoever wants to leave this family cannot expect to do away with all its responsibilities while keeping the privileges,' she argued. She saw no way for the UK decision to be reversed: 'we all need to look at the reality of the situation. It is not the hour for wishful thinking.' Merkel also agreed with Renzi and French President François Hollande that there would be no formal or informal talks with the UK on its exit terms until Article 50 had been triggered.

Despite this stipulation, it seemed in the first days after the referendum that there was wide scope for initiatives on both sides. Members of the EU had an economic and strategic interest in keeping Britain, if not as an EU member, at least in a close association. It was also in the interests of all sides that there should be a strong relationship in security and defence. There was a possibility that the eventual settlement with the EU could be submitted to a new referendum. But such thoughts were speculative. Meanwhile, European leaders would face their own pressures. Le Pen, who was polling as the favourite to win the 2017 presidential election, stepped up her calls for France to hold a referendum on EU membership.

The British referendum created a fluid situation in which there remained a great deal to play for. The vote was yet another factor threatening to drive Europe apart, challenging leaders to find new solutions in the interests of European prosperity and security.

Migration to Europe

If Britons felt undermined by migrants from within the EU, the influx of refugees from outside it caused significant anxiety elsewhere in Europe. But there was a humanitarian response, even though the sheer number of daily arrivals caused chaos. Many governmental and non-governmental bodies, as well as international organisations, played important roles helping refugees and beginning the process of integration. The shock caused by mass fatalities, such as the death by drowning of more than 1,200 people en route to Italy in April 2015 alone, prompted an expansion of maritime operations that rescued many people at sea, and were still doing so by mid-2016. Photographs of a three-year-old Syrian boy whose body washed up on a Turkish beach in September 2015 intensified popular pressure for more effective responses to the crisis. His family had been trying to make the 4-kilometre journey from Turkey to the Greek island of Kos.

The Italian and Greek systems for handling refugees were stretched to breaking point, and their task was complicated by the fact that many migrants wished to immediately push northwards. Under the EU's Dublin Regulation, the country in which a refugee first arrives is responsible for processing his or her application for asylum. Yet, in many cases, migrants were not registered in their first country of arrival and sought to cross borders towards their desired destinations. A considerable number of them registered for asylum in Hungary, which in June 2015 suspended its Dublin obligation to take back asylum seekers who had registered but then gone elsewhere and been rejected. This move, which Budapest made on the argument that its systems were overburdened, was the first significant breakdown of EU immigration rules as a result of the influx.

Several EU countries tightened their border controls. With hundreds of thousands of migrants travelling north from Greece, Orbán ordered the construction of a fence along Hungary's 175km border with Serbia, which is not an EU member. This had the effect of barring entry to those who did not wish to register for asylum in Hungary, redirecting them to Croatia, which promptly moved them on to Hungary and Slovenia. Both Hungary and Slovenia then built razor-wire fences on their borders with Croatia – despite the fact that all three are EU members. As winter set in, while EU nations bickered, columns of refugees were trudging north along roads and across fields, or else becoming stranded in camps.

The immediate reason for the pressures on these countries was the accommodative stance adopted by Germany and Sweden. Merkel's announcement that Germany would welcome Syrian refugees was a striking move, particularly given that her leadership of the euro-zone's response to a five-year debt crisis had been marked by careful steps. The chancellor's decision was announced on 25 August 2015 by the Federal Office for Migration and Refugees, which stated on Twitter that 'we are at present largely no longer enforcing Dublin procedures for Syrian citizens.' Merkel called on other EU members to fulfil their asylum responsibilities, warning that the 26-nation Schengen agreement would otherwise be at risk: 'if Europe fails on the question of refugees, if this close link with universal civil rights is broken, then it won't be the Europe we wished for.' In Sweden, Prime Minister Stefan Löfven similarly called on Europe to do more, arguing that 'we need to decide right now what kind of Europe we are going to be. My Europe takes in refugees. My Europe doesn't build walls.'

By the end of 2015, the scale of the migrant influx had become clear. Around 1.3m people had applied for asylum in the EU during the year, double the number in 2014. More than half of first-time applicants came from three countries embroiled in large-scale conflicts: Syria (29%), Afghanistan (14%) and Iraq (10%). The vast majority of migrants applied for asylum in Germany (35%), followed by Hungary (14%), Sweden (12%), Austria (6.8%) and Italy (6.6%). Of the hundreds of thousands who arrived in Greece, only 11,370 registered for asylum there in 2015. Berlin said that around 1.1m asylum seekers actually arrived in Germany during the year – more than double the figure published by the statistics agency Eurostat, with the discrepancy apparently explained by the time taken to complete registration processes.

According to Eurostat figures, EU countries were accepting almost all applications for asylum from Syrians, and very high percentages from Eritreans and Iraqis. Acceptance rates for people from Afghanistan, Iran, Somalia and Sudan were significantly lower, but still above 50%. Those for other countries were much lower. The figures showed that 10% of all first-time applications came from citizens of Albania and Kosovo, but that only 2% of these were accepted. This meant that a sizeable number of those who arrived in Europe in 2015 would be returned to their home countries.

The displacement of people to Europe needs to be put into perspec-tive. There have been far larger movements of people in the world and within Europe itself, including in the years after the Second World War. The number of Syrians coming to Europe is far fewer than the 5m who remain in camps in Turkey, Lebanon and Jordan, with little near-term prospect of finding worthwhile employment or improving their lives. Net migration, of which the refugee influx is a part, may over several years add a few million people to the EU's population, which had reached 508m by the end of 2014. For instance, according to Eurostat, migration accounted for 85% of the 1.3m increase in the EU's population in 2014. European nations have the capacity to absorb flows of migrants, and have long been doing so: at the beginning of 2015, the EU was home to 34.3m people who were born outside the Union. Given European countries' ageing populations, migrants are needed to fill jobs and fuel economic growth. Although young men made up a high proportion of the migrant influx in 2015, many of the Syrians who arrived were middle-class professionals. In Germany, Sweden and other countries, there were major efforts to integrate migrants through measures such as language and cultural training, as well as employment- and housing-assistance programmes (even if such schemes could be frustratingly slow for those involved).

While the influx stirred xenophobic reactions and political opposition, these developments should not be overstated: in Germany, Merkel appeared to be acquiescing to popular pressure when she opened the borders. Nonetheless, she was criticised by the Christian Social Union (CSU), the Bavaria-based conservative party that has long been the partner of her Christian Democratic Union. Horst Seehofer, the CSU leader, warned that 'without restrictions on immigration, Germany and all of Europe will collapse spectacularly.' However, by mid-2016, Merkel's authority did not appear to have been seriously dented. Despite the rise of Alternative für Deutschland, a right-wing eurosceptic party, a strongly pro-European consensus and an accommodative attitude towards migrants appeared to be holding in Germany.

Anti-immigration feeling contributed to strong showings in opinion polls by right-wing parties in other countries. But in France, for example, the National Front had only two seats in the 577-member National Assembly. In Poland, immigration was but one of many factors that contributed to the October 2015 election victory of the right-wing Law and Justice Party. Still, the criticisms levelled at Germany and the EU by leaders such as Hungary's Orbán underlined the strength of feelings on immigration, especially in some Eastern European countries that had little experience of integrating non-European migrants. In an article published in *Frankfurter Allgemeine Zeitung* in February 2016, Orbán contended that 'the European continent is threatened by an ever-swelling modern-day Great Migration of peoples'. Yet he made clear his commitment to Schengen, which he perceived as being 'among Europe's greatest achievements'. His focus was on the need to protect the EU's external borders – a sentiment with which many European leaders would agree. Hungary's dissension therefore had strict limits.

European leaders tried to develop solutions that could reduce the migrant influx. Merkel struck a deal with Ahmet Davutoglu – then Turkey's prime minister – that became the basis for a controversial agreement between the EU and Turkey reached on 18 March 2016. Under the accord, Turkey would take back any asylum seekers that landed in Greece, and would receive €6 billion to help it cope with the 2.7m Syrians in Turkey. Turkish citizens would be able to travel to the EU without a visa, and discussions on Turkey's EU membership would be given renewed attention. For each Syrian returned to Turkey, the EU would accept a Syrian from a Turkish camp. To enable the returns, the EU would classify the country as safe for refugees – an assertion challenged by humanitarian organisations.

This had the immediate effect of all but halting the trafficking of people across the Aegean Sea. Nevertheless, the agreement was fragile. Turkey failed to meet the EU's conditions for visa-free travel, which required the reform of Turkish counter-terrorism laws. While Brussels symbolically opened negotiations on one of the 35 chapters of Turkey's accession process, the country had little prospect of admittance.

Meanwhile, the EU sought to preclude a repeat of the arguments that plagued its handling of the migrant influx. It was working on reforms of the Dublin Regulation, in part by creating a 'fairness mechanism' that would be triggered if a country received a disproportionate number of arrivals, sharing responsibility for handling them across the EU. Brussels also offered incentives to Middle East and African countries to reduce migration to Europe. Nonetheless, the flow of people across the Mediterranean to Italy continued and, with conflicts and economic decline rife in the Middle East and Africa, there remained a strong possibility of further displacement. The imposition of border controls within the EU, and bitter disputes between its members, had seriously damaged European unity.

European project in question

The first European reaction to the British referendum was for the foreign ministers of the six founding member states to meet symbolically in Berlin. But the EU had become much larger and more complex since the visionary early days. Then, a Franco-German axis had been at the heart of the project. Today, Germany is the clear – if reluctant – leader of the Union. The departure of the UK would enhance Germany's position, but the EU itself would be weaker.

The British referendum brought into renewed focus a familiar issue: the EU's perceived democratic deficit. The growth of euroscepticism suggests that governments will need to address it more explicitly. Indeed, the EU seemed distant to the citizens of its member countries due to the complex structure of its institutions; the power and lack of accountability of its officials; its obscure processes for choosing commissioners, as well as bloc leaders within the European Parliament; and the opaque roles of national and European parliaments in making EU-wide laws. The British referendum suggested that the power of national parliaments needed to be reasserted.

The feeling that the EU has outpaced its electorates is not a new one. In 2005, a so-called EU constitution was rejected by French and Dutch voters in referendums. Tony Blair, then British prime minister, told the European Parliament that rejection of the constitution was 'merely the vehicle for the people to register a wider and deeper discontent with the state of affairs in Europe'. Leaders, he said, needed to address worries about globalisation and jobs: 'the people are blowing the trumpets round the city walls. Are we listening?' Subsequent crises re-emphasised the need for the greater responsiveness he recommended.

The eurozone crisis was another development that indicated that the EU had run ahead of itself. The euro – the common currency now used by 19 countries – had been created without the mechanisms to ensure its survival. The EU rushed to build them as, led by Germany, it bailed out Greece, Ireland, Portugal, Spain and Cyprus. Economists pointed out that monetary union required fiscal union if it was to last. Eurozone leaders subsequently agreed on a fiscal compact that put limits on budget deficits and debts. However, the eurozone has fallen far short of establishing a fiscal union: France's budget deficit remains above the 3%-of-GDP ceiling of the fiscal compact, and Italy won exemption from the debt-reduction target. With Europe having muddled through the crisis, it seemed that no further moves towards fiscal union were being contemplated.

In fact, following the setbacks of preceding years, the EU appeared to be moving away from the super-state demonised by the UK's Leave campaigners. Instead, the Union was perhaps mutating into a more pragmatic association, albeit one backed up by a substantial body of EU laws and principles. The examples of Greece, the refugee crisis and the British referendum showed that there was much work to be done in explaining the purpose of the EU to its citizens.

Adaptation in Europe's security structures

Europe's security turned more perilous in the year to mid-2016, as internal political weakness combined with persistent external threats and challenges. The UK's referendum vote to leave the EU was interpreted across the continent as a major blow to the liberal international order – of which European integration had been an important building block for nearly 60 years. In an advisory referendum held less than three months earlier, Dutch voters had rejected the EU–Ukraine Association Agreement, undermining the attempts of EU member states to form a coherent foreign policy. The episodes suggested that two important EU and NATO member states suffered from a deep division between the political establishment and voters disenchanted by their weak political and economic prospects. High-casualty Islamist terrorist attacks in Belgium and France highlighted Europe's vulnerability to instability and violence originating on its southern border. Meanwhile, Russia continued to advance its assertive foreign-policy posture, mixing military modernisation with armed intervention in Syria and direct support for separatist militants in eastern Ukraine.

Seeking to address these challenges, EU and NATO heads of state and government began to renovate the strategic foundations of their main multinational frameworks. At its summit meeting held in Wales in September 2014, NATO adopted a raft of measures to reassure its eastern members that they would be protected against Russian aggression, following Moscow's hybrid campaign against Ukraine. The Alliance used another summit, held in Warsaw on 8–9 July 2016, to chart an ambitious course for its long-term adaptation towards strengthened deterrence and greater stability in Europe. The spending cuts that had dominated European defence budgets since the onset of the 2008 financial crisis appeared to bottom out in 2015. According to NATO estimates, 2016 would bring a 3–4% increase in defence spending among the Alliance's European members. Encouraged by the projection, NATO Secretary-General Jens Stoltenberg suggested that defence expenditure had 'turned a corner'. Taking into account GDP growth, Europe's NATO members had maintained the same position that they had in 2014 – when they agreed to spend 2% of their GDP on defence by 2024, but were around US$100bn short of meeting this goal. Nonetheless, changing threat perceptions seemed to have begun to affect spending patterns.

At the Warsaw summit, NATO declared that the major objectives of its 2014 Readiness Action Plan had been achieved. Indeed, Stoltenberg declared on the margins of the meeting that the Alliance had 'delivered the biggest reinforcement of our collective defence in a generation'. Core aspects of the move included the expansion of the NATO Response Force (NRF) from roughly 13,000 personnel to more than 40,000, and the creation of the Very High Readiness Joint Task Force – a 5,000-strong formation within the NRF, elements of which can deploy in two or three days. To assist with the reception of forces in case of reinforcement, NATO set up force-integration units (essentially, small headquarters) in Bulgaria, Estonia, Hungary, Latvia, Lithuania, Poland, Romania and Slovakia. However, the renewed emphasis on rapid response and mobility created unforeseen problems of its own, beyond the readiness of forces. NATO planners quickly realised that it would take them approximately four weeks to gather the permits to move forces across European borders in peacetime, making it near-impossible to rapidly deploy in a crisis that fell short of war. By June 2016, this time had reportedly been reduced to five days – a clear improvement, but not the 48–72 hours NATO was aiming for.

A new element in NATO's approach, formalised at the Warsaw summit, was the so-called 'enhanced forward presence', which required the deployment of one multinational battalion each to Estonia, Latvia, Lithuania and Poland. Canada, Germany, the UK and the United States will be the respective framework nations for these formations, meaning that they will provide the core capabilities and enablers that will be augmented by other Alliance members. The precise capability mixture was left to these countries. By July 2016, the deployment was supposed to be sustainable on a rotational basis, involving combat-ready forces, but it remained unclear what the precise composition of these units would be, and what the rotational roster would look like. Involving approximately 1,000 troops each, the four battalions of the enhanced forward presence created a tripwire that would allow for an 'immediate Allied response to any aggression', according to the Warsaw summit communiqué.

In this context, NATO tried to fill major gaps left by the 2014 Wales summit. There, NATO had largely overlooked the fact that Russia was building its capabilities – including air defence, coastal defence, electronic warfare and ballistic missiles – in Kaliningrad, Crimea and, later, Syria. Alliance planners began to fear an anti-access/area-denial (A2/AD) challenge, potentially constraining or preventing the movement of NATO rapidly to reinforce an eastern member state under attack. Whereas the Wales meeting focused only on high readiness and rapid response, in Warsaw NATO also prioritised the development of heavy high-end forces. Presumably, these forces would be able to punch through the A2/AD bubbles Russia was deemed to have established. Likewise, NATO signalled its intent by strengthening its language on deterrence, which was based on a mixture of nuclear, conventional and missile-defence capabilities. At the Warsaw summit, NATO declared initial operating capability had been reached for its ballistic-missile defence (BMD) system involving US forward-deployed *Aegis*-equipped destroyers to Spain, an early-warning radar in Turkey and a BMD site in Romania. Another BMD site in Poland was under development.

NATO also tried to provide conceptual frameworks for dealing with hybrid threats, as well as guiding activities to address challenges stemming from the arc of instability to the south of Europe. Open-source information remains vague on both counts. However, NATO clarified that a hybrid campaign launched by an opponent against a member of the Alliance could trigger its Article 5 collective-defence commitment. The announcement was likely inspired by a desire to strengthen NATO's ability to exert control over the escalatory dynamic in a hybrid attack. Likewise, stressing that the first line of defence against hybrid attack would always be the member state in question, NATO established guidelines and requirements to strengthen national resilience and civil preparedness at a defence ministers' meeting in June 2016. A largely overlooked development at the Warsaw summit involved the overhaul of NATO's intelligence structures, marked by the establishment of a new joint intelligence and security division overseen by an assistant secretary-general. Intelligence, anticipation and understanding feature strongly in the Alliance's approach to challenges from the south, and the language that it adopted on these matters seemed to be strongly influenced by ideas presented in France's 2013 defence White Paper.

Despite establishing a strategic partnership in 2002, NATO and the EU had long been hampered in their efforts to collaborate by an unresolved political dispute. The disagreement centred on the EU's decision to grant membership to Cyprus in 2004, which prompted Turkey to effectively block meaningful exchange between the organisations. Thus, collaboration occurred in informal settings, and was often propelled forward by personal relationships rather than institutional dynamics. At the 2016 Warsaw summit, the president of the European Council, the president of the European Commission and the NATO secretary-general signed a joint declaration designed to 'give new impetus and new substance' to the strategic partnership. The move was overdue, given the deteriorating security environment faced by members of NATO and the EU, as well as the complementary capacities the organisations could provide in addressing problems such as hybrid threats. The declaration emphasised the importance of several areas, including early warning, intelligence sharing, strategic communications, cyber security and coordinated exercises. Unlike previous statements, it provides clearer tasking to bureaucrats to report progress in the strategic partnership to their political leaders – thereby signalling that the measure has high-level political support.

Federica Mogherini, the EU foreign minister, had made a significant effort to draft the Union's global strategy on foreign and security policy (EUGS), which was presented to EU heads of state and government on 28 June 2016. The inspiration for the document was the internal and external crises confronting the EU. Mogherini wrote: 'our Union is under threat. Our European project which has brought unprecedented peace, prosperity and democracy is being questioned.' She decided to present the strategy despite the outcome of the UK referendum, which had already delayed the process. The document replaces the ambitious language of its 2003 predecessor with a more measured call for 'principled pragmatism' as the guideline for the EU's external engagement. In a sense, the EUGS can be interpreted as lowering ambitions that had proven unachievable in the preceding decade. Within this more realistic framework, the strategy defines the security of European citizens, resilience, integrated conflict management, cooperative regional orders and progress on global governance as its five priorities. While these core interests could undermine any intended realism due to their potentially limitless scope, the strategy attempts to clarify them. For example, in its passage on support for cooperative regional orders, the EUGS acknowledges that these orders may take many forms, specifying that the EU will not 'strive to export our model, but rather seek reciprocal inspiration from different regional experiences'. This continues a theme Mogherini stressed in her speech at the 2015 IISS Shangri-La Dialogue, in which she explained that it was in Europe's and Asia's 'reciprocal interest to invest even more ... in the work we can jointly do for the security of our people'.

Perhaps surprisingly, the EUGS includes a lengthy section on defence, codifying many of the ideas that had dominated the discourse among experts and politicians in the preceding decade. It describes defence cooperation among EU members as creating 'interoperability, effectiveness, efficiency, and trust: it increases the output of defence spending'. The strategy makes the case for harmonised defence-planning cycles among EU member states, and suggests that defence cooperation must become the norm in Europe (while avoiding integrationist language in this sensitive area). However, the EUGS imprecisely handles notions of deterrence, full-spectrum defence and the protection of the Union. The use of these terms could be interpreted as beginning the development of a security and defence role that goes beyond the aims of the EU's Common Security and Defence Policy. Although such a move might be appropriate in light of evolving challenges, the EUGS fails to provide corresponding guidelines. While several EU member states had pushed in the first half of 2016 for the Union to develop a White Paper on defence, the EUGS contained no mandate for doing so. There seemed to be a willingness and even preparedness for such a step at the institutional level, including within the EU Military Staff and the European External Action Service generally, as well as the European Commission. But the political signal to press ahead had not been given.

The unstable international security environment exerted evolutionary pressure on NATO and the EU, triggering significant shifts in their strategic assumptions and defence plans. For both organisations, adaptation to new threats will take many years. And, given the EU's internal problems, it seems likely that most member states would focus their defence policies on NATO.

Terrorism in Europe

Since the end of the Second World War, many European nations have experienced terrorist attacks. Palestinian rejectionist groups, ethno-separatist organisations such as the Provisional Irish Republican Army and the Basque Euskadi ta Askatasuna, as well as anarcho-syndical-ist movements such as the German Red Army Faction and the Italian Red Brigades, have all caused significant casualties and other damage. More recently, transnational jihadist group al-Qaeda targeted Europe in several large-scale operations, notably the attacks in Madrid in 2004 and in London the following year – with the security services thwarting many more plots of similar ambition. But the terrorist threat in Europe arguably reached an unprecedented level in the year to mid-2016. This was due to the activities of adherents to, and sympathisers of, ISIS, a new and more violent al-Qaeda offshoot that originated in Iraq's sectarian politics and the Syrian civil war.

The forerunner of ISIS is al-Qaeda in Iraq (AQI), an affiliate set up by Abu Musab al-Zarqawi following the US-led invasion of the country in

2003. A petty criminal from Jordan, Zarqawi rapidly established a reputation for such extreme brutality that even al-Qaeda's central leadership was moved to urge him – unsuccessfully – to rein in his organisation's excesses. American special forces killed Zarqawi in late 2006, and the subsequent 'surge' orchestrated by US General David Petraeus reduced AQI to a rump organisation. But the unashamedly sectarian policies pursued by then-prime minister Nuri al-Maliki squandered the gains of the surge and alienated Iraq's Sunni population, creating the conditions for a resurgence of AQI that was assisted by former Ba'athist Iraqi intelligence officers.

In 2014 the organisation that was to become ISIS gained global attention by dramatically taking the Iraqi city of Mosul and threatening to move on Baghdad. The group also came to occupy a significant swathe of territory in northern and eastern Syria, from where it proclaimed the formation of a 'caliphate', setting it at odds with al-Qaeda. The creation of the caliphate proved to be a significant draw for extremists around the world, and by the end of 2015 an estimated 30,000 foreign fighters had made their way to Syria to join ISIS. Approximately 5,000 of these fighters came from Western Europe, 75% of them from just four states: France, the UK, Germany and Belgium. And fears that some of these fighters would return home to undertake terrorist attacks soon proved well founded.

The January 2015 attack on the Paris office of satirical French magazine *Charlie Hebdo*, which resulted in 13 deaths, came shortly before shootings at a Jewish supermarket in the city. The assaults were a harbinger of things to come. Throughout 2015, European intelligence and security services maintained a high tempo of arrests as they thwarted further ISIS-inspired plots; arrested individuals involved in proselytising, recruiting and fundraising for the group; and prevented would-be jihadists, including a significant proportion of young women, from travelling to Syria to take part in the conflict there. European governments struggled to contain a flood of social-media posts by ISIS supporters, including many from young European jihadists who had joined the Syrian war.

The drumbeat of ISIS-related threats became louder and more insistent. It became known that the group had established a department for external-attack planning, with the aim of promoting terrorist operations in the West. The resulting plots focused in particular on countries that had taken part in military operations against ISIS, which had the effect of first containing the group's efforts to expand its territory and then of degrading its economic resources and decapitating its leadership. Following the failure of several planned operations, ISIS struck again in Paris in November 2015, carrying out a series of coordinated attacks that killed 130 people and injured more than 300 others. The operations were planned in Belgium and, although French police killed their architect and leader Abdelhamid Abaaoud in a raid on a Paris safe house several days later, the hunt for the remaining attackers lasted several months. In March 2016, a joint Franco-Belgian investigation closed in on the suspects, who were hiding in the Brussels district of Molenbeek, a predominantly Islamic enclave. The surviving jihadists, who had been planning another attack in France, instead carried out a suicide bombing at Brussels airport and the Maelbeek metro station in central Brussels, killing 32 people and injuring more than 300 others.

The Paris attacks epitomised the changing threat posed by ISIS. They were planned in Brussels and involved several individuals who, like Abaaoud, had served jail sentences for jihadist activities and were on police watch lists. Other members of the network had a background in petty criminality, and it was through their criminal connections that they had acquired the weapons used in the attacks. Different parts of the network were responsible for providing logistical support, including car hire and the rental of safe houses. Operational security was tight, with the jihadists using multiple pay-as-you-go mobile phones once before discarding them. And, during the attacks, the jihadists showed a capacity for improvisation and manoeuvre that testified to the training some of them had received in Syria.

The arrest of what appeared to be the last two surviving members of the network suggested that that specific threat had been neutralised. But many young or recently converted European Muslims remained susceptible to ISIS propaganda. Territorial losses suffered by ISIS in Syria and Iraq resulted in a tenfold decline in foreign fighters travelling to the countries in the first half of 2016. Nonetheless, Europe generally, and the ghettoised Muslim areas of France and Belgium in particular, were home to more radicalised young Muslims than the police and security services could hope to keep track of. Meanwhile, it appeared that, as the fortunes of ISIS declined, al-Qaeda underwent something of a resurgence, moving back into Afghanistan after the NATO drawdown there, and reinforcing its already strong presence in Yemen. Europe therefore potentially faced a dual threat from an ISIS desperate to demonstrate its continuing relevance and an al-Qaeda for which the 'far enemy' – Western democracies – continued to be the main target. Further terrorist attacks in Europe seemed not just likely but inevitable.

Following the November attack in Paris, the French government declared a state of emergency that was extended to cover the Euro 2016 football tournament, held in June and July. This gave rise to extensive police raids and the closure of some mosques and Muslim-owned businesses, actions decried by human-rights groups as unnecessary and counterproductive as they threatened to further alienate an Islamic community that already felt disenfranchised, and that distrusted the authorities. Meanwhile, France's security service, long seen as one of Europe's most professional, quietly admitted to its partners that it had lost control of the situation. Nonetheless, the assaults in France and Belgium catalysed closer European inter-agency collaboration on counter-terrorism, particularly in data-sharing.

©IISS

Atlantic Ocean

Pacific Ocean

MEXICO

Mexico City ■

THE BAHAMAS

Havana ■
CUBA

BELIZE

DOMINICAN
REPUBLIC

JAMAICA   HAITI
Belmopan ■   ■ Santo Domingo

GUATEMALA
Tegucigalpa   Kingston ■
Guatemala City ■   Port-au-
Prince

EL SALVADOR   HONDURAS
San Salvador

NICARAGUA
COSTA RICA

Managua   ■ Panama
City   Caracas ■   TRINIDAD & TOBAGO

San José   Georgetown ■
VENEZUELA   Paramaribo
PANAMA   ■ Cayenne

GUYANA
Bogotá ■   SURINAME
FRENCH GUYANA
COLOMBIA

Quito ■
ECUADOR

B R A Z I L

PERU

■ Lima

■ Brasília
La Paz ■

BOLIVIA

PARAGUAY
■ Asunción

CHILE

URUGUAY
Santiago ■   Buenos Aires ■   ■
Montevideo

ARGENTINA

■ Capital   ⌇ Borders

0   1,000 miles

0   1,000km

Falkland Islands (UK)

South Georgia (UK)

Chapter 10

Latin America

For Latin America, the year to mid-2016 formed part of a difficult economic and political period, as the sharp economic downturn that began three years earlier only became worse. Having averaged annual GDP growth of 4.3% for seven years, the region's economy fell into recession in 2015 and 2016, weighed down by Brazil, Argentina and Venezuela. These headwinds severely hobbled political leaders who had become accustomed to riding a wave of prosperity. As economies floundered, voters grew frustrated with their governments. Presidential approval ratings fell sharply across the region, and incumbent parties began to lose key elections or were removed from power altogether.

In Argentina, Mauricio Macri, a centre-right businessman and the mayor of Buenos Aires, succeeded the leftist Cristina Fernández de Kirchner following elections in November 2015. In congressional elections held in Venezuela the following month, the socialist party of President Nicolás Maduro – Hugo Chávez's successor – lost in a landslide, with the opposition picking up an astounding two-thirds of the seats. In Bolivia, Evo Morales, the country's socialist president and first indigenous leader, lost a February 2016 referendum on whether he could run for a fourth term – although many expected him to try again. In Ecuador, President Rafael Correa, a left-leaning, US-trained economist, announced that he would not run for re-election after his term ended. In Peru, the 77-year-old Pedro Pablo Kuczynski, a market-friendly fiscal conservative, social liberal and US-trained economist, won the 5 June presidential run-off election to replace the unpopular Ollanta Humala.

The most dramatic fall from grace, however, came from one of Latin America's great political success stories: the Brazilian Workers' Party (PT), which since 2003 had presided over an unprecedented era of economic growth and social progress. The downturn hit harder in Brazil than anywhere else on the continent, with the exception of Venezuela. The Brazilian economy – the largest in Latin America – shrank by nearly 4% in 2015 and was expected to record a similar decline in 2016. Inflation and unemployment rates both approached 10%. At the same time, the massive Lava Jato (Car Wash) investigation implicated much of the political class in a sprawling web of corruption centred on the state oil company, Petrobras. The dual political and economic crises were more than President Dilma Rousseff could manage, and she was dramatically forced from office on 12 May 2016. Her removal was technically a suspension, in the face of an impeachment trial for using funds from state banks to mask budget shortfalls and the dire state of the economy in an election year. But the impeachment process was political: her approval rating had fallen below 10% and her enemies – including members of the fractious Congress and her more centrist vice-president and successor, Michel Temer – took the opportunity to oust her. Nonetheless, the interim Temer presidency did little to restore legitimacy to the broken political system. There were strong indications that Brazilian politics and markets would remain turbulent for years to come.

These rapid changes created a striking shift in Latin America's strategic landscape, which had been fairly consistent for more than a decade. From the early 2000s on, left-leaning movements had dominated the political scene. Their leaders combined ambitious social policies with resistance to globalisation (even as globalisation boosted their economies through voracious demand for commodities) and the influence of the United States.

Yet this leftist trend was far from monolithic, with many countries – most importantly, Colombia and Mexico – breaking the mould. Moreover, there was a good deal of ideological and strategic variation among states. The leftist movement was also far less of a strategic alliance than any its proponents claimed or its opponents feared. And yet, even if this consensus was not the sweeping tide of socialism as some in Washington suspected, the ideological trend stabilised the region's political alignments and interests somewhat. To be sure, the past 15 years have seen a proliferation of new regional organisations, such as the Union of South American Nations (UNASUR) and the Community of Latin American and Caribbean States (CELAC). Some are active to this day, as shown by UNASUR mediation in Venezuela and the activities that followed the 2015 China–CELAC Forum. But most of these new efforts are political rather than institutional, as they lack developed secretariats and focus only on occasional summits. By and large, with strong economies and ambitious domestic agendas, Latin American countries have prioritised domestic social issues.

Now, amid this cascade of political changes, the region is hard to categorise in strategic, economic and political terms. Latin America has splintered, and some of its leaders are experimenting with new strategies. Staunch anti-American voices have diminished considerably, and some countries are seeking new forms of engagement with the US and the rest of the world. Moreover, Latin America remains largely free of inter-state conflict. Instead, most countries struggle against widespread violence, drug trafficking and other criminality at home – albeit of a kind involving groups with transnational networks. As a result, the strategic relationships between Latin American countries tend to be diplomatic and economic rather than security-oriented. The region consistently has some of the lowest levels of military expenditure in the world, especially when measured as a percentage of GDP. The last inter-state conflict in the region occurred in 1995, when Ecuador and Peru engaged in a month-long border skirmish. Prior to that, the most recent full-scale war had been Argentina's invasion of the Falkland Islands in 1982. Aside from the modest contributions to the coalition in Iraq in 2003 made by El Salvador, Honduras, Nicaragua and the Dominican Republic, Latin American military deployments oversees have been almost exclusively under UN peacekeeping banners. As a result, it is unclear how Latin America's changing political dynamics will affect security in the Western Hemisphere.

Against this backdrop, the relationship between the US and Latin America is also changing, if to an uncertain degree. The continuing process of rapprochement between the US and Cuba paid strategic dividends for the Obama administration, effectively removing a perpetual irritant in hemispheric relations. That Washington no longer regards Cuba as a national-security problem has important implications for cooperation and engagement in the Caribbean and wider Latin America. President Barack Obama was widely praised for making a historic trip to Cuba and Argentina in March 2016, softening a long-standing animosity in the former and building the foundation for a strong new partnership in the latter. Meanwhile, due to a renewed effort to promote economic development and security in Central America under the Alliance for Prosperity, the US engaged with the region more than it had at any moment since the 1980s. As countries in the Northern Triangle (El Salvador, Guatemala and Honduras) struggled to prevent a further deterioration of their security and economic outlooks, Washington hoped to prevent a recurrence of the 2014 child-migrant crisis, and to address its root causes.

Observers in Washington also grew more concerned about the state of human rights and law enforcement in Mexico, as the country's security services continued to fend off accusations of torture, extrajudicial killings and other human-rights violations. The case of the 43 students who disappeared in Ayotzinapa in September 2014 remained a flash point for public protest. This was especially true after April 2016, when an independent international group of experts published a report highly critical of the government's handling of the incident. Nonetheless, there was persistently strong cooperation between Washington and the Mexican government, with the latter preparing to extradite notorious drug lord Joaquín 'El Chapo' Guzmán to the US. Guzmán had been captured in Sinaloa in January 2016 after he broke out of a Mexican prison – his second such escape – through an elaborate, mile-long tunnel the year before. The US was also deeply engaged in the push for a negotiated settlement to the only armed conflict in South America: Colombia's long-standing battle against the Marxist guerrillas of FARC. Within the talks, which were held in Havana, the interests of the US aligned with those of Cuba. Finally, the perpetual Latin American concern of narcotics trafficking and transnational organised crime stayed at the forefront of most diplomatic agendas, although there were signs that the hardline global consensus on drug prohibition and enforcement was fraying, even in the US. However, while the rhetoric of counter-narcotics efforts was changing – spurred in part by attempts to legalise marijuana in the US – their policy-execution strategy was unaltered, and continued to centre on operations by the US Southern Command and other military organisations.

There were also some negative trends in relations between the US and Latin America as new concerns arose. Venezuela's troubled economy and contentious political sphere moved ever closer to collapse, a development that threatened to inflict enormous damage on the region as a whole, especially Colombia. Moreover, outside powers were largely unable to prevent continued deterioration in Haiti, Latin America's poorest country. While the first round of the Haitian presidential elections was held in 2015, the run-off was postponed due to serious problems with the electoral process. Neither the beleaguered Provisional Electoral Council nor the weak transitional government seemed capable of restoring even the most basic political stability or legitimacy, suggesting that there would be a prolonged period of uncertainty. And, perhaps most crucially, the rest of the hemisphere (not least Mexico) watched with growing apprehension as populist billionaire Donald Trump secured the Republican nomination for the US presidential elections. This raised the prospect of Obama's successor being elected on a platform that was openly unfriendly to Latin Americans, particularly those who had emigrated to the US.

Deepening political strife and the rise of new leaders

The sea change in Latin American political orientations – which several observers described as 'the death of the Latin American left' or the 'end of the pink tide' – is best explained by economic discontent leading to far more constrained political circumstances. Even newly elected centrist or right-leaning leaders would have to contend with difficult economic conditions. Moreover, these dynamics vary considerably among different countries.

Venezuela

In the most dramatic case, Venezuela, political and economic tensions grew as the price of the country's oil collapsed from well over US$100 a barrel in 2014 to barely US$25 in 2015. Economic growth, citizens' incomes and government revenue plummeted alongside it. The country's budget deficit also rose to more than 20% of GDP, according to many estimates – with some analysts arguing that the increase was as high as 100%. The fall was dramatic: Venezuela had run a budget surplus as recently as 2007. Instead of slashing spending and reforming a bloated and corrupt state, President Maduro's government attempted to plug the gap by printing money. Inflation topped 500%, and was projected to reach 700% by the end of 2016. Price controls and fixed exchange rates meant that, while nominally pegged at 10 bolivars to the dollar, black-market exchange rates rose to more than 1,100 bolivars to the dollar. It appeared that a default was all but inevitable.

The economic crisis had severe humanitarian consequences. While for several years black-market redistribution was able to provide most Venezuelans with the basic goods they needed, by mid-2016 even that market began to run dry. A lack of imports and faltering domestic production led to widespread shortages in goods. The international community was particularly worried about a shortfall in medical supplies. Venezuelan hospitals and pharmacies were forced to operate without vital medicines, basic medical equipment and often even electricity or water.

Venezuelans channelled their frustrations with deteriorating conditions in the country into the 6 December congressional elections. With a huge turnout, opposition party the Democratic Unity Roundtable (MUD) won a supermajority of 112 out of 164 seats. This impressive showing gave the MUD almost complete control over the legislative branch, re-igniting its hopes for political change. The new opposition legislators declared their intention to remove Maduro from office through a constitutional change or a recall referendum.

However, the other two branches of government, both firmly controlled by Maduro and his supporters, stymied the opposition's momentum. The Supreme Court promptly deemed as unconstitutional many legislative efforts, including an amnesty law aimed at freeing opposition leader Leopoldo López and other political prisoners. Meanwhile, the president continued to strengthen his control over the economy through declarations of a state of emergency in January and May, allowing him to counter what he called 'foreign threats' by controlling prices, quashing protests and seizing factories. The government also blocked the opposition's efforts to organise a recall through a variety of decrees, court decisions and bureaucratic manoeuvres.

Governments and human-rights organisations across the region also became anxious about creeping authoritarianism in Venezuela, as well as disregard for human rights by the economically embattled socialist government. The Organization of American States, led by Secretary-General Luis Almagro, took up the issue, as some of its members demanded that Venezuela be expelled for violating the Inter-American Democratic Charter. But the strategic implications of a potential trigger event in Venezuela – a coup, a popular uprising, a crackdown on opposition figures or simply an explosion of random violence and looting – would also go beyond democratic and human-rights concerns. Instability in Venezuela could have contagion effects for regional security and global energy markets. Colombia and several countries in Central America had already begun to experience negative effects from organised crime and drug trafficking originating in Venezuela. Venezuelan criminal organisations were relatively safe from prosecution, as their Colombian counterparts had been in the 1990s. This was due to weak institutions, endemic corruption and criminals' entanglement with government officials. Were Venezuela to collapse, it could become a haven for drug producers and traffickers, as well as guerrilla fighters and members of organised-crime groups – a problem that would especially affect neighbouring Colombia.

Venezuela is the world's tenth-largest oil producer and home to proven oil reserves larger than those of any other country. As such, further decay of its energy infrastructure and production capacity could remove its oil from world markets for many years, and could cause energy shortages in many countries, particularly those in Central America and the Caribbean. While Venezuela's subsidies to Caribbean countries through the Petrocaribe programme had already been significantly reduced – and a low oil price made the programme less important – sharper cuts could be economically damaging, not least for Cuba, which is still considerably reliant on Venezuelan support. Even China would feel the effects of a collapse or default, having loaned Venezuela more than US$65 billion since 2006, much of which is to be repaid by preferential oil shipments over a long period of time.

Brazil

Brazil also experienced sustained economic and political turbulence in the year to mid-2016. In 2015 the dual crises of the massive Petrobras corruption scandal and a rapidly decelerating economy threatened to end Brazil's rise as a major power. By the following year, the economic and political situation was in free fall.

After suffering a contraction of 3.8% in 2015, the Brazilian economy was expected to shrink by a similar amount in 2016, with no growth expected until at least 2018. This would have a significant impact on the middle and lower classes – above all, on the millions of Brazilians who had recently been lifted out of poverty. Despite high expectations, much of the new middle class remained highly vulnerable. But with the overall fiscal deficit as high as 12–13% of GDP, there was a building consensus that the government should urgently cut spending, reduce social programmes and implement ambitious reforms to restart growth. Weighed down by persistently low commodity prices, the economy needed to diversify. Throughout 2015, Joaquim Levy, President Rousseff's market-friendly finance minister, was the face of this effort. He was widely seen as attempting to balance an ambitious austerity programme with concerns from within the PT that cuts to spending and social programmes could disproportionately impact economically vulnerable groups. By December, in the face of mounting tensions and resistance from Rousseff's party, Levy – a well-known fiscal hawk – was increasingly at odds with the president and Congress. He resigned on 18 December and was replaced by the former minister of planning, Nelson Barbosa, who was seen as friendlier to the left's concerns about protecting social programmes. For much of the private sector, this was a critical signal that Levy's austerity drive lacked support within the administration. As a consequence, there were widespread fears that Rousseff had wavered in her commitment to reform by bowing to political pressure.

Adding to her problems, Rousseff faced allegations of malfeasance. Unlike the leaders of most other Brazilian parties, she had not been directly linked with the Petrobras scandal, although much of the population believed that, as president and former chair of the company's board, she should have been aware of its conduct – guilty, at the very least, of incompetence. Instead of attempting to impeach her on this count, opposition leaders accused Rousseff of violating Brazil's fiscal-responsibility laws. They alleged that, in the lead-up to the 2014 elections, her administration siphoned funds from state-run banks to cover holes in the budget and to bolster the economy. In the process, so the argument went, she disguised the economy's underlying weakness, postponed difficult financial decisions and magnified the effects of the inevitable crash. Under Brazilian law, this kind of creative accounting – known colloquially as *pedaladas* (peddling) – is prohibited in most cases as a 'crime of responsibility' (political negligence for which one can be held liable, regardless of intent). According to the *Financial Times*, the government shuffled around US$17bn from the banks onto its own books during this period.

President Rousseff's allies were correct in arguing that such practices were common in Brazil, and had been regularly used by past governments. 'I may have made mistakes but I did not commit any crime', Rousseff declared. Still, with protests spreading across the country and her support in Congress dwindling, the campaign to impeach her gathered momentum. She was suspended on 12 May and, legally required to step aside during the 180-day trial, was replaced by Temer.

The impeachment appeared to be a fundamentally political affair. A product of Brazil's heavily coalition-based political system, Temer represented the centrist Brazilian Democratic Movement Party and, by the time of the trial, he had become a staunch political enemy of Rousseff. Although some on the left decried the impeachment as a legislative *coup d'état*, Temer's rise to the presidency was greeted with little overt resistance either inside or outside the country. Nonetheless, there was a palpable sense of unease, with governments across Latin America regarding Temer's ascent as, at least, worrying and problematic. The swiftness of his rise was less an expression of popularity – one poll conducted at the time found that just 2% of Brazilians would vote for him in a new election – than of pervasive disenchantment with Rousseff's government and the status quo.

Even with an array of early missteps and scandals, many in Brazil and abroad hoped that Temer's presidency would mark a new, more pragmatic era in Brazilian governance. Expectations rose that he would move quickly to cut spending, liberalise the economy and pursue more open trade policies. José Serra, the new foreign minister, quickly made clear his intention to liberalise trade policy, stating that the government aimed to 'upgrade' Mercosur (designed to create a single market for Brazil, Argentina, Paraguay, Uruguay and Venezuela) into a 'real trade bloc'. He also expressed a desire to pursue new bilateral trade deals and to 'expand commerce with traditional partners such as Europe, the United States and Japan'. This outlook, together with Temer's purported skill in steering reforms through a fractious Congress, raised the possibility that gradual economic progress and self-reinforcing political legitimacy could come hand in hand.

However, the crisis inflicted considerable damage on Brazilian democracy as a whole. Voter discontent was at its highest levels since democratisation in the late 1980s, and there were significant threats to the cohesion that had held governing coalitions together for nearly a generation.

Argentina

President Fernández had a difficult last year in office. The Argentine economy had struggled since 2013 – as had others in Latin America – and it experienced almost no growth during the period, even briefly dipping into recession in 2014. Due to loose monetary policy and a primary deficit of around 5.4% of GDP, inflation rose fast – reaching 30% in early 2016 by many estimates (there was a lack of reliable data on inflation, as the national statistics institute was allegedly politicised under Fernández). The government also fixed exchange rates, creating a large currency black market. And, although Buenos Aires did not officially recognise rising prices and the weakness of the peso, voters did, with opinion polls identifying inflation as their chief concern.

Throughout all of this, the country's long-running legal battle with bondholders – dating from its 2001 default – lingered in US courts, becoming ever more antagonistic and political. Fernández dismissed these bondholders as *buitres* (vultures). But the lawsuit held Argentina in a state of default, effectively locking it out of international credit markets.

Despite the economic malaise, there were predictions that the Peronist political movement behind Fernández and her anointed successor – Daniel Scioli, the powerful governor of Buenos Aires Province – would win the presidential elections. Polls showed Scioli easily ahead of the other two main candidates: Macri and Sergio Massa, a former Fernández ally who led a coalition of dissident Peronists. Scioli promised some continuity with Fernández, while Macri pledged ambitious changes and Massa promoted a gradualist path somewhere in the middle. While Scioli won the 25 October first round, his 38% share of the vote was not enough to avoid a run-off with Macri one month later.

In a sweeping and surprising turn, Macri won the second round with slightly more than 51% of the vote. In doing so, he became Argentina's first non-Peronist president in 14 years and the first from neither the Peronist party nor its Radical counterpart since 1916. After taking office on 10 December, he moved quickly to reverse major policy courses taken by his predecessor. Within a week, he had lifted controls on the exchange rate, letting the peso float freely for the first time in years – resulting in a 30% devaluation. He also immediately removed or reduced export taxes on a broad range of agricultural goods, Argentina's main products. High export taxes, intended to control domestic food prices, had been consistently criticised by economists as counterproductive and a drain on the economy. He also took rapid steps to clean up the national statistics institute and to produce clear, unbiased economic data. 'Argentina is no longer lying about its statistics', claimed Macri's new finance minister, Alfonso Prat-Gay.

The Macri administration subsequently began to tackle many of the more difficult parts of its economic-reform agenda, moving at what the *Wall Street Journal* called a 'dizzying pace'. This included slashing burgeoning energy subsidies and (according to Macri's critics) cutting up to 10,000 public-sector jobs. Crucially, the government announced on 29 February a US$9.3bn deal to end the stand-off with the bondholders, ending one of the longest government-debt negotiations in history. This freed Argentina to again borrow money in international markets and, perhaps more importantly, signalled to foreign investors that the country was entering a new, friendlier economic era.

The Macri government accomplished all of this even while Fernández's party controlled the majority of seats in the Senate. To gain legislative support for most of his reforms, he built coalitions and struck deals with opposition leaders. His success was a testament to the government's broad desire for change in its approach towards the economy. Indeed, approval ratings for Macri and most of his cabinet remained relatively high throughout the first half of 2016. Argentines seemed to agree that the promise of long-term growth was worth the hardship of austerity in the short term. Nonetheless, their continued support likely rested on the administration's ability to deliver some tangible results within its first year. Macri's reforms, particularly his abolition of government subsidies, had enormous immediate effects – most of them negative – for many of Argentina's most vulnerable people. Between a weak economy and cuts to government programmes, thousands fell below the poverty line. The risks of a public backlash were substantial, and grew as reform proceeded.

Changing political alignment

Latin America's strategic outlook grew more unsettled in the year. As political and economic crises destabilised Brazil and Venezuela – and the latter was increasingly unable to lead a leftist 'Bolivarian' coalition against perceived capitalist and imperialist influences in the region – neighbouring states became ever more concerned about spillover effects. Meanwhile, economic, political and security challenges elsewhere in Latin America – particularly in Mexico and Central America – largely outweighed new opportunities for cooperation and integration. While recognising the importance of collaboration rhetorically, governments primarily focused on national agendas.

The US, by contrast, seemed to reach an inflection point in its relationships with Latin American countries, as opportunities emerged for establishing deeper, more productive ties. Firstly, and most visibly, the trend towards political pragmatism in the region created a considerable diplomatic opening for Washington. At the same time, reasonable economic growth of 2.4% in 2015 made the US an attractive partner. Moreover, Latin America's alternatives diminished as China lost some of its appetite for commodities and European economies remained stagnant. For new political leaders such as Temer, who was determined to return Brazil to a sound economic footing, partnership with the US was an obvious choice. This dynamic also appeared among previously antagonistic governments – including those in Bolivia, Nicaragua and Ecuador – whose anti-US rhetoric dwindled as they faced increasing economic headwinds. In short, a lack of options rendered Latin American states less able to spurn the US.

Nowhere was this more obvious than in Argentina, where Macri clearly stated his intention to work closely with Washington. Speaking at the World Economic Forum's January 2016 meeting in Davos, he declared that Argentina was 'ready to build a pragmatic, intelligent and productive relationship among our countries', citing climate change, drug trafficking, terrorism and corruption as areas of potential collaboration with the US. Macri delivered this speech in English – an act that was a clear statement in itself.

Obama responded positively, announcing that he would conduct a state visit to Argentina the following March. The Obamas were greeted in Buenos Aires, quite literally, with open arms. The meetings, photo opportunities and press conferences were visibly warm and jovial. In a clear attempt to bolster Macri's reform agenda, Obama praised him as 'a man in a hurry' and claimed 'Argentina is re-assuming its traditional leadership role in the region and around the world'. Moreover, both leaders agreed that the visit marked a new, mature relationship. The US was clearly relieved to see an end to the Kirchner years, which were characterised by perpetual strain, frustration and mistrust.

The year to mid-2016 also seemed to mark a paradigm shift on the part of the US, especially in terms of its Cold War history in Latin America. Obama received some criticism from human-rights groups for conducting his trip to Argentina during the 40th anniversary of the 1976 military *coup d'état* that, supported by Washington, ushered in a brutal dictatorship. But, in a goodwill gesture, the Obama administration acknowledged these criticisms, announcing that it would make a new effort to declassify Cold War-era documents detailing US involvement in Argentina. The White House hoped to use the moment to move even further away from past chapters of relations between the US and Latin America.

President Obama's landmark trip to Cuba, prior to reaching Argentina, made this post-Cold War mentality even clearer. As the first US president to visit the island since 1928, Obama aimed to cement Washington's policy changes on Cuba – which he had announced jointly with President Raúl Castro in December 2014 – and to open a new diplomatic era in the Western Hemisphere. 'I have come here to bury the last remnant of the Cold War in the Americas,' said Obama in a 35-minute speech in Havana on Cuba's future, the virtues of democracy and human rights, and the shared history of the two countries. Raúl Castro and other prominent Cuban political leaders were in the audience, and the remarks were broadcast live and uncensored across the island. During the trip, Obama also held a joint press conference with the Cuban president – marking the first time that the latter had answered questions from journalists – toured old Havana, met with Cuban dissidents and entrepreneurs, and attended an exhibition baseball game between the Tampa Bay Rays and the Cuban national team.

Some critics argued that the visit failed to produce any substantive advances in Cuban democracy and human rights, either before or afterwards. If anything, Havana displayed its intransigence by arresting dozens of protesters on the eve of Obama's visit. Still, there was only relatively subdued political opposition in the US to the historic trip, which had seemed unthinkable only a few years earlier. Polls consistently showed that the vast majority of US voters approved of the visit, just as they continued to support broader changes towards Cuba.

However, the road to full normalisation of relations between the two countries remained long and complicated. While Obama sought to further erode the US embargo on Cuba, the power to lift it altogether fell on Congress, which was unlikely to act on the matter until after the 2016 elections. The process of rebuilding economic, diplomatic and interpersonal ties had only just begun. And, just as importantly, Cuba faced arduous economic and political reform at home to rejoin not just the US but the rest of the world as well. Obama argued that Washington should be detached from this process, making it harder for the Castro brothers to present their authoritarian rule as a protection against US hegemony. 'El futuro de Cuba tiene que estar en las manos del pueblo cubano,' he said. 'Cuba's future must be in the hands of the Cuban people.'

To be sure, much of this new orientation was a product of Obama's personal approach to foreign policy. His preference for engagement and 'moving beyond' the conflicts of the past was visible around the world, from his 2009 Nobel Prize acceptance speech to the nuclear accord with Iran. Moreover, Obama's image as a youthful, charismatic African-American president – his approval ratings among Latin Americans were consistently much higher than those of their own presidents – helped build the narrative of a new era. As such, the durability of this shift probably depended on his successor.

Hillary Clinton, the Democratic nominee, seemed likely to continue Obama's legacy in Latin America. While her tenure as secretary of state lacked notable initiatives there, her overall outlook on the region is much the same as Obama's. Despite some criticisms – especially around her role in not labelling the 2009 ouster of Honduran President Manuel Zelaya as a coup – Clinton's support for policies such as that for ending the Cuban embargo implied relative continuity, although it appeared she would make more strenuous demands for reform.

Trump's approach could scarcely have been more different. Announcing his candidacy with a speech that accused Mexico of sending 'drugs', 'crime' and 'rapists' into the US, Trump made an antagonistic stance towards that country a centrepiece of his campaign. He pledged to build a wall along the southern US border, which runs for nearly 2,000 miles, and to 'have Mexico pay for that wall'. Former Mexican presidents responded strongly, comparing Trump to Hitler and arguing that his candidacy had already damaged the image of the US abroad. In another incident, Trump ejected Hispanic journalist Jorge Ramos from a press conference with the words 'go back to Univision', a reference to the influential Spanish-language media network. Trump also received widespread criticism from Democrats and Republicans for attacking the Mexican heritage of a federal judge presiding over a civil case against Trump University. Under a Trump presidency, relations with Mexico would likely be strained. Even if he did not follow through on his promises, he would have to work hard to repair ties with offended Mexicans. Although Trump was one of only two Republican candidates open to Obama's Cuba policy (the other was the libertarian-leaning Senator Rand Paul), that fact was largely lost in the noise. Moreover, many in

Mexico and the rest of Latin America saw Trump's rise as a racist and xenophobic threat, and were shocked by the vulgarity of his political appeal. On issues of trade, counter-narcotics, immigration, development assistance and security cooperation, relationships with Latin America were likely to be complicated by a Trump victory.

Colombia grasps at peace, but the drug war continues

While most of Latin America has been formally at peace for decades – affected by pervasive criminal violence rather than insurgency or inter-state conflict – there has been one exception to this trend: Colombia. The complex, half-century war between the Colombian government and various armed guerrilla groups moved closer to a negotiated settlement in the year to mid-2016, as the approximately 7,000 members of the main insurgent group, FARC, largely held to a unilateral ceasefire. The coalescing accord between the sides had the potential to end a brutal phase in Colombia's history, but the progress towards peace appeared under threat as the original deadline for concluding the negotiations, 23 March 2016, came and went. The negotiators in Havana had reached agreements on almost all of the main issues, including the thorny subject of transitional justice – in which crimes committed during the conflict would go before a special tribunal and, assuming the defendants cooperated and admitted their responsibility, be punished essentially by house arrest. Yet the talks stalled on setting out the process for disarming the insurgents.

The fundamental disagreement was over the size of the 'concentration zones' in which demobilisation would take place. Government security forces would withdraw from these areas and guard their borders, while FARC guerrillas would gather there to disarm under the oversight of UN observers, before reintegrating into civilian life. The government wanted these zones to be restricted, isolated rural areas that acted only as trans-action points. In contrast, FARC saw them as larger territories that could serve as bases for future, non-violent political activity. The dispute also underlined broader differences on security and demobilisation. When FARC fighters disarm, they will be vulnerable to retaliatory attacks by criminal groups and ideological remnants of right-wing paramilitaries now known as *bacrim* (criminal bands), and will thus be dependent on government security forces for protection. Naturally, they have grown skittish. Many Colombians are deeply sceptical of FARC's intentions, particularly whether its members truly plan to disarm and abandon criminal activity such as drug trafficking.

These tensions boiled over in February 2016, when FARC leaders on a break from the negotiations were videotaped and photographed carrying out 'armed campaigning' in rural areas. Images of heavily armed rebel leaders mingling with voters and giving speeches swept across Colombian television and social media, infuriating some voters and political leaders. This delayed the process even further. But finally, on 23 June 2016, negotiators announced a breakthrough on the remaining issues and both sides signed a historic bilateral ceasefire. Many hoped that the date would mark the beginning of peace in Colombia.

However, the setbacks created political challenges for President Juan Manuel Santos, whose approval ratings plummeted as low as 21%. Colombian voters grew increasingly sceptical of the peace process itself, as well as the overall trajectory of the country as the economy slowed. Former president Alvaro Uribe, who presided over previous demobilisation agreements, led the opposition to the deal and to Santos, rallying supporters across the country. This had implications for the peace process, as Santos promised that any finalised agreement with FARC would be put to a national referendum. While polls showed a slight majority of Colombians still planning to vote for the accord, the margin grew thinner by the month. Partly because of these concerns, Santos dramatically reshuffled his cabinet in April, appointing a more politically, racially and regionally diverse team – a move some observers saw as designed to ensure that the referendum would pass and that the accord would be implemented effectively.

The government also began to turn its focus towards the post-conflict situation. In the wake of demobilisation, FARC would leave behind large swathes of territory lacking a state presence. To ensure that the void left by the guerrillas was not filled by other rebels or armed criminal groups – which could potentially include former FARC fighters – the government planned an ambitious set of development initiatives. To assist this drive to build schools and other infrastructure, and to encourage economic activity, the Obama administration proposed a new phase for the ongoing Plan Colombia – renamed 'Peace Colombia' – which had provided more than US$10bn in security and counter-narcotics funding over 15 years. Starting in fiscal year 2017, this US$450m package would help Colombia to, in the words of the White House, 'win the peace'. But it remained unclear whether the country would actually receive the funding, as it was subject to congressional approval and, presumably, the outcome of the 2016 US elections.

Washington was primarily concerned with the implementation of transitional justice and the progress of counter-narcotics programmes in Colombia. Even as Bogotá worked towards ending the armed conflict, the underlying illicit-drug trade continued with just as much, if not more, intensity. Coca production in Colombia soared in 2015 and 2016, with overall cultivation rising by at least 44%. Colombia once again became the world's top coca producer, surpassing Peru and Bolivia. This led the Santos administration to reverse its earlier decision to suspend aerial-eradication efforts, which had been halted over concerns that the chemicals used were carcinogens. Many of the government's critics stated that the rise in coca production reflected the underlying weakness of the peace process, arguing that the deal with FARC undermined Colombia's decades-long struggle to overcome the drug problem and re-establish the rule of law. Santos gave a much-publicised speech at the United Nations in April, during the second special session of the General Assembly designed to assess global counter-narcotics strategies. There, he stated that the 'war on drugs' had been a failure and that it was 'time to opt for a different treatment'.

This paralleled a growing debate across the Western Hemisphere over the merits of the war on drugs. After decades, little progress had been made and aspects of the struggle showed signs of deterioration. There were widespread doubts about the capacity of long-standing drug policies to yield positive, sustained results – but there was no consensus on alternative approaches. More than ever, cracks appeared in what was once a relatively monolithic and steadfast global consensus on drug policy. The UN meeting had been called largely due to pressure from Colombia, Mexico and Guatemala. The resulting discussions led to few tangible changes in global policy conventions, mostly because of resistance from China, Russia and some developing countries, which defended their hardline punishments for drug crimes, including the death penalty. Nonetheless, the meeting revealed a growing separation between national approaches, as the final document called for 'sufficient flexibility for [states] to design and implement national drug policies according to their priorities and needs'. With Uruguay having legalised marijuana and several other Latin American countries considering similar measures, this was likely the tip of the iceberg. Above all, this fragmentation was evident in the US, which had long been the chief proponent of a prohibitionist and punitive approach to drug crime. While the federal government had not changed its position, a wave of legalisation movements in states and even the District of Columbia dramatically undermined the US negotiating position. Thus, the trend towards more flexible counter-narcotics programmes seemed set to continue, especially as US politics experienced a discernible rhetorical shift on the issue. However, the shift was yet to have a significant impact on the illegal drug trade.

Central America on the brink

As the international community began to debate the war on drugs, the countries in Central America's Northern Triangle (El Salvador, Guatemala and Honduras) suffered disproportionately from the narcotics trade, struggling to enforce even the most basic rule of law. Their homicide rates remained among the highest in the world. Honduras experienced 57 killings, and Guatemala 36, for every 100,000 people in 2015 (although there were suggestions that the figure for Guatemala was an underestimate). El Salvador was more violent than any other country in the Americas – and, arguably, any state not at war – with a homicide rate in excess of 100 per 100,000 people. The more than 6,600 murders reported in 2015 were largely caused by the country's burgeoning gang war, driven by the increasing size and brutality of the *maras* – transnational criminal syndicates involved in activities such as extortion, theft and kidnapping, as well as the trafficking of guns, drugs and people. Many of the gangs formed in prisons and among immigrant communities in the US, but spread – in part due to deportations – back to El Salvador, flourishing amid the chaos created by the country's civil war. It is estimated that there are 70,000 active gang members in the country, split mainly between two rival groups.

A main cause of this deterioration was the collapse of El Salvador's 2012–13 gang truce, which had cut homicide rates in half. In 2016, there emerged evidence that the truce was facilitated by agreements with the government of Mauricio Funes, who had served as president between 2009 and 2014. His successor and former vice-president, Salvador Sánchez Cerén, largely rejected the truce. The new government instead embraced an approach similar to the *mano dura* (strong hand) policies of previous, more conservative leaderships. According to most analysts, these efforts by the Sánchez Cerén government have been unsuccessful, with violence still rising, prison populations swelling and the gangs growing more powerful. The attorney general began to target members of the Funes administration due to allegations that the truce had been the product of illegal coordination with criminal groups. By mid-2016, there was even speculation that the defence minister, General Munguía Payés, a key figure in the truce, would be stripped of his immunity and arrested.

Meanwhile, Guatemala and Honduras experienced persistent corruption, insecurity and economic weakness. Primarily motivated by the child-migrant crisis of 2014 – which was a direct product of these conditions – the US began to develop a more active and engaged role in Central America. On the recommendation of Vice President Joe Biden, the Obama administration requested a new US$1bn aid package to support the Alliance for Prosperity, a joint development and security effort with Northern Triangle states coordinated by the Inter-American Development Bank. Eventually, Congress approved annual funding of US$750m over three years. This assistance was directed not just at supporting security, as US aid had generally done in the past, but also at promoting new economic activity and investment in long-term growth, as well as institutional support to promote accountability and the rule of law. Washington hoped that long-term financial support for Central America could play a role similar to that which it had in Colombia in the 2000s, edging the three countries back from the brink.

The fight against corruption in Central America was most evident in the activities of the UN International Commission against Impunity in Guatemala (CICIG), an independent judicial-support mechanism. The commission helped oust President Otto Pérez Molina as part of a sweeping corruption investigation in 2015, and continued its work unabated after the inauguration of his replacement, Jimmy Morales, a former comedian who had campaigned on an anti-corruption platform. The international community was also involved in an attempt to replicate the CICIG's success in Honduras, with the Mission to Support the Fight against Corruption and Impunity in Honduras, sponsored by the Organization of American States. However, the mission lacked much of the authority and resources of the CICIG, even from the beginning, and as such there were doubts about whether it could succeed.

In all, the Northern Triangle countries faced challenges that were perhaps even greater than those of Colombia in the 1990s and 2000s. Resolving their endemic problems – stemming from organised crime, drug trafficking, and institutional and economic weakness – would require broad, long-term international engagement. And it remained unclear whether Central American governments had both the capacity and the political will to pursue serious economic and institutional reforms, and to confront rampant crime and insecurity.

A trying, pivotal year

The year to mid-2016 held limited cause for optimism in Latin America. While economic conditions varied sharply among countries, the overall picture was the worst that it had been for many years. Moreover, governance problems grew worse in all but a few countries. The flood of corruption scandals that began in 2014 continued to drive widespread disillusionment with government institutions and the political process. Little was done to address environmental challenges such as a crippling drought that left northern Andean countries on the verge of massive power shortages and blackouts. An earthquake in Ecuador in April delivered another blow to the country's already troubled economy. Haiti, by far the most distressed and impoverished state in the region, lacked a fully functioning government for several months. Brazil – Latin America's largest country, and home to over 30% of the region's population and 40% of its economic activity – slipped further into a political and economic crisis of enormous scale.

Some of the year's most high-profile developments were important in the sense that they clarified the region's troubles. From the Petrobras scandal in Brazil to the erosion of the Maduro government in Venezuela and the weakening rule of law in Central America, these difficulties were caused by long-term structural factors – and, in that sense, had been all but certain to emerge eventually. Arguably, there was simply a convergence of economic and political errors at the same moment. In the broad arc of events, the downfall of left-leaning governments across the region came to seem inevitable, due to their over-reliance on favourable economic winds and failure to prepare for hard times. Latin American leaders had too often missed the chance to build on a sharp rise in prosperity by diversifying economically.

However, some governments began to make significant progress towards addressing persistent problems. By mid-2016, Macri's reforms seemed likely to improve Argentina's institutions and economy, all while maintaining considerable popular support. Anti-corruption movements in Brazil, Guatemala, Chile, Honduras and other countries continued to grow stronger as citizens demanded new levels of accountability and transparency. At the same time, the relationship between the US and Latin America gave reason for cautious optimism. There were an increasing number of opportunities for mutual engagement, albeit of a kind that depended on the continuation of positive trends in the region, the outcome of the US presidential elections and, above all, the ability of the countries involved to find common ground.

Chapter 11

North America

The year to mid-2016 portended change, possibly radical, in the United States, as President Barack Obama's second term neared an end and the Republican Party settled on a presidential candidate dramatically different to any it had fielded in the previous century or more. The year delivered actual change in Canada, with the return to power of the Liberal Party, after almost a decade, under the leadership of a charismatic young prime minister.

A change of direction for Canada?

Canada's Liberal Party, led by Justin Trudeau, formed a majority government following the October 2015 general elections, ending the rule of Conservative leader Stephen Harper. Trudeau, son of the former Liberal leader and prime minister Pierre Trudeau, campaigned on the promise of 'real change', calculating that Canadians had grown tired of the Conservative emphasis on lower taxes, small government and a militaristic foreign policy. The electorate also opted for a change in leadership style, with the younger, more outgoing Trudeau providing a break from the introverted Harper.

At a victory party the day after the election, Trudeau addressed what he said were global concerns that Canada had lost its 'compassionate and constructive voice' under the previous government. 'I have a simple message for you on behalf of 35 million Canadians', he said. 'We're

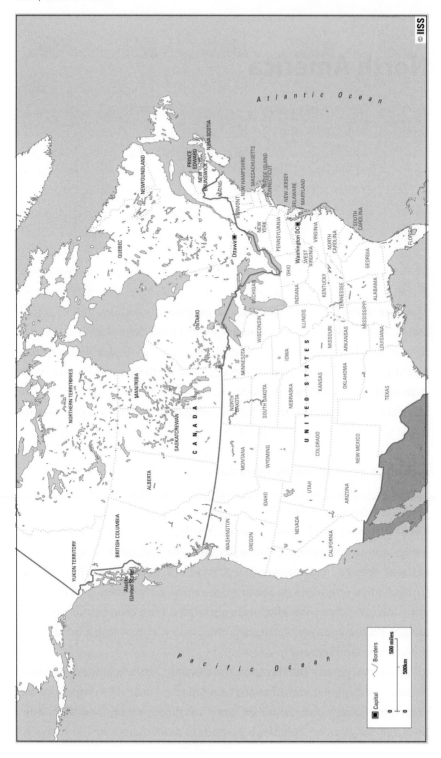

back.' The statement appeared to signal a return to the largely bipartisan foreign policy that prevailed under governments of both political stripes until the Conservatives came to power in 2006. This traditional policy emphasised close and productive relations with the United States, Canada's largest trading partner; strong support for multilateral organisations such as the United Nations, NATO, the Commonwealth and the Organisation Internationale de la Francophonie; a healthy relationship with Western Europe, coupled with the exploitation of economic opportunities in Asia; a balanced approach to the Israel–Palestine conflict; and modest engagement with Africa and Latin America.

The Harper government had diverged from this tradition in small but meaningful ways. Relations with Washington cooled after President Obama rejected an application to construct the Keystone XL pipeline, designed to carry crude oil from Harper's home province of Alberta to refineries in the southern US. And Harper dismissed many multilateral bodies, including the UN General Assembly, as talking shops, electing not to appear before them on several occasions. The General Assembly repaid the slight in 2010, when it elected Portugal rather than Canada to fill one of the non-permanent seats on the UN Security Council. Ottawa had always supported Israel's right to exist, but it became actively pro-Israel in Middle East matters under Harper. He drastically curtailed Canada's engagement with Africa. And his government withdrew the country from the Kyoto Protocol on climate change, while refusing to contemplate the introduction of a carbon tax due to the energy industry's importance to the economy.

The election of a Liberal government therefore marked a distinct change in tone. By mid-2016, the Liberals had taken a significantly different approach to taxation, the environment (particularly climate change), marijuana legalisation and engagement with the UN. The warming of US–Canada relations became apparent after Trudeau visited Washington in March and Obama travelled to Ottawa in June, with the president making a rare address to the Canadian Parliament. Trudeau also stated that he wished for Canada to become 'an active and constructive member of the United Nations and other multilateral organisations'. Yet it remained unclear whether there would be a comparable shift in Canada's approach to defence, relations with non-Western powers,

immigration or overseas development, as the government was conducting public consultations before releasing its policies on these areas. Trade
policy was largely unchanged, as the Trudeau administration sought to
quickly ratify the free-trade deal with the European Union negotiated
under Harper.

Although Canada weathered the financial crisis that began in 2008
better than most developed countries, with its banks and housing market
emerging intact, more recently it was affected by the global downturn.
Real GDP growth fell from 2.5% in 2014 to 1.1% in 2015, and only a
partial improvement is expected for 2016 and 2017. In a sharp departure from the previous government, the Liberal government cut taxes for
the middle class and increased spending, resulting in projected federal
budget deficits of C$30 billion (US$23bn) in 2016–17 and 2017–18. Much
of the new spending is dedicated to domestic infrastructure projects and
green technology, leaving the government little room to spend more on
defence, overseas development or other foreign initiatives. Canada spent
around 1% of GDP on defence in 2015, well below the agreed NATO
target of 2%. This left the country vulnerable to the charge that it was not
pulling its weight in the Alliance.

Canada, under Harper, had also been criticised for failing to act on
climate change. Catherine McKenna, head of the newly renamed environment and climate-change ministry, pledged in November 2015 to
address these concerns, stating that there would be 'no more delays,
no more denials. We need to act.' The following month, Trudeau led
a multiparty Canadian delegation to the UN Framework Convention
on Climate Change's 21st session of the Conference of the Parties. He
signed the deal agreed at the meeting, along with 173 other countries
and the EU, in April 2016. Moreover, Trudeau said that Canada would
spend C$2.65bn (US$2bn) over five years to help developing countries
tackle climate change. Responsibility for setting Canada's environmental
policy is partly shared between its federal and provincial governments.
As the Harper administration refused to impose a carbon tax, the country's ten provinces and three territories were left to act on the issue as
they saw fit. Some of them, such as British Columbia, imposed a broad,
revenue-neutral carbon tax. Neighbouring Alberta, which has a large oil
and gas industry, set a narrow carbon levy that will be replaced by a

broader one in January 2017. Ontario and Quebec, the two most populous provinces, are implementing a system of cap and trade.

Having advocated the measure during the election campaign, the Liberals worked to establish a framework that included a national carbon price, but that allowed the provinces to choose how it was paid. By mid-2016, the federal government was still negotiating with them on this price, and Trudeau said that he would impose one if no agreement was reached. The issue was particularly delicate because, as McKenna pointed out, it threatened to undermine national unity. As a result, the effort to reach a deal tested the prime minister's will to improve the relationship between the federal government and the provinces – some of which had been irritated by the Trudeau administration's decision to revisit environmental assessments for major natural-resources projects.

Further afield, the rapport between Trudeau and Obama would no longer affect relations between their countries after early 2017, when the next US president was scheduled to take office. Both contenders in the November 2016 US elections had made protectionist statements, voicing their desire to either renegotiate (Donald Trump) or adjust (Hillary Clinton) the North American Free Trade Agreement with Canada and Mexico. Canada is heavily dependent on trade with the US, which in 2015 purchased 77% of its goods exports and supplied 53% of its goods imports. (Trade accounts for 66% of Canada's GDP, compared with 28% for the US.) Bilateral relations would quickly sour under a protectionist American administration. Nonetheless, Trudeau's pledge to legalise marijuana is unlikely to cause friction, because both US presidential candidates favour the policy.

Canada's relationship with Mexico has also warmed considerably since the Liberals came to power. This is largely because Trudeau has promised to lift a visa requirement for visiting Mexicans, imposed by the previous government in 2009 following a surge in bogus refugee claims from the country. Canada and Mexico have limited economic relations, trading little with each other. Yet they found common cause in negotiations for the Trans-Pacific Partnership (TPP), a 12-nation agreement that has been signed but not ratified, and may do so again if the US becomes more protectionist under its next president.

Ottawa's developing foreign policy

The Trudeau government had yet to engage meaningfully with China or Russia, largely due to its major review of policies on defence, international aid and development, agriculture, electoral reform and immigration. As a consequence, much Liberal foreign policy was inchoate.

During and after the 2015 election campaign, Trudeau indicated his preference for pursuing national interests without the use of force, and multilateralism over the bilateralism of his predecessor. Delivering the throne speech in late 2015, Canada's governor general stated that 'the Government will renew Canada's commitment to United Nations peace-keeping operations, and will continue to work with its allies in the fight against terrorism'. Peacekeeping, a potent symbol of Canadian identity, was also mentioned in the mandate letter for Stéphane Dion, the foreign minister. The document instructed him to work with the minister of defence 'to increase Canada's support for United Nations peace operations and its mediation, conflict-prevention, and post-conflict reconstruction efforts'.

Canada stayed out of the 2003 Iraq War but invested heavily in Afghanistan, leaving the latter country in 2014 after a 12-year mission. Canada has also contributed to the campaign against the Islamic State, also known as ISIS or ISIL, in the Middle East, as well as the NATO-led mission to meet the rising Russian challenge in Eastern Europe. Although the Trudeau government had not yet formulated a new defence policy, it moved in February 2016 to end combat missions in Syria and Iraq, recalling its six fighter jets from the US-led coalition. However, Canada maintained the deployment of surveillance and refuelling aircraft to the coalition, and tripled to more than 800 the number of Canadian troops training and assisting Kurdish fighters in northern Iraq. In June, Canada agreed to send 450 soldiers and armoured vehicles to Latvia as part of a NATO mission to bolster the Alliance's presence in the Baltic states. The announcement came after Obama made a plea for more support in his address to the Canadian House of Commons, telling parliamentarians that 'the world needs more Canada'. But defence spending was likely to be constrained by the government's large budget deficit, and there were no plans to increase the size of the armed forces. This suggested that resources for new missions would have to be reassigned from existing operations.

Trudeau also planned to re-establish relations with Iran, following the closure in 2012 of the Canadian Embassy in Tehran and the expulsion of Iranian diplomats from Canada. He also intended to maintain a relationship with Moscow, despite Russia's actions in Ukraine. 'I'm of the school of international relations that says it's important to talk to each other,' Trudeau said in 2014. 'It's especially important to talk to regimes you disagree with.' Dion made the same point in a speech outlining his approach to foreign policy. 'Unilateralism is not the Canadian way,' he commented, adding: 'Canada has been at its most effective when we have engaged in even the most difficult circumstances.' In another break from the previous government, Canadian diplomats have been told that they no longer need to clear everything they say with Ottawa in advance. The government has also permitted scientists to publicly discuss findings from government-funded research.

The two constants between Liberal and Conservative policymakers appear to be trade and immigration policy. As part of a strategy to diversify Canadian trade, the Conservative government negotiated the EU–Canada Comprehensive Economic and Trade Agreement. It was due to be signed in October 2016, with ratification planned for early 2017. However, it was caught up in the turmoil caused by the British vote to leave the EU, and its prospects were uncertain. Undeterred, the Liberal government battled to proceed to ratification as soon as possible. Yet that seemed unlikely to occur in the foreseeable future, after the European Commission decided in early July 2016 that, as a mixed agreement, it would require ratification by all EU member states.

The TPP was also in limbo, pending the approval of the US Congress. If this fails to emerge before Obama steps down, the deal is likely to fail, as both US presidential candidates oppose it. The Liberal government has not stated its policy on the TPP, and is likely waiting to see what transpires in Washington before taking a firm position.

In the last two decades, under governments of both political stripes, Canada has accepted an average of around 250,000 immigrants as permanent residents per year. People born abroad comprised around 21% of the population in 2011. While the Conservatives favoured economic immigrants and the Liberals wished to accept more refugees, both parties agreed on their importance to the economy. Canada has perhaps the only conservative party in the Western world that favours high immigration, a policy that has broad popular support. The target for 2016 is 300,000, up from 280,000 the previous year. The government plans to accept 45,000 refugees in 2016. Trudeau was particularly focused on Syrian refugees, and even personally greeted some of them as they entered Canada. Around 29,000 Syrians arrived in the country between November 2015 and mid-2016.

The Liberals had therefore sketched the broad outlines of their foreign policy, leaving the details to be filled in after the public consultations were completed. The early indications were that the new government planned to return Canada to its enthusiastic multilateralism, favouring free trade and globalisation. This trajectory sharply contrasted with that of many Western states, not least the US.

The United States: a volatile country

By mid-2016, Donald Trump was the Republican nominee in the US presidential elections, and it was possible, if unlikely, that he would win the contest. Whatever the outcome of the November vote, however, his nomination by one of the two major parties was a signal event in American history. Political commentators struggled to express its magnitude. 'The degree to which, by changing the Republican Party, he will also permanently deform American politics can only be speculated upon', *Slate* magazine's Isaac Chotiner wrote, 'but his primary victory will, decades from now, likely be seen as one of the defining events of 21st-century America'. Writing in *New York Magazine*, Andrew Sullivan sought to explain Trump's ascent by referencing a passage in Plato's *Republic* on why democracy leads, with deceptive ease, to tyranny. Sullivan concluded that, 'in terms of our liberal democracy and constitutional order, Trump is an extinction-level event. It's long past time we started treating him as such.'

The simple reason for this alarm was that a major-party nomination for a man of his temperament and world view was unprecedented in the last century, and perhaps in the history of the United States. In place of ideology, Trump projected narcissism – which, to the extent that it had ideological content, consisted of visceral nationalism and authoritarianism. His years-long promotion of 'birtherism' – a movement based on the idea that President Barack Obama was not born in the US – should have been a clue. Yet the June 2015 announcement of his bid for the Republican nomination nonetheless shocked:

> When do we beat Mexico at the border? They're laughing at us, at our stupidity. And now they are beating us economically. They are not our friend, believe me. But they're killing us economically. The US has become a dumping ground for everybody else's problems … It's true, and these are the best and the finest. When Mexico sends its people, they're not sending their best. They're not sending you. They're not sending you. They're sending people that have lots of problems, and they're bringing those problems with us. They're bringing drugs. They're bringing crime. They're rapists. And some, I assume, are good people.

These words were a prelude to his first and signature campaign promise: to build a massive wall along the US–Mexico border, and to force Mexico to pay for it. Several months later, Trump revealed his plan for extorting these funds. As president, he would threaten to cut off the flow of remittances from the US to Mexico – that is, to induce a failed state on America's southern border if Mexico did not bend to his will.

From this beginning, Trump rolled through primary or caucus victories in 37 of the 50 states. His rhetoric became more unhinged, yet he paid little, if any, penalty among Republican voters. He claimed, falsely, to have seen thousands of New Jersey Muslims celebrating the destruction of the Twin Towers on 9/11 from across the Hudson. When a *New York Times* reporter who had written on police and FBI investigations into rumours about a small number of celebrations insisted that no such parties had taken place, Trump publicly mocked that reporter's physical disability. After the December 2015 San Bernardino killings, in which an American-born citizen of Pakistani descent and his Pakistan-born wife killed 14 people with semi-automatic pistols and rifles, Trump promised that his administration would ban all Muslims from entering the US. He also promised to reinstate torture as US policy, emphasising that the methods would need to go well beyond the water-boarding adopted, and then renounced, in the aftermath of 9/11. And he suggested that the US could only deter terrorism by killing terrorists' family members. Concerned, apparently, that a general promise of war crimes was still too vague, Trump excited his crowd at one South Carolina campaign rally with an almost certainly apocryphal story about General John Pershing. In Trump's telling, Pershing dealt with a rebellion in the Philippines in the early twentieth century by lining up 50 Muslim insurgents, before shooting 49 of them with bullets dipped in pigs' blood. Moreover, Trump ritually invoked, and his supporters often used, violence against protesters, many of whom were black. 'I loved the old days,' the candidate said as one protestor was removed from his event. 'You know what they used to do to guys like that when they were in a place like this? They'd be carried out on a stretcher, folks.'

On 4 May 2016, Trump's last standing rival for the nomination, hard-right Texas Senator Ted Cruz, lost the Indiana primary and pulled out of the race. It would take another month for Trump to acquire a majority of delegates to bring to the July nominating convention, but at this point his path was clear. Yet during this period two realities became apparent: firstly, the demagoguery that appealed to a plurality of Republican voters (and Republican-leaning independents voting in some primaries) was harder to sell to a more diverse national electorate; secondly, demagoguery was central to Trump's world view and personality, and he could not discard it in a strategic pivot towards a more presidential persona. Trump appeared unable to acquire the tone and campaign organisation that might establish him as a credible challenger. At about this time, Federal District Judge Gonzalo Curiel denied Trump a summary judgment and unsealed depositions on two class-action lawsuits against the outlandish Trump University. Trump responded at campaign rallies and in a *Wall Street Journal* interview that Curiel, born in Indiana, was inherently biased because of his 'Mexican heritage', adding: 'I'm building a wall. It's an inherent conflict of interest.' The statement came at a moment when some Republican politicians were reluctantly beginning to officially endorse the presumed nominee. One of them was House Speaker Paul Ryan, who said in June that Trump's attack was 'the textbook definition of a racist comment', but that he still had more in common with Trump than Clinton, and that he would therefore continue to back him. That same month, after a gunman killed 49 people at a gay nightclub in Orlando, Florida, Trump first congratulated himself on Twitter for having warned of such attacks, then insinuated that President

Obama was actively in league with members of the Islamic State, also known as ISIS or ISIL.

The rhetorical anarchy combined with organisational chaos. In fact, only a month before Trump's nomination at the Republican National Convention in Cleveland, it remained unclear whether he had a campaign organisation. In late June, campaign-finance reports revealed that his campaign had US$1.3 million in the bank – compared to the Clinton campaign's US$42.3m. At around the same time, it was reported that he had 70 paid staff members nationwide, compared to Clinton's 700.

Yet, despite this apparent meltdown, polls published a week before the Republican convention showed Trump again drawing even with Hillary Clinton, who had been wounded in her primary campaign against self-described 'democratic socialist' Bernie Sanders and struggled to appeal to his younger, more leftist (and generally whiter) supporters. Polling experts cautioned that such movements in the weeks before the party summits were unreliable. Nonetheless, there remained a significant possibility of a Trump presidency.

Demagoguery and authoritarianism

How had this moment arrived? It was, to be sure, a time of convulsive reaction in many developed democracies, as seen in Britain's narrow but decisive referendum vote to leave the European Union, and surging support for far-right and anti-immigrant parties in France, Austria, the Netherlands and elsewhere. The broad explanation for all of these developments was a response by aggrieved middle classes against the disruptions of globalisation. The opening of borders and transcendence of national sovereignty had increased overall wealth, but in a manner that polarised societies rather than binding them together. The increasing imbalance in the distribution of wealth exacerbated a sense of stagnation and vulnerability for white- and blue-collar workers, whose confidence in stable and adequate employment was being steadily undermined. One much-cited academic study found that the mortality rate for non-Hispanic white Americans between 45 and 54 years of age – which had declined until 1998 in line with that in other wealthy countries – had risen by half a percentage point per year since the turn of the century. This astonishing development, redolent of post-Soviet Russia, was at odds with the continued decline in mortality rates in other Western democracies and, indeed, among US Hispanics. The causes, according to the study, included alcohol and opiate abuse, as well as suicide. The researchers also found evidence of a broader link to job insecurity.

As an explanation for Trump's rise, the insecurities of globalisation had the advantage of fitting well with one of his genuine political heterodoxies: he was the first major-party presidential nominee since the Second World War to have espoused trade protectionism. And the significant constituency for protectionism had long been unrepresented by American politicians. The anti-globalisation argument also seemed plausible in explaining the unexpected success of Sanders in his campaign against Clinton for the Democratic nomination. Sanders lost, but Clinton was forced to take his campaign seriously, and to move her platform leftwards to win over disaffected Sanders supporters. Moreover, although Trump espoused a tax plan that constituted a significant upward redistribution of income – a key tenet of conservative orthodoxy – he also occasionally adopted heterodox positions, such as hostility to foreign trade. The latter issue seemed to resonate with those lower-middle-class whites who resented multiracial liberalism but were unmoved by established conservative causes: low marginal tax rates; a minimal welfare state; free markets; and, at least implicitly, a large supply of cheap immigrant labour.

Broken party?

The disruptions of globalisation were a pervasive problem for Western democracy. The US also faced the more specific challenge of a Republican Party that appeared to be in many respects broken. The party's most superficial flaw was tactical: during its primary campaign, a range of relatively conventional politicians continued to target each other rather than appreciate and focus on the threat posed by Trump. This complacency ran through the pitches made by Cruz; former Florida governor Jeb Bush; Florida Senator Marco Rubio; New Jersey Governor Chris Christie; former head of Hewlett-Packard Carly Fiorina; Wisconsin Governor Scott Walker; Ohio Governor John Kasich; and nine other candidates. Hence, they waited too long to secure their place as the establishment favourite who would finally stop Trump. But the party

enabled Trump's rise in much deeper ways. Conservative public intellectual Robert Kagan wrote that 'a plague has descended on the party
in the form of the most successful demagogue-charlatan in the history
of U.S. politics'. Trump, Kagan wrote, was the natural consequence of
the 'party's wild obstructionism — the repeated threats to shut down
the government over policy and legislative disagreements, the persistent calls for nullification of Supreme Court decisions, the insistence that
compromise was betrayal, the internal coups against party leaders who
refused to join the general demolition'.

The current of Republican right-wing radicalism went back to the
'movement conservatism' that powered Barry Goldwater's 1964 capture
of the Republican presidential nomination, which resulted in Democrat
Lyndon Johnson's landslide victory. Ronald Reagan was a creature of
the movement, but both his persona and his presidency were generally
pragmatic. So were those of the traditional New England moderate,
George H.W. Bush. It was arguably in reaction to the election of Bill
Clinton that right-wing radicalism really took off. During Clinton's
presidency, the *Contract with America*, brainchild of Georgia congress-
man Newt Gingrich, became the foundational text of the first Republican
majority in the House of Representatives since the 1950s. This document
promised a 'historic change [that] would be the end of government that
is too big, too intrusive, and too easy with the public's money … the
beginning of a Congress that respects the values and shares the faith
of the American family'. Gingrich had already promised a 'civil war'
against liberals, saying in a 1988 speech to the Heritage Foundation that
'this war has to be fought with a scale and a duration and a savagery that
is only true of civil wars.' In 1990 his political action committee advised
Republican candidates to 'speak like Newt', by describing Democrats
with words such as 'decay, traitors, radical, sick, destroy, pathetic,
corrupt and shame'. It was an approach that gave spirit to the subsequent impeachment proceedings against President Bill Clinton.

Republicans continued to put forward conventional conservatives,
if not moderates, as their presidential nominees: Bob Dole, George W.
Bush, John McCain and Mitt Romney. George W. Bush led the US in the
radical misadventure of Iraq and authorised forms of torture for terrorist suspects. He later appeared, in behaviour if not words, to recognise

that it had been a mistake to authorise torture, and he remained faithful to other fundamental liberal principles. Paramount among these was the recognition of the danger of an anti-Muslim backlash after 9/11, which he worked to prevent. No significant backlash occurred on Bush's watch. But it started, almost inexplicably, with an angry reaction to the 2010 proposal to build a 'Ground Zero mosque' in New York – even if the building was in fact an ecumenical centre located away from Ground Zero. (Gingrich took an agitating lead in the movement, which stopped the project.) This Islamophobia was one ingredient in the dark brew of Tea Party reaction to the 2008 financial crash, the ensuing prolonged recession and the election of a black president whose middle name was 'Hussein'. The Tea Party Republicans had a lot of anger to spend, and they advanced impressively in Congress two years after Obama's election, and again two years after his re-election; Cruz and Rubio were among the new right-wing senators and representatives elected in these surges.

Rubio's trajectory showed how much the Republican Party had been transformed in the seven years since Bush had left office. Bush won 44% of the Hispanic vote in his 2004 re-election. The result encouraged Bush's political strategist Karl Rove to imagine that American Hispanics – Catholic and family-oriented – were open to a strategic bid from the more conservative major party. Rove may have been missing the fact that, even if socially conservative, Hispanics were generally supportive of statist solutions, such as a generous welfare state. In any event, such philosophical questions were subsumed under the growing nativism of Rove's party. In 2012 Romney tried to appease this nativism by promising policies that would lead to the 'self-deportation' of illegal immigrants. This idea did not go over well with Hispanics, and Romney's share of their vote fell to 27%. Having expected to win the presidency in 2012 following what they regarded as the manifest failure of Obama's first term, Republican leaders tried to focus on their Hispanic problem. An 'autopsy' commissioned by the Republican National Committee reached the common-sense conclusion that, 'if Hispanics think we don't want them here, they will close their ears to our policies.'

This was the context for the hopes invested in the Cuban-American Rubio as a 2016 candidate, and for Rubio's participation in a bipartisan 'gang of eight' senators who sought to fashion a compromise on immigration reform that would help bring America's estimated 11m undocumented immigrants out of the legal shadows. But the effort fell apart in the face of another angry reaction from the Republicans' Tea Party base. Although Rubio subsequently repudiated the draft plan, he was unable to compete with Trump's promise that – far from normalising the immigrants' status – he would create a new force to systematically, aggressively deport them. Implementing the plan would incur hundreds of billions of dollars in administrative expenses and many hundreds of billions more in broader economic costs. In human-rights terms, it implied greater brutality than the internment of Japanese-Americans during the Second World War.

Also telling was the gap between Bush's and Rubio's – not to mention Trump's – approaches to the much smaller community of American Muslims. Six days after 9/11, the deeply religious Bush had sought to project ecumenical reassurance by visiting the Islamic Center of Washington DC. Obama adopted similarly inclusive rhetoric, but did not visit a mosque until the last year of his presidency. When he eventually did, Obama told Muslims in Baltimore that 'you're not Muslim or American, you're Muslim and American.' Rubio on the campaign trail called this another example of the president 'pitting people against each other', adding: 'I can't stand that.'

This puzzling statement requires some explanation. A central Republican argument, repeated by many of Rubio's competitors in the presidential primary, was that Democrats were the true racists because they lacked the Republicans' principled colour-blindness. It was true that the Democratic Party had been structured as a coalition of identity-conscious groups including Hispanics and blacks. Republicans could count on a majority of the non-Hispanic white vote – which they needed due to their relative lack of popularity among the rest of the electorate. But the claim of colour-blindness encountered more fundamental problems. It has been impossible to ignore the racial divide that coincides with ideological disagreements, and that has constituted the central drama of American history. To the poisonous legacy of slavery there is now added the cultural, economic and religious panic induced by Hispanic immigration and growth, and by the association of Islam with jihadist terrorism. At least part of Trump's appeal was undeniably racist, as Ryan, the highest-ranking Republican official in the country, had acknowledged and lamented. Ryan did not, however, acknowledge the historical reality that the Republican Party for half a century had strategically positioned itself as the home for whites disaffected by the civil-rights advances of blacks and other minorities. This positioning did not require personal racism on the part of any particular Republican leader, but it was striking that, at the historical moment when an African-American president demonstrated impressive progress, the racial element in Republican politics had become more explicit. Hence, the transparent efforts of many Republican-controlled states to enact voting restrictions that disproportionately penalised blacks under the flimsy pretext of fighting 'voter fraud' (a virtually non-existent problem). Hence, too, the fact that Mitt Romney, who forthrightly condemned Trump's bigoted appeals in 2016, had four years earlier embraced Trump's endorsement and ignored the racist content of his alleging a vast conspiracy to cover up Obama's supposed foreign birth. It was Kagan, again, who implored his fellow Republicans to look into the mirror and realise that Trump's bigotry had been 'enabled' by the party's attacks on immigrants, its trafficking in Islamophobia and its propagation of 'Obama hatred, a racially tinged derangement syndrome that made any charge plausible and any opposition justified'.

There did not appear to be enough racially aggrieved whites to win the 2016 election; but if it turned out that there were, it would probably be for the last time. And so, whatever the outcome of the general election, Trump had the potential to project havoc into Republican presidential prospects for decades to come. As a consequence of his campaign, Hispanics could be lost to the Republican Party for another half-century, just as most African-Americans have resolutely shunned the GOP in the 52 years since Goldwater opposed the passage of the Civil Rights Act.

Obama's legacy

America's first black president entered office as an avatar of hope for finally transcending America's racial divides. He also put himself forward as a pragmatic figure who could reverse the country's ideological polarisation; indeed, this was his promise in the keynote speech to the 2004 Democratic convention that first brought him to national attention.

In policy terms, his presidency achieved a great deal, but both projects of transcendence would have to be judged failures. In ideological terms, the liberal policy achievements collided with a Republican Party moving sharply to the right. In racial terms, the subtext of the reaction was made explicit by the rise of Trump. And the hopes embodied in Obama's election and re-election did not always correspond to the reality of life for black Americans. Black men were incarcerated at astonishingly high rates, often for drug offences for which their white counterparts received a lighter sentence. The experience of black men also included more intrusive and aggressive handling by the police, which in extreme cases resulted in violence and death. Whether they were shot by police at a higher rate than whites was a matter of statistical dispute, but this anecdotal narrative had suddenly become observable through the widespread use of smartphone cameras.

The narrative and the imagery that supported it were disseminated across the internet, inspiring Black Lives Matter, a campaign reminiscent of the civil-rights movement that came a half-century earlier. Yet there were also echoes of the armed violence of the 1960s. In July 2016, an African-American army veteran shot and killed five police officers in Dallas. Days later, another African-American veteran shot and killed three officers in Baton Rouge. Before being killed himself in a parking garage, the first man had expressed his hatred of whites and his determination to kill white police. Both cities had been the scenes of Black Lives Matter demonstrations that month.

This violence compounded the racial tensions of the election campaign. It came around a year after white supremacist Dylann Roof allegedly walked into a venerated black church in Charleston during a service; after chatting with congregants, he shot to death nine of them, including the senior pastor. Roof's crime acted as a reminder that the US security services have deemed right-wing terrorism a danger on par with the jihadist threat. However, this particular act of terrorism had one surprising consequence: it led several white southern politicians to repudiate the Confederate flag that remained an official motif in many southern states – a flag that Roof had embraced and African-Americans had long resented as an expression of atavistic pride in slavery, segregation and white supremacy.

'God works in mysterious ways', said President Obama, in Charleston to eulogise the victims, as he reflected on this loosening of devotion to the Confederate flag and other displays of solidarity inspired by Roof's attack. By this point, Obama had made many statements in the aftermath of mass shootings during his presidency, but few offered any glimmer of hope that America might significantly amend its gun-control laws. In December 2012, after a disturbed 20-year-old man shot and killed 20 children and six adults at Sandy Hook Elementary School in Newtown, Connecticut, it was imagined that lawmakers might finally enact some restrictions on at least the types of semi-automatic weapons with large magazines that facilitated mass killings. But unfettered access to most types of firearms, however unnecessary for civilian purposes, was a talisman of identity for politicians representing rural and southern whites. Efforts by urban liberals to impose gun-control measures were interpreted as a cultural assault on a way of life; moreover, mainstream Republicans often turned to the argument that a constitutional right to bear arms was still needed as a guard against federal tyranny. Even the most obvious intersection of lone-wolf jihadist terrorism and easy access to guns was unpersuasive to gun-rights advocates. The *reductio ad absurdum* of this discourse came on the day after the Baton Rouge police shootings, when the leader of a Cleveland, Ohio, police union asked Governor Kasich to suspend the 'open carry' law that permitted ideologues and vigilantes of every persuasion to parade loaded firearms on the city's streets. Kasich replied that he lacked such authority under the law. Only the US Secret Service succeeded in drawing a line of sorts: no weapons would be permitted in the convention hall where Trump was to be nominated.

Political choices were stark. Obama was the first Northern liberal to win the presidency since John F. Kennedy. Obama came to office in a time of economic crisis and near-catastrophe, and with slim Democratic majorities in both houses of Congress he was able to apply the traditional liberal remedy of stimulus spending, together with financial and industrial rescue packages. In expanding access to health insurance, he completed a liberal agenda that Harry Truman had proposed six decades earlier. He used his executive powers to regulate carbon emissions and to exercise considerable discretion regarding the status of illegal immigrants. All of these measures offended the philosophical principles of a Republican Party that had moved significantly to the right.

But Obama's approach was also incrementalist and, in a philosophical sense, conservative, in a way that tended to disappoint the political left, which included a large share of young Americans. Opinion polls indicated that, too young to have a living memory of the Cold War, they were unconstrained by the political paradigms established in the Reagan era. Theirs may have been the first generation since the Second World War to be unpersuaded by the virtues of capitalism and untroubled by the idea of socialism – at least in abstract terms. The generation-defining experience of the 2008 financial crash and subsequent recession no doubt played a role in this, as did the disastrous consequences of the 2003 Iraq War.

Thus, the political battle to inherit and define Obama's legacy was waged in distinctly leftist territory. Hillary Clinton might not have assumed an easy path to the nomination that Obama had denied her eight years before, but she probably did not imagine that her most formidable rival would be a 74-year-old, Brooklyn-accented democratic socialist who had honeymooned in the Soviet Union. And although Clinton – Obama's clear favourite – won the primary contest, its tumult indicated a continuation of the centre–left ideological struggles that had defined her and her husband's careers. Hillary Clinton was a Republican when she entered Wellesley College in 1965; she was moving gradually to the left when she attended the Republican Convention in Miami that nominated Richard Nixon. The Democratic Party to which she moved was in turmoil. After Nixon narrowly defeated then-vice president Hubert Humphrey, the Democrats experienced a convulsion that writer Peter Beinart compares to the more recent Tea Party conquest of the Republican Party:

> Between 1968 and 1972, grassroots activists – many of them incubated in the anti-war movement – took over the Democratic Party, state by state. In 1970, activists rewrote Michigan's party platform so that it advocated reparations to North Vietnam. In Washington state, they demanded amnesty for draft evaders and a ban on the building of missiles.

George McGovern, the Democratic nominee in 1972, was really a conventional Midwestern liberal in the mould of Humphrey – and a Second World War hero to boot – but he was driven left by the zeal of this movement and his own anger about the senseless war in Vietnam. Nixon, running for re-election, trounced the Democrat, who lost every state except Massachusetts.

The Democrats' next nominee, Jimmy Carter, came from the right of his party, although from the left of the great civil-rights struggle in his native South. After Carter lost his re-election bid to Reagan, the Democrats put forward two sedate Northern liberals, Walter Mondale and Michael Dukakis. And after both lost, the southerner Bill Clinton led his party in accepting that it would have to engage in the national debate on terms that had been set by Reagan. This required greater engagement with middle-class anxieties about urban crime, and an effort to purge the party of residual pacifism. Clinton was lucky on both counts. Crime fell sharply for reasons mainly unrelated to policy, and he inherited a uniquely benign international environment.

Nearing 70, Hillary Clinton assumed the leadership of her party carrying the weight and assumptions of these earlier struggles. One of her burdens is that she was the target of what could be called witch-hunts from the early 1990s – as a modern career woman and thus the first non-traditional first lady in the White House, she jarred a lot of nerves and assumptions. Among the investigations into her real-estate investments and legal-records billing in Arkansas, there came absurd suggestions – taken seriously by some Republicans at the time – that Vince Foster, a friend and White House aide who committed suicide, had actually been murdered by the Clintons. The investigation eventually uncovered President Clinton's sexual relationship with intern Monica Lewinsky.

A generation later, congressional Republicans conducted a lengthy investigation into the deaths of American diplomats and security personnel during an assault on their Benghazi compound by jihadists and assorted thugs, following the fall of Libyan leader Muammar Gadhafi. The operating theory of this investigation was never entirely clear: one theme was a charge that the Obama administration was politically and ideologically reluctant to label the attackers 'terrorists', although the president had quickly called it an 'act of terror'. As secretary of state,

Hillary Clinton had overall responsibility for security in the compound, and Republican investigators clearly hoped to derail her candidacy. This hope appeared to have been stymied by her commanding performance in responding to the investigative committee's questions for 11 hours.

Nonetheless, the Benghazi committee uncovered one piece of damaging information: Clinton's use, as secretary of state, of a private email account and server in lieu of her State Department address. The security implications of this were minimal but, given the ingrained tendency of many US government agencies to classify too much information, it was probably inevitable that some technically classified emails would be transmitted on this system. The FBI duly investigated, and rumours of Clinton's imminent indictment were rife. In the event, FBI Director James Comey concluded that 'no reasonable prosecutor would bring such a case'. But he also said that Clinton had been 'extremely reckless' in her handling of the matter. Polls taken shortly after he made these statements indicated that they had undermined her support among a majority of voters, who deemed her dishonest and untrustworthy.

Still, going into the party conventions, her modest polling lead over Trump was evidence that, as journalist Josh Marshall put it, 'the communities and demographic subgroupings that Clinton is able to appeal to are larger than Trump's'. This was significant for the future of American politics. Demographic trends pointed to a citizenry that was becoming more diverse and liberal, as was suggested by the re-election of an African-American president. Indeed, Obama was leaving office with approval ratings comparable to Reagan's 28 years earlier. However, the US remained deeply polarised. The Republicans had ridden a large and adamant conservative minority to strong positions in state legislatures and both houses of Congress. Moreover, Donald Trump had, on his way to winning the GOP nomination, consistently defied pollsters' best estimates of his vote ceiling. The struggle for America's future was not over.

Washington's foreign-policy choices

Obama announced Hillary Clinton as his choice for secretary of state on 18 November 2008, to widespread predictions that their bitter campaigns against each other would preclude a functioning relationship. Less evident in those predictions was an idea of what, in substantive

terms, might divide the two. They had traduced each other's judgement – Obama attacking Clinton's vote to authorise force against Iraq
in 2002, and Clinton running a famous advertisement implying that
a 46-year-old, first-term senator would be temperamentally unfit to
answer an early-morning call bringing news of an international crisis.
Nonetheless, on the afternoon of 1 May 2011, Obama and Clinton were
photographed sitting drawn-faced in a crowded White House conference room, watching footage of US Navy SEALs carry out an operation
to kill Osama bin Laden. Campaign-trail differences could be ascribed to
temperament and the demands of a primary season; the two had proved
similar enough in judgement and political direction to form an effective
working partnership.

Yet, on the crucial matter of Iraq, Obama's expression of temperament had been in itself an act of ideology: instinctive caution serving as
a rebuke to the confidence implicit in Bush-era pre-emption. His 2002
speech in Chicago provided a preview of a remarkably settled view of
the world. The core slogan of the Obama doctrine was there, in sanitised
form: 'what I am opposed to is a dumb war. What I am opposed to is a
rash war.' More importantly, so was the core of the future president's
aversion to direct military intervention:

> I know that even a successful war against Iraq will require a U.S. occupation of
> undetermined length, at undetermined cost, with undetermined consequences.
> I know that an invasion of Iraq without a clear rationale and without strong
> international support will only fan the flames of the Middle East, and encour-
> age the worst, rather than best, impulses of the Arab world, and strengthen the
> recruitment arm of al-Qaida.

Obama's pessimism about the efficacy of the use of force – rather than
his diagnosis of the character of Saddam Hussein's regime – separated
him from Hillary Clinton over Iraq, and would continue to do so when
she served as his secretary of state. In the Obama administration's debate
over a surge of troops into Afghanistan in 2009, Clinton reportedly
pushed for the full 40,000 advocated by General Stanley McChrystal,
and regretted Obama's announcement of a July 2011 withdrawal date.
She is credited with persuading the president first to intervene in Libya

in 2011, and then to give secular rebels lethal assistance. She was also reportedly an early advocate of arming rebels in Syria and, after leaving office, described the failure to strengthen moderate rebel forces as having created 'a big vacuum, which the jihadists have now filled'.

Obama outlined the intellectual framework for his military reticence in an interview with Jeffrey Goldberg of the *Atlantic*. The president provided a vigorous defence of the decision not to strike Syria in 2013 after the Syrian regime's use of chemical weapons on Ghouta, a breach of the 'red line' he had drawn the previous year. In Obama's reading, a Syria disarmed of its chemical weapons was of greater value than the supposed deterrent effect, to the regime, of retaliatory airstrikes that would have been unlikely to destroy all of Assad's chemical weapons or his capacity to use them. The radicalism of the justification lay not in the cost–benefit analysis, but in the narrowness of its frame: Obama rejected the idea that he owed payment to American deterrent credibility, either against future users of chemical weapons or against aggressors elsewhere. He ascribed that expectation to a Washington foreign-policy 'playbook', designed to be followed unthinkingly; his deputy national-security adviser, Ben Rhodes, called the keepers of that playbook 'the blob' in a popular, if wildly misadvised, interview with the *New York Times*.

Although her instincts were probably more hawkish than Obama's, it was unclear where Hillary Clinton as president would depart sharply from his foreign policy. Obama's marquee achievement was a nuclear agreement with Iran that resulted in the shipment of most nuclear material out of the country, and the imposition of strict limits on, and tight inspections of, its uranium-enrichment activities – in exchange for sanctions relief. In addition to this diplomatic achievement, Obama won a major political victory when Israeli Prime Minister Benjamin Netanyahu failed in late 2015 to persuade enough Democratic senators to thwart the deal. Clinton's top aide, Jake Sullivan, had travelled to Oman for the initial secret diplomacy that produced a breakthrough with Iran, and so Clinton herself had some ownership of the achievement, even if it was her successor, John Kerry, who most doggedly negotiated it. There are likely to be many threats to the nuclear deal in coming years: on the Iranian side, anger and disappointment that sanctions relief failed to end

Iran's economic isolation (partly because banks and other businesses are wary that the sanctions will be reinstated). On the American side, a large body of opponents to the agreement could point to unchanged Iranian behaviour and rhetoric in Syria, against Israel and in the development of missile technology.

A President Clinton, however, would likely do what she could to preserve the deal. And, while she might be marginally more assertive towards Russian behaviour in Syria and Eastern Europe, or towards Chinese predations in the South China Sea, circumstance and philosophical inclination would make hers, in foreign as well as domestic policy, an Obama third term.

The imagined President Trump could not be more different. The admiration he expressed for the tough leadership of Russian President Vladimir Putin appeared genuine. This was less a matter of an inclination towards appeasement than a manifest disinterest in the norms of democracy. Trump would enter office as the only genuinely isolationist president since the nineteenth century; although not, as a rule, philosophically inclined, he expressed a coherent world view of international relations as fiercely zero sum. In this view, NATO was an inherently bad deal for the US because the country was defending European allies who had little capacity to reciprocate, and who were unwilling to adequately pay for their protection. Likewise, maintaining a nuclear umbrella over South Korea and Japan seemed to be a foolish and dangerous entanglement when those countries could just as well develop and deploy nuclear weapons themselves. And, of course, 'isolationism' was a mild term for what Trump conceived as the proper relationship between the US and its southern neighbour.

Yet the departure offered by Trump was more fundamental and organic than specific foreign policies. His election would constitute a sea change in the Western liberal order. He is a familiar character from history. His American antecedents include Henry Ford, Charles Lindbergh, Father Coughlin and George Wallace. In contemporary Europe, the late Jörg Haider of Austria's Freedom Party offered a similar mix of xenophobia, media savvy, appeal to middle-class anxieties, and attacks on the complacency and corruption of establishment political parties. Haider's successor, Heinz-Christian Strache, ploughs the same swampy fields, as have France's Jean-Marie Le Pen and his daughter Marine (who succeeded him as head of the National Front).

The major difference is that the European far-rightists are mainly third-party forces, challenging but not supplanting their establishment rivals. Italy's Silvio Berlusconi, a Trump-like demagogue, was an exception, and both Poland and Hungary are today governed by rightist, illiberal parties. The general pattern in Western Europe, however, has been that while far-right parties pose significant dangers, the mainstream also has had a way of uniting to fight back. This could be seen in 2002, when French socialists fell behind Jacques Chirac in the second round of the presidential vote rather than risk a National Front victory.

In early 2016, *Washington Post* columnist Anne Applebaum speculated that the international system might be two or three elections away from the demise of the West. With the help of another terrorist attack or major scandal, Trump could become president of the US and Marine Le Pen the leader of France. Britain could leave the EU (as it eventually voted to do) and broader commitment to alliances and principles could fade away.

Even if Trump falls short in November and Marine Le Pen is defeated, damage has already been done through the normalisation of illiberal discourse. Terrorism has played a role: the political norms of Western democracies are affected by the ability of solitary terrorists to render public spaces insecure (this is one reason why the work of security services is a front-line defence of democratic values).

But the judgement and temperament of politicians is also critical. On 14 July, a Tunisian-born Frenchman killed more than 80 people by aiming his truck down a crowded quay in Nice. Gingrich, apparently still hoping to become Trump's vice-presidential running mate, reacted on Fox News with the following words: 'Western civilisation is in a war. We should frankly test every person here who is of Muslim background, and if they believe in Sharia they should be deported.' Generously, he added that 'modern Muslims who have given up Sharia' could remain as citizens. 'But we need to be fairly relentless about defining who our enemies are.' Gingrich concluded, his voice dripping with disgust: 'this is the fault of Western elites who lack the guts to do what is right, to do what is necessary, and to tell us the truth, and that starts with Barack Obama.'

Although it was doubtful that Gingrich understood what it meant to 'believe in' or to 'have given up Sharia', he was at least consistent in offering an authoritarian alternative to American traditions of religious tolerance. Trump, meanwhile, was just making things up. Following the killings of police officers in Dallas, he repeated in numerous venues the wholly fabricated claim that 'somebody called for a moment of silence to this maniac that shot the five police'. At a campaign rally in Indiana he said: 'the other night you had 11 cities potentially in a blow-up stage. Marches all over the United States – and tough marches. Anger. Hatred. Hatred! Started by a maniac! And some people ask for a moment of silence for him. For the killer!'

When Trump had made similar assertions about New Jersey Muslims' purported celebration of 9/11, news organisations took care to observe that the claims were false. By mid-2016, fabrications had become the norm, and were ever less newsworthy.

Index